Selected Writings
of Speranza
& William Wilde

edited by

EIBHEAR
WALSHE

Boston College
Irish Studies

Boston College is one of the world's leading centers for Irish Studies. The Boston College Irish Studies Series publishes monographs and edited collections that reflect the research strengths of the center and highlight the rare editions and manuscript collections of the Burns Library. Each book in the series contributes to a notion of Irish Studies that is capacious and open to comparative study with other cultures.

The Irish Studies Faculty at Boston College, with the Director of Irish Studies as chair serve as the Advisory Board for the series.

Selected
Writings
of Speranza
& William Wilde

edited by
EIBHEAR
WALSHE

CLEMSON
UNIVERSITY
PRESS

First Edition, 2020
This paperback edition published 2025

ISBN: 978-1-949979-25-1 (hardback)
ISBN: 978-1-63804-173-3 (paperback)
eISBN: 978-1-949979-26-8 (e-book)

Published by Clemson University Press
in association with Liverpool University Press

For information about Clemson University Press,
please visit our website at www.clemson.edu/press.

Names: Wilde, Lady, 1821-1896. Works. Selections. | Wilde, W. R. (William
    Robert), 1815-1876. Works. Selections. | Walshe, Eibhear, editor.
Title: Selected writings of Speranza and William Wilde / edited by Eibhear Walshe.
Description: First edition. | Clemson, [S.C.] : Clemson University Press in
    association with Liverpool University Press, 2020. | Series: Boston
    College Irish studies | Includes bibliographical references and index. |
    Summary: "This book is the first, groundbreaking edition of writing of
    Speranza (1826-1898) and William Wilde (1815-1874), selected poems,
    translations, travel writings, medical observations, literary criticism,
    folklore and political commentary, reclaiming the writings of Jane and
    William Wilde as part of the public history of Ireland in the nineteenth
    century"-- Provided by publisher.
Identifiers: LCCN 2019048282 (print) | LCCN 2019048283 (ebook) | ISBN
    9781949979251 (hardback) | ISBN 9781949979268 (pdf)
Classification: LCC PR5809 .A6 2020 (print) | LCC PR5809 (ebook) | DDC
    828/.809--dc23
LC record available at https://lccn.loc.gov/2019048282
LC ebook record available at https://lccn.loc.gov/2019048283

Typeset in Minion Pro by Carnegie Book Production.

For Saul Perez

Contents

II   1860–1880: Merrion Square

III   1880–1893: Speranza in London

Acknowledgments

In the course of preparing this fascinating collection of writings, I was greatly helped by a number of people, and I would like to record my gratitude here to James H. Murphy of Boston College for all his help and encouragement when I began to plan the project, and also to Teresa Caneda-Cabrera of the University of Vigo and all my colleagues on her wonderful project "Inconvenient Truths: Cultural Practices of Silence in Contemporary Irish Fiction," funded by the Spanish Ministerio de Economía y Competitividad, for their excellent feedback.

For invaluable work in preparing the text, I thank Donald O'Driscoll and Flicka Small in Cork very much for all their assistance, and Ciaran Wallace in Dublin, Liverpool University Press, and Clemson University Press – in particular, Alison Mero and John Morgenstern. My great thanks also to Wildean scholars Noreen Doody, Michael Cronin, and Maureen O'Connor, and also to my colleagues Lee Jenkins, Anne Fitzgerald, and Claire Connolly in the School of English at University College, Cork, Ireland.

I would like to thank Glenn Dunne of the National Library of Ireland for the cover images and also acknowledge the assistance of a CACSSS UCC Publication Grant, a CACSSS UCC research grant, and the School of English Research Grant and Publication funds.

Finally, I would like to dedicate this book to Saul Perez, with my love.

Introduction:
Speranza and William Wilde

"A Name They Had Made Noble"

She and my father had bequeathed me a name they had made
noble and honoured, not merely in literature, art, archaeology,
and science, but in the public history of my own country, in its
evolution as a nation.

Oscar Wilde, *De Profundis*[1]

Lady Wilde's writings are forgotten, and deservedly so.

Eric Lambert, *Mad with Much Heart*[2]

Oscar Wilde's praise for his parents' scholarship was no pious
gesture of filial loyalty. Speranza and William Wilde were
indeed central to cultural and political life in nineteenth-
century Ireland. When Wilde wrote these words in prison in 1897, he was
at the lowest point of disgrace in his career and keenly aware that his own
downfall would cause damage to his parents' reputation. Speranza and
William Wilde, famous and respected in their own lifetimes, were either
neglected or scorned in the years after Wilde's imprisonment in 1895 and
their writings largely forgotten. Subsequently, the gradual recovery of his

1

own reputation over the twentieth century and into the twenty-first has enabled the parallel recovery of their lost status. My purpose in this book is to reclaim the intellectual legacy of Jane and William Wilde and situate them within the public history of Ireland in the nineteenth century. This volume of their selected writings reassesses their intellectual and aesthetic achievements and explores the nature of their legacy.

This edited collection builds on my research for my 2011 book *Oscar's Shadow*, where I traced the ways in which Oscar Wilde's name became problematic in Irish public discourse. I argued in that book that his downfall directly influenced the way in which the reputation of his distinguished parents, Jane and William Wilde, was also damaged. As writers, intellectuals, and Irish nationalists, Speranza and William Wilde were key figures for the awakening of the Celtic Imagination in the latter part of the nineteenth century, with their innovative work as scholars, folklorists, and cultural historians. They were concerned with an impressive range of intellectual discourses – Irish poetry, European travel writing, archaeology, medicine, literature, cultural politics, and folklore. Witty, opinionated, and learned, Speranza and William Wilde merit reappraisal. Key to this volume is the representation of their interests in social observation, medical practice, and the recovery of Irish archaeology and folklore, placing these two Victorian Irish at the center of an impressive web of international scholarship. Their social writings reach beyond Ireland and the question of Irish independence to interrogate parallel questions in their contemporary European cultures and societies.

In Oscar's words above, "made" is the key term. Speranza and William Wilde were self-invented, both as writers and as cultural figures. Both were on the rise socially by dint of their writings and their intellect, particularly William, who began life in a quiet town in Roscommon and ended his days in Merrion Square, one of the best addresses in Dublin. Speranza (and William to a lesser degree) broke away from the mainstream political beliefs of their Protestant heritage but occupied the ambivalent position of being empathetic to Irish rebellion while also attending Dublin Castle. Living between two political worlds, Irish nationalism and the British establishment in Ireland, honored within one but supporting the other, they thrived on ambiguity. This made them keen observers of their society and its modes of self-expression and identity. Although not themselves Irish scholars (William could understand spoken Irish and later his grandson Vyvyan Holland remembered Oscar singing Irish songs to him as a child, songs Oscar had learnt from William),[3] their imaginative use of their research into folklore was transformative in terms of the literature of Irish cultural nationalism later in the nineteenth century. They both drew from the same body of learning on early Irish cultures and legends and saw this learning as a resistance to the British Empire, fearing that this indigenous Irish culture would be lost. William had first-hand experience of the Irish Famine of the mid-1840s in his role as a doctor, and, in her poems, Speranza directly imagined the dire consequences of this famine, with immediacy and terror in her writings, urging resistance, rebellion, outright revolution. At the same time, often using his own money, William worked hard to catalogue vanishing Irish historical artifacts and to preserve vital archaeological and folkloric traditions on the verge of extinction. On a personal level, they succeeded in becoming public figures, central to wealthy Dublin literary society yet managing to defy respectability and conformity, often challenging bourgeois norms of social behavior, both within their marriage and in their writings.

Speranza was keenly aware of the potential contradictions of her own political position and indeed relished them. Keen to establish her nationalist credentials, given her position as a middle-class Irish Protestant, she recounts this anecdote about her Wexford grandfather and the rebellion of 1798:

> On the day the rebels entered Wexford, the rector Archdeacon Elgee assembled a few of his parishioners in the church to partake of the sacrament together, knowing that a dreadful death awaited them. On his return, the rebels were already forcing their way into his house; they seized him, and the pikes were already at his breast, when a man stepped forth and told of some great act of kindness which the Archdeacon had shown his family. In an instant, the feeling changed, and the leader gave orders that the Archdeacon and all that belonged to him should be held safe from harm.[4]

In her essay on Daniel O'Connell, she argued that, "At all times, there is a much stronger affinity between Protestantism and the Republican form of government than between the Catholic and Republicanism."[5] Both William and Jane saw Irish folklore, archaeology, history, and literature the primary expression of colonial protest and self-preservation. In her essay, "The American Irish," Speranza claims, "When laws forbid a people to arm, they can only speak or sing. Words become their weapons and the Irish armoury is always bright and bouncy."[6] Colm Tóibín makes the shrewd observation about Speranza and William that

> This idea of unstable and gnarled allegiance, of some beliefs in a sort of veneer, was something that would become, in turn, an essential element in the life of Sir William Wilde himself and the lives of his wife and son. It is their very instability and unpredictability from which they would get much of their notoriety and power. No one was ever sure what they believed in, where their loyalty lay.[7]

I would argue that this unpredictability enriched their writings, giving them insight into the complex cultural questions they addressed. It would also enrich the writings of their son, an Irishman reinventing himself within London high society. Their self-invention made them flexible in their opinions and sharpened their skills of observation. It empowered their scholarship, both as independent writers before their marriage and then in their time together. Later, after his death, Speranza would use much of William's scholarship in her publications on Irish folklore, making them key to her own reinvention as an Irish writer in London.

By the time they married in November 1851, both Speranza and William Wilde were, each of them, well-established scholars and writers in their own right and Speranza a popular literary presence in Ireland. Jane Frances Elgee was born to a prosperous middle-class Church of Ireland family in Dublin in 1821,[8] and, despite her apolitical upbringing, became a key figure within Irish cultural nationalism, a poetic voice for revolution and dissent at a young age and against the wishes of her family. She was largely self-taught and became a scholar and translator of repute in

French, German, and Latin. She began contributing poetry to *The Nation*, a radical journal for the Young Irelanders, the younger Irish republicans intent on armed rebellion and the overthrow of British rule in Ireland. She adopted the pen name Speranza, the Italian for hope, as a protection against the disapproval of her middle-class Protestant family, and was first published in February 1846, with a translation of a German poem called "The Holy War."

Later, she was to write of this period of Irish history in her essay "Irish Martyrs and Patriots": "A delirium of patriotic excitement raged through the land as these young orators and poets flashed the full light of their genius on the wrongs, the hopes, and the old heroic memories of their country; even the upper classes in Ireland awoke for the first time to the sense of the nobleness of a life devoted to national regeneration." This was a time of great excitement and fulfillment for the young writer and she told a correspondent in December 1848 that "I should like to rage through life – this orthodox creeping is too tame for me – ah this wild rebellious nature of mine. I wish I could satiate it with Empires though a St Helena were the end."[9] When she began to submit her poems, the editor of *The Nation*, Charles Gavan Duffy, had not then met the author in person, and in his memoirs recalled his impressions at their first meeting: "a tall girl ... whose stately carriage and figure, flashing brown eyes and features cast in an heroic mould, seemed fit for the genius of poetry, or the spirit of revolution."[10] In February 1849, Duffy was put on trial for publishing a seditious call to arms and revolution, "Jacta Alea Est – The Die is Cast". In fact, Speranza herself had been the author of this piece, and she was reported to have stood up in the body of the court during the trail and declared loudly, "I am the culprit, if culprit there be." However, it was said that the judge refused to listen to her and thus *The Nation* trial fell apart. In later life, she said that this incident never actually happened, but she enjoyed the sense of drama that the legend invoked. After this close brush with British justice, Speranza continued writing her nationalist verse unchecked and she became an established and respected figure within Irish literary circles.

Antiquarian and oculist, William Wilde was already a renowned medical scientist and travel writer when he and Speranza met and married in 1851. He was born in Castlerea, Roscommon, in 1815, and began his medical training in Dublin at seventeen, specializing as an aurist (with regard to diseases of the ear) and oculist. Then, in 1837, he made a yacht voyage in the Levant in charge of an invalid patient, Robert Meiklan, a member of the Royal Yacht Squadron. The resulting account of the trip, his first travel book, was an immediate success and established his reputation as a writer. In 1844, he founded the St. Mark's Ophthalmic Hospital in Dublin, spending over one thousand pounds of his own money, and developed a lucrative and demanding private medical practice. At the same time, he found time to publish works on medicine, Irish antiquities, and general literature, and his work on the census of 1851 was ground-breaking. Peter Froggatt comments: "the whole exercise showed Wilde's grasp of statistical principles, unusual at the time, and his demoniacal energy, drive and ingenuity."[11] This energy and drive meant that by the age of thirty William was a member of the Imperial Society of Physicians in Vienna and in 1853 had published another successful book, this time on Austria. His *Boyne and Blackwater* was published in 1850 and he had also become one of the most active members of the Royal Irish Academy, creating the first catalogues of their collections.

It is not clear exactly how William and Speranza met, but they were part of the same literary and intellectual circles in Dublin. We do know that William quotes one of her verses in *Boyne and Blackwater*, and in turn Speranza reviewed his work admiringly. They married in 1851 and it was clearly a partnership based on respect for each other's stature and learning, as well as affection and loyalty. In a letter to her friend John Hilson in Scotland, in 1852, the year after she married, Speranza describes William as "a celebrity – a man eminent in his profession, of acute intellect and much learning, the best conversationalist in our metropolis." She goes on with characteristic honesty to confess to his "strange, hypochondrichal [sic] home nature which the world never sees ... when I ask him what could make him happy, he answers death and yet the next hour if any excitement arouses him he will throw himself into the rush of life."[12] Their marriage was, on the whole, a successful one, based on mutual respect and weathering the loss of their beloved daughter, the existence of William's children before he married, and the scandal of a court case. Their own children – Willie, Oscar, and Isola – were born over the next ten years. They lived at first in Westland Row, but moved to Merrion Square in 1855. William bought summer homes near Cong and at Illaunroe in Connemara to pursue his interest in folklore and archaeology. He seems to have spoken Irish as he addressed the people of the Aran Islands when he went there in September 1852 with the Academy. From their home in Westland Row, and then later in the impressive house at 1 Merrion Square, Speranza and William Wilde pursued their literary and scientific careers and became part of a wide circle of international writers, scientists, and political figures, including Petrie, Edgeworth, and Carlyle. Between 1857 and 1862, William compiled and published three volumes of the *Catalogue of the Antiquities at the Royal Irish Academy*, under great difficulty and sometimes at his own expense. At one point, exasperated by the unwillingness of the Royal Irish Academy to continue paying, he resigned his membership, but was persuaded to return the following year. He also continued to publish essays and observations on deafness and the nature of diseases of the ear. Speranza's Saturday afternoon literary salons attracted many of the most celebrated intellectuals of the day, and she continued her poetry and her translations, with *The Wanderer*, translated from the French of Alphonse de Lamartine, in 1851, and *The Glacier Land* by Alexander Dumas père the following year, and then a volume of her collected poetry published in 1864. William was appointed Surgeon Oculist in Ordinary to the Queen in Ireland and, for his work on the Census Reports from 1851 onwards, he was knighted in 1864. Other honors included an honorary degree from the University of Uppsala, the Order of the Polar Star from the King of Sweden, and Honorary Membership of the Antiquities Society of Berlin.

A scandal rocked Dublin and brought the Wildes great national and international attention, when, in 1864, Speranza was sued for libel by a young woman, Mary Travers, possibly William Wilde's lover. On December 12, 1864, the case of Travers versus Wilde opened in the old Four Courts in Dublin. The Travers libel case attracted widespread public interest and amusement as the private life and letters of the Wildes became public property.[13] One of Oscar Wilde's first biographers, Robert Sherard, wrote: "Lady Wilde's serenity and tolerance reached a level which none but great philosophers have attained."[14] In a letter to her friend, the Swedish feminist and writer Rosalie Olivecrona, she wrote on January 1, 1865:

> You, of course know by this of the disagreeable law affair in which we have been involved ... The simple solution to the affair is this – this Miss Travers is half mad ... Sir William will not be injured by it and the best proof is that his professional hours never were so occupied as now ... all is over now and our enemy has been signally defeated in her efforts to injure us.[15]

William's career continued to prosper when he published his book on *Lough Corrib* and in 1873 the Royal Irish Academy awarded him the Cunningham Gold Medal. However, his health and the family finances began to fail, and William died in Dublin on April 19, 1876, aged 61, and was buried in Mount Jerome Cemetery. Speranza was left in great difficulty but loyally made no complaint, and even finished his last book, on Gabriel Beranger, with a glowing and tender tribute to him.

With William's death, finances became difficult for his widow and sons and they sold the house in Merrion Square. Speranza made her new life in London with her sons Willie and Oscar, running a successful literary salon in Chelsea, visited by Shaw and Yeats and many others. At the time, Yeats wrote fondly of his visits to her gatherings there on Saturdays for the American press and told his readers that, "When one listened to her and remembers that Sir William Wilde was in his day a famous raconteur, one finds it no way wonderful that Oscar Wilde should be the most finished talker of our time."[16] In London her writing flourished and she made a precarious living as a freelance journalist, writing for many popular magazines and attempting to get a government pension, despite her rebellious past. Her *Ancient Legends, Mystic Charms, and Superstitions of Ireland*, published in 1887, provided lively and influential materials for many of those writers central to the Celtic Revival. During Oscar's own trials in 1895, Speranza was cast as the prime motivation behind Oscar's decision, after his first trial, to stay on in the Cadogan Hotel and face arrest and imprisonment for gross indecency, despite been given a chance by the police to flee to France. Yeats wrote in his 1914 autobiographies, "I heard later, from whom I forget now, that Lady Wilde had said, 'If you stay, even if you go to prison, you will always be my son, it will make no difference to my affection but if you go, I will never speak to you again.'"[17] Speranza died in January 1896, while Oscar was still in prison, her heart broken, in poor circumstances, and both her sons ruined; her grave in Kensal Green, London is now lost.

Biographical Views of the Wildes

One of the direct consequences of Oscar Wilde's disgrace was the destruction of his parents' literary reputations. Held in high esteem in their lifetimes for their scholarship and literary talents, they lost most of their intellectual credibility with their son's fall from favor in the years after his death in 1900. Notably, Speranza was to bear the brunt of this misogyny and homophobia. In her lifetime, Charles Gavan Duffy called her "A substantial force in Irish politics, and a woman of genius."[18] Little wonder, novelist William Carleton, a man who admired the "great ocean of her soul," described Speranza as "the most extraordinary prodigy of a female that this country, or perhaps any other has produced."[19] All respect disappeared, however, in the twentieth century, and instead there were many destructive homophobic biographical accounts of William and Speranza. Underlying these was unease with Oscar's sexuality. This led to the eclipsing of her standing as a writer and scholar, making her a scapegoat for his criminalized sexuality. Homophobia and misogyny informed much of the discussion of her life, her work, even her body. Her public persona, celebrated in her lifetime, was now reconstructed as an overpowering maternal influence that effeminized her son and rendered him homosexual.

Much of this came from one particular biographical source – George Bernard Shaw. Shaw's account of her in London became a template for those biographers wishing to undermine her.[20] Shaw knew the Wilde family when growing up in Dublin, and later, by his own account, was treated with great kindness by Speranza in her literary gatherings in London when he was young and poor and struggling to find himself as a writer. In later life, Shaw repaid Speranza's kindness badly in his writings on the family, and with his theories on Oscar's sexuality and Speranza's culpability. The key document from Shaw is a letter to Frank Harris, published as part of Harris's biography of Oscar in 1916, and given great weight, as Shaw had known the family reasonably well. Partly, Shaw found it necessary to distance himself from any understanding of homosexuality: "I don't quite know why, for my toleration of his perversity and recognition of the fact that it does not imply any general depravity or coarseness of character is an acquirement through observation and reflection. I have all the normal repugnance to homosexuality – if it is really normal which nowadays one is sometimes provoked into doubting."[21]

In his letter to Harris, man to man, Shaw offers a biological explanation for Wilde's so-called aberrant sexuality by expounding the unsupported theory that Speranza was suffering from an abnormal physical condition called gigantism and that Wilde had inherited her physical abnormality, remade as homosexuality, and was thus sexually monstrous. Shaw provides no medical proof for this theory, apart from the evidence of his own eyes, and no other contemporary account mentions this condition. However, he clearly feels the need to demonize the sexuality that led Wilde to prison, seeing the grotesque body of the mother as the perverting influence on normative heterosexuality.[22] Shaw set a tone for later works and for the consequent erosion of her intellectual reputation.

An exception was *Victorian Doctor*, a biography of William published in 1942 by T. G. Wilson, an admiring account of both Wildes, which opens with the statement that "Posterity has not done justice to Sir William Wilde,"[23] and evinces a clear sense of respect and liking for Speranza throughout, calling her the "Madame Roland of the Irish Gironde," and commending her "capacity for loyalty."[24] However, many later biographers failed to pick up this line of respectful characterization. Horace Wyndham's 1951 study, *Speranza: A Biography of Lady Wilde*, saw itself as sympathetic to her fate, yet, in reality, consistently undermined her scholarly standing: "the trouble with Lady Wilde was that where her output was concerned, she wandered (and often floundered) in too many fields."[25] Having maligned the diversity of her interests, Wyndham goes on to make the contradictory complaint that, "unfortunately, she professed to value intellectual culture not only above all else, but as the only object in life; and this grave mistake brought upon her tragic consequences."[26] Speranza was damned in this biographer's eyes by both the energy and the range of her intellectual interests; yet also damned, it seems, by having an interest in the cerebral at all. Wyndham concludes his biography with the judgment that: "If, during her seventy years, she did many a foolish thing, and some that were regrettable, she never did a mean one. Hence, when the final balance is struck, and the debits and credits adjusted, it will be found that the balance on the whole is in favour of Speranza, Lady Wilde."[27] Believing himself to be sympathetic, Wyndham erodes any respect for her intellect by praising her character rather than examining her seriousness as a scholar and a poet.

Perhaps the most venomous account of the family came in 1952 from the Belfast playwright St John Ervine, a biographer of Shaw, who asserts that "neither of the Wildes had any sanctity to dispense." The cruelty of his approach can be seen in this casual aside. "Their second son Oscar was damned on the day that he was born and would have done better to have died in childhood as his sister Isola, who followed him, did."[28]

Another nasty account of the Wildes came in 1967 with Eric Lambert's *Mad with Much Heart*, which showed little evidence of heart on the part of the author. Lambert opens with the line that Oscar was, "Foredoomed by his parentage,"[29] and goes on to say that "the fatal flaw of the Wildes was moral courage." Not the most accurate of scholars himself, Lambert seems to think Speranza was from Wexford. Again, with no evidence, he asserts that Speranza felt little sorrow at the sudden death of her daughter Isola at nine years of age, despite evidence of her deep anguish, as seen in her letter to her Swedish friend Froken Lotten von Kraemer, included in this collection. Lambert's is a coarse, salacious study, motivated by his unpleasant sexual prurience and his dislike of Speranza.

In the same year, 1967, their biographer Terence de Vere White, acknowledging that "they had acquired something of the inevitability and pathos of the routine vaudeville act," perpetuated much of this prejudice himself, writing that William Wilde's enthusiasms "had an intellectual basis, while his wife's were emotional: they went with her craving for sensation."[30] He calls Speranza a pantomime queen, but, despite himself, does manage to show some admiration for her famine poetry. White follows on Shaw's pathological explanation for Oscar's homosexuality, continuing to see it as an aberration and a freak of nature that needed to be accounted for by his parents' abnormalities. "His [William Wilde's] reputation for lechery and his wife's gigantism have provided an explanation for Oscar's homosexual tendencies."[31]

Despite societal changes in England and Ireland, representations of Speranza continued to fall along these misogynistic lines. In 1989, Terry Eagleton's play, *Saint Oscar*, was produced by Field Day, a theatre company with a clear political link with Irish cultural nationalism. Eagleton brings Wilde back to life, making him the central character. The play is structured around a series of encounters between Oscar and key figures in his life, like Bosie and Edward Carson, and Speranza is the first person Oscar confronts. As a representation of their actual relationship, it is far from the recorded biographical reality of mutual respect and affection. Here, there is a real sense of resentment on Oscar's side against his mother, and a kind of shrewd undermining of her son on her side. As I wrote in my book *Oscar's Shadow*, the opening scene of the play is in line with many earlier, more hostile versions of Wilde's life, where the over-mothering of Speranza is held accountable for the "unnatural" homosexuality of her son. In an effort to come to terms with Wilde's sexuality, Eagleton relies on an androgynous notion of sexuality. In doing so he falls back on a retrograde feminizing of the homoerotic and a discourse of the monstrous to represent sexual otherness. As the play opens, Wilde describes his birth as "a monstrous birth. When they pulled me out they screamed and tried to kill me on the spot. A cock and a cunt together, the one tucked neatly within the other." It is Speranza who is blamed for this hermaphrodite birth, as Wilde accuses her with: "Who was it unmanned me?" He goes on to explain: "Don't you see, mother, something went awry with me within the furry walls of your womb. Your little boy is flawed, botched, unfinished. I had my own body but I was too greedy for flesh. I wanted yours, too. The two don't mix well."[32]

The scene between Speranza and Oscar which opens the play is an antagonistic one, where they snipe at each other's literary reputations, "I'm into comedy, she is into farce."[33] Yet, in some of their arguments, a more nuanced version of the complications of Speranza's political role in Ireland is suggested. At one point, she tells him that she was never afraid to appear a fool, despite the contradictions of her political stance: a rebel who attended Dublin Castle soirées, a poet of the famine victims who had tenants herself. As Eagleton's Speranza proudly tells him, "Better a rich rebel than no rebel at all."[34] Oscar, stung by this, accuses her of "unmanning" him. He rejects her dangerous attraction to the myth of blood sacrifice at the core of Irish Republicanism, but she, in turn, warns him that his snobbish interest in British society will mean that Britain's laws and moral double standards will trip him up and lead him to disaster. The real merit of the play is the way Eagleton dramatizes the conflict between their two opposing political stances as writers. He asks the useful question: why did Oscar write so few direct essays or reviews about Ireland? Given his parents' keen interest in their own country in their writings, was he perhaps seeking new territory, allowing him to use Ireland indirectly within his work?

Within the past fifty years, Wildean scholarship has reconsidered all aspects of his corpus. As laws changed and social perceptions altered, first Wilde's sexuality, then his Irishness, and finally the vital importance of his family identity have been acknowledged. As a result, Richard Ellmann in his 1987 biography of Oscar is more even-handed, telling his readers that the unpleasant stories around Speranza and William came from the undeniable fact that "success promotes malice,"[35] and sensibly dismisses the idea that Speranza was responsible for Oscar's sexuality. "However accommodating it is to see a maternal smothering of masculinity as having contributed to his homosexuality, there is reason to be sceptical."[36] Coakley's 1994 study, *Oscar Wilde: The Importance of Being Irish*, re-establishes his father and mother's scholarly reputation and treats them with respect: "Sir William and Lady Wilde shared a love of learning and their son inherited this trait from them."[37] Coakley makes the point that Speranza was an active feminist, the first signature on a petition demanding women be allowed to study in Trinity College in 1892, and quotes many admiring contemporary accounts of her salon in Merrion Square. Coakley, a professor of medicine, dismisses Shaw's gigantism theory as being without any medical proof. Joy Melville's 1994 biography, despite being called *Mother of Oscar*, is an impressive work of reclamation for this "outstandingly erudite, witty eccentric and gifted woman," and sets the tone for much of the serious and weighty scholarship to follow.[38]

The essay on Wilde by Colm Tóibín in his 2002 collection, *Love in a Dark Time*, was a timely and original one. Unusually for an Irish commentator writing on Wilde, Tóibín cites Sir William as the crucial parental influence that made Wilde decide to prosecute Queensbury. "The Wildes were part of a small breed of Irish Protestants. … Their addiction to the cause of Irish freedom gave them an edge, lifted them out of their own circumstances and gave them astonishing individuality, and independence of mind."[39] Tóibín highlights Wilde's respect for Speranza – much needed after all the sneering or grotesque accounts of his mother that had appeared. "In all of Oscar Wilde's letters in which he refers to his mother, there is not one word of mockery or disloyalty. Mostly he refers to her not as his mother but as Lady Wilde."[40] He also makes the point that all negative portraits of Speranza appear after Wilde's trials and disgrace. Before 1895, contemporary accounts of her are respectful and admiring of her scholarship and her literary standing.

Towards the end of the twentieth century, with more enlightened views on homosexuality becoming part of public discourse, the reputation of the Wildes waxed again and the Irish element of their scholarship was rediscovered. Renewed scholarly interest in the Wildes included conferences at Trinity College Dublin, the Royal College of Surgeons, Dublin, and the Royal Irish Academy, and studies like *The Fall of the House of Wilde*, *The Wilde Legacy*, and the recent publication of several volumes of Speranza's letters and a critical biography by Karen Tipper. Tipper has been a valuable source of scholarship in the revival of Speranza's academic reputation, with several edited volumes of her letters now available in print. Tipper's 2002 biography is an important one as it considers Speranza's writing life in great detail and looks at her work as a nationalist, poet, teacher, and woman of letters. Tipper makes the point that Speranza's intellect and her assertiveness have been largely unacknowledged, and the sufferings of her life as somehow taken for granted or dismissed.[41]

Finally, to conclude this section on biography, in the excellent *The Fall of the House of Wilde*, Emer O'Sullivan makes her argument plain: "In many biographies of Oscar Wilde, Jane and William are not given their due. This does not square with the eminence Jane and William enjoyed in Ireland. Neither does it fit in with Oscar's view of them."[42] O'Sullivan places them within the correct context when she argues that "the political and cultural campaign William and Speranza fought was fought again years later, in 1916, with bloody results."[43] Eleanor Fitzsimons's *Wilde's*

Women, published in 2015, further reclaimed Speranza as "an incomparable role model." On the whole, it provided a sympathetic and nuanced account of Speranza, celebrating her scholarship and her tolerance, but sometimes in ambiguous terms – wondering if, while she loved her children, she also "may have set both up for a fall."[44] Overall, recent years have restored Speranza's and William's status and have provided an accurate account of their scholarship.

The Structure of This Anthology

Few embraced the cosmopolitanism of the time as thoroughly as the Wildes ... The notion of pluralism is at the heart of all of their ideas. The belief not merely in the multiplicity but also of the incommensurability of the values of different cultures and societies.[45]

Emer O'Sullivan

His wife's nationalism pronounced itself in poetry, Wilde's in recognising, salvaging and bringing forth – editing – all that constitutes the acta and the annals of the Irish nation.[46]

Michael O'Doherty

In selecting the texts for this edition, I have followed a chronological structure to illustrate the parallel writing careers of Speranza and William before their marriage and then interwoven their shared interests and concerns during their twenty-five years or so together. Speranza's reinvention of herself as a writer in London after William's death meant that we have a great deal of her writings to choose from and therefore this selection of their work has more of her texts. To demonstrate the range of their intellectual interests, included are some of William's medical writings on Austria, as well as the opening section of Speranza's translation of *Sidonia the Sorceress*, an influential text. By and large, the anthology features extracts from their essays, travel writings, lectures on Ireland and Irish questions, folklore collections, and, in addition, a number of Speranza's poems and letters.

It is clear that they shared a range of interests, as Speranza was a polymath – "My favourite study was languages. I succeeded in mastering ten of the European languages. Till my eighteenth year I never wrote anything. All my time was given to study."[47] But William seems also to have a command of French and German, as well as a working facility with spoken Irish. As well as observing the links between them, it is also worth considering the differences between two writers broadly in sympathy with the same political aims: self-rule for Ireland and a more enlightened approach to public governance. Speranza in her call to arms, "Jacta Alea Est," included here, and her essay on Irish Patriots, sees violent rebellion as necessary for Ireland's regaining of self-respect:

> To die for Ireland! Yes; have we not sworn it in a thousand passionate words by our poets and orators – in our grave resolves of councils, leagues and confederations? Now is the moment to test whether you value most freedom or life. Now is the moment to strike, and by striking save, and the day after the victory, it will be time enough to count your dead.

Also included is an extract from her entertaining travel book *Drift-wood from Scandanavia*, as well as William's travel writings on the Mediterranean and on Austria. One critic, Michael Cronin, sees a link with her writings on the position of women and the implicitly feminist project of women's travel writing. Cronin writes:

> In an essay entitled "The Bondage of Women", Jane Wilde inveighs against the social and economic subjugation of women ... Above all, her view of patriarchy is that it fears more than anything else, the *mobility* of women, this dangerous, illicit, unchaperoned wandering from their assigned place in the social and economic order. Some women chose to break these fetters by engaging in the physical act of travelling and Jane Wilde does indeed produce her own travel account in 1884 entitled *Driftwood from Scandinavia*.[48]

In addition, her poetry of the Famine is featured, praised in contemporary critical discussions for its sense of immediacy and empathy for the victims of famine. As a writer, Speranza was determined to represent the immediate and disastrous consequences of the Famine. In her poem, "The Famine Year," published in January 1847, she laments:

> Weary men, what reap ye? – Golden corn for the stranger.
> What sow ye? – Human corpses that wait for the avenger.
> Fainting forms, hunger-stricken, what see you in the offing?
> Stately ships to bear our food away, amid the stranger's scoffing.
> There's a proud array of soldiers – what do they need round your door?
> They guard our masters' granaries from the thin hands of the poor
> Pale mothers, wherefore weeping? – Would to God that we were dead –
> Our children swoon before us, and we cannot give them bread.

In the words of the critic Amy Martin, "Elgee uses a sophisticated exploration of gender and family to represent dehumanisation,"[49] and she goes on to write that, "At the same time, Elgee resists narratives of blame, or lapsing into stereotypes of Irish men as feminized, violent or culturally deviant."[50] Contemporary literary criticism celebrates Speranza's famine writing, where, in the words of Matthew Campbell, "Her poems on the famine not merely intrude, they are focussed on the experience with an effect which approached shock, drawing into verse images of horror garnered from newspaper sketches and journalistic reports."[51] Contemporary Irish poet Eiléan Ní Chuilleanáin suggests that

> Within the Irish political canon of her century, she is a match perhaps for Thomas Davis but not for Allingham or Ferguson, certainly not for Mangan. Her language and her metre are quite different. They are energetic … Speranza needs something to slow her down and in fact the most successful of her poems with their long lines and strong pauses have a drag on them, a drag of feeling as much as metre in "The Famine Year" and in the poem on Henry and John Sheares. Some of the extra weight that ballasts those two poems come from their sense of real history.[52]

William's views on the famine were also influential: well-informed by first-hand experience and observation, but very different from Speranza's and in stark contrast to the imaginative weight of protest seen in her poetry. William was not as ardently nationalist as Speranza, although in favor of Home Rule. In the words of the historian Laurence Geary: "Wilde intuited correctly the famine's catastrophic dimensions,"[53] being, amongst other things, in charge of the census in 1851, which gave him the chance to catalogue the worst consequences. In addition, he edited the *Dublin Quarterly Journal of Medical Science* from 1846 until 1849. He was at the forefront of medical observation during the Famine and afterwards, and ran a questionnaire in August 1848 amongst doctors, cataloguing diseases that had occurred as a result of the Famine. In his essay "The Food of the Irish," published in 1854 in the *Dublin University Magazine*, William makes the controversial point that, "On the whole, Irish agriculture has been greatly benefitted by the Famine."[54] William, unlike Speranza, defends government policy in this essay, arguing that many more people would have died without their intervention. Furthermore, in his lecture, twelve years later, called *Ireland Past and Present*, delivered in 1864, he makes the uncomfortable and provocative point to his prosperous Dublin audience that: "Had not events to which I have glanced in a previous part of this lecture taken place, some of us would not have had as good dinners as we seem to have enjoyed today"; and he goes on to make the controversial point: "We have, it is true, lost a great many people: whether however they are *so far* an eventual loss to Ireland is questionable." William, as a doctor, was interested in the medical and scientific questions that arose from the calamity of the famine, and, as a result, is pragmatic in his approach. He concluded that lecture with a tilt at armed rebellion. "We may talk rebellion in our assemblies … I for one hold that there is still a good time coming not for 'old' or 'young' Ireland but for New Ireland." William's gentle dismissal of Young Irelanders seems not to have dismayed Speranza, who wrote with pride of his performance in this lecture and was delighted at his knighthood.

Equally of interest in terms of contemporary criticism are Speranza's translations before and after marriage. Michael Cronin makes the point that her introduction to rebellion came via translation and that her translations made links between Irish nationalist revolt and those of other countries, particularly France. Her translations and her travel writing kept Ireland connected to Europe and provided a pan-European dimension to her Irish Nationalism. As biographers attest, Speranza had French, German, Italian, some Latin and Greek, and later taught herself Swedish. Included is a short extract from her most influential translation, *Sidonia the Sorceress*, which Oscar Wilde later was to claim was his favorite book to read as a child. Michael Cronin notes the profound impact that the translation, produced by a woman who had never been to a German-speaking country, was to have well beyond the period of its immediate publication. The English writer and critic Edmund Gosse noted that, "this German romance did not begin to exist until an Irishwoman revealed it to a select English circle." Dante Gabriel Rossetti was particularly taken by Elgee's translation and he talked incessantly about it to his other Pre-Raphaelite friends. Edward Burne-Jones produced a noted portrait of Sidonia in 1860 and in 1893 William Morris sought permission through Oscar Wilde for his Kelmscott Press to republish the translation, which Morris described as "an almost faultless reproduction of the past, its action really alive."[55]

Also included are her essays on Thomas Moore and Irish Leaders and Martyrs and her poem on Daniel O'Connell, evidence of one of her key political interests, particularly her interest in O'Connell. As a younger revolutionary, Speranza could have been dismissive of the elder statesman but she is perceptive as to the shifting and ambivalent position O'Connell found himself in. Her essay on O'Connell is discussed by the contemporary critic Marjorie Howe, who argues that, "For Wilde, O'Connell's life was part of the incomplete process of resistance as well as an image of its successful completion. It embodied a history of suffering and defeat and provided a diagram of Victorian revolution."[56] From a different perspective, Speranza saw the ambivalence of O'Connell's position and was, unusually for her generation, sympathetic to it and to the sense that O'Connell was caught in a difficult position. As Karen Tipper observes, Speranza in her essay on O'Connell makes a point of "championing his strengths,"[57] but Tipper argues that Speranza is not totally uncritical of O'Connell.

> Above all she cannot support his decision to seek Repeal only through constitutional means at the expense, ever, of human rights. While she can state that "the horrible excesses of anarchy, disguised under the mask of freedom," he witnessed in France no doubt contributed to his lifelong "earnest, undeviating advocacy

of religion, peace and order" she herself never relinquished the belief that the use of the sword was warranted in the face of unrelenting injustice and oppression.[58]

Both wrote about Dean Swift and William quotes an anecdote about her great grandfather, Thomas Kingsbury, a friend of Swift and President of the Royal College of Physicians. This common preoccupation with Swift brings out the differences in their imagination in a pointed way. William wants to dispel medical misinformation about Swift's supposed madness. He was dispassionate in his account of the tortured relationship between Swift and Stella, justifying Swift's withdrawal from her life just before her death, writing that "We can perfectly understand how a person of Swift's peculiar temperament, and past sixty years of age, should be unwilling to witness the last moments of one so dear to him as Stella," as if this was perfectly normal.[59] On the other hand, Speranza is interested in the divisive and turbulent nature of literary genius and the cost for women:

A great prophet of our own day has said: … "The great man does in truth belong to his own age, but he belongs likewise to all ages, otherwise he is not great. What was transitory in him passes away, but the immortal part remains, the significance of which is inexhaustible." It is this "inexhaustible significance" of Swift's best thoughts that make them for ever worth re-interpreting in the new forms of a new age.

But, above all, the love-drama of Swift's life has helped to make his name immortal.[60]

Also included are extracts from William and Speranza's folklore collecting, key to the Celtic Revival, illustrating the links between the two and the ways in which their writings influenced and informed each other's work. William published his *Irish Popular Superstitions* in 1852, more of a childhood memoir than an anthology of Irish folklore. In his introduction, he suggests that the recent Famine, the "Great convulsion," along with the consequent damage to family life and to social customs, had endangered the preservation of popular superstitions and folklore, what he calls "the bond that knit the peasant to the soil," and his collection sought to preserve a vanishing culture. His interest in fairy lore, in Mayday superstitions and festivals, and in fairy archaeology is represented in his own collection and then reproduced when Speranza published her two collections, *Ancient Legends, Mystic Charms, and Superstitions of Ireland* in 1887 and *Ancient Cures, Charms and Usages of Ireland* in 1890. In her introduction, she tells the reader that "these narrations were taken down by competent persons skilled in both languages" – which meant William – and argues, like him, that "In a few years such a collection will be impossible."[61] Both were aware of the urgency of their collecting in preserving lost traditions.

There was for me in compiling this collection a parallel sense of urgency in recovering their writings after such a long period of silence. Now, in the twenty-first century, the words of Speranza and William Wilde are speaking again with all the power and wit that animated these two influential Irish writers and shaped the culture of their country in such a profound and lasting way.

Eibhear Walshe
University College Cork
Ireland

I   1840–1860:
Words Become Their Weapons

CHAPTER ONE

William Wilde, *The Narrative of a Voyage to Madeira, Tenerife, and Along the Shores of the Mediterranean*, 1840

William Wilde's first publication was this two-volume travel book, a lively and observant account of his eight-month-long journey in the company of an invalid, Robert Meiklan, a member of the Royal Yacht Squadron. William had himself been ill with a fever and took this opportunity to travel. Although having never been at sea before, they left Dublin on September 24, 1837 and set off to Galicia and onward to Lisbon, where William opened the tomb of a king. The next parts of the book chart his time in Madeira, Tenerife, Algiers, Sicily, Egypt, Rhodes, Cyprus, and Syria and onwards to Palestine and Greece. This is very much a young man's book, for, despite his ill health, William scales the Great Pyramid, almost falling into danger, and climbs the volcanic Mount Teide in Tenerife. The man of science is very much in evidence in his observations, medical and social, but he also noted much of the political worlds he observed, something he repeats in his later travel writings. The book was a huge success and William was paid £250 outright.

In this extract, William Wilde visits Jerusalem.

Jerusalem

Jaffa March, 1838

At length we arrived at an old marabut, where the country became more level, but still presenting the same stony character and here we caught the first glimpse of Jerusalem, at about a mile's distance. The first object which attracted our attention, was a line of dead wall, flanked by two or three square towers, above which could be distinguished a few domes and minarets. Such is the appearance which the city presents when seen from this point. Beyond the city, on the eastern side, rose a three-capt hill, whose highest point was surmounted by a white dome and one or two straggling buildings; its sides, which were studded with low shrubby plants, exhibited a brown and rugged aspect. This is the memorable Mount of Olives. Our party reined their horses and stood in motionless silence for some minutes gazing on the scene. The expectations we had formed respecting the appearance of Jerusalem were disappointed, but our enthusiasm had not, in the least degree, abated. For myself, I confess, that as I gazed upon the north-western angle of that solitary wall, sorrow came over my heart; no living thing could be seen on the intervening ground; nothing stirred, and solitude seemed to reign within its walls. It was then approaching towards the close of day, and everything we saw appeared lone and desolate; so quiet and solitary did the city appear, that it looked as if its inhabitants had been asleep for years, and that we had come to awaken them from their slumbers. As we approached the city, the line of wall which we had first seen, opened out and extended to the right. We passed the upper pool of Gihon, and met a few Arab crones going with their pitchers on their heads to draw water from a neighbouring well. They appeared like so many of those witches described in works of fiction, coming forth to meet us from the silent city. Turning a sharp angle of the wall, we reached a large massive square building, commonly called the castle of David, and now the citadel of the modern city. To the left of it is the Jaffa gate, which was guarded by a few Egyptian soldiers who offered no obstruction to our entrance.

We rode on through a narrow street with a low dead wall on either side. On our left lay a piece of waste ground, covered with old walls, broken cisterns, and prickly pears of an enormous size, jumbled together. On our right, the apertures in the broken wall afforded us occasional glimpses of the minarets and domes that rise throughout the lower and more populous parts of the city. A few minutes more conducted us to the Latin convent, which we entered by an arched gateway that rang with the sound of our arms and the horses' hoofs which echoing through the old building, aroused its inmates; presently, we found ourselves in a square court, from whose surrounding windows, numbers of bearded monks peered forth, astonished at our appearance, and wondering who the party could be that had created such an unusual stir within their solitary dwelling ...

A letter from Signor Campanelli, procured us the services and kind assistance of Father Benjamin, the curate of the convent. He generally acted as our guide. The curé was a kind, goodnatured creature, but extremely dirty in his habits. He had been but a few years in the country, and had not yet told his tale often enough to believe it himself; for, on questioning him as to the accuracy of many of the sacred places, he usually finished his speech with, "But I am sure it is all tradition." His evening visits to us were often very acceptable, for he generally produced from underneath his cloak a bottle of good wine, much better than that supplied to us by the convent.

After dinner, we proceeded to pay our respects to the superior of the convent, and in passing to his apartment we were conducted through a long gallery, on either side of which were ranged the cells of the Padres, numbers of whom stood waiting at their doors to catch a chance word; to know our country, and hear something of what was going forward in Europe. The reception-room we found a very comfortable apartment, with some good old paintings. It was partly hung with tapestry, and a deewan ran along two sides of the room. The superior was a stout, intelligent-looking Italian, about forty years of age; courteous, well-bred, and apparently well skilled in the art of pleasing. He appeared to be well acquainted with the general affairs of Europe; and hearing that we had been lately in Spain, seemed particularly anxious to learn the success of Don Carlos, in whom he seemed to be deeply interested. In the course of conversation, he learned that I was an Irishman, and instantly inquired after Daniel O'Connell, and asked if the bishops of Ireland were not now a very learned body. Being an Irishman seemed to raise me not a little in his estimation, perhaps from his supposing that I must, of necessity, be also a Roman Catholic, as it is considered in several places abroad, that none others are to be found in Ireland; and, I attribute the attention I received in visiting many places of worship here, to this circumstance. The superior invited us to partake of lemonade and brandy flavored with aniseed, which brought to our recollection the day we spent at Mafra. The secretary of the superior, I found a good botanist, and a man of more taste and refinement than we were led to believe could exist among the Terra Santa friars. We returned to our hospicé, and thus ended our first evening in Jerusalem.

Having taken up our residence in the Holy City, I here close my diary for the present, and instead of dragging my readers from place to place, and enumerating all that we saw and heard, I choose rather to compress my notes of the week which I spent here, into distinct sections upon some of the most remarkable places and objects which have been least dwelt upon or described by recent travellers.

One of the places first visited by the traveller or the pilgrim, is the holy sepulchre; and here I generally spent an hour daily during our sojourn at Jerusalem – for all must be willing to accept the invitation – "Come and see where they have laid Him." Our way from the Latin convent to the sepulchre led *down* through a tolerably wide street, having high dead walls on either side, with low massive doors at intervals, leading into the courts and houses within. Turning to the right, at the end of this street, we proceeded through one of the smaller bazaars, generally filled with ragged Arab women, the vendors of vegetables and snails, the latter of which are much eaten here, especially during the season of Lent. Pursuing this path for a short distance, our attention was attracted to a crowd of people of different nations, hastening towards a narrow lane upon the left. Mixing with these, we found both sides of the lane crowded with shops for the sale of wearing apparel, crosses, rosaries, and such other sacred ware. Several crooked turnings, and a steep descent, conducted us into a large square court in front of the church of the holy sepulchre. Part of this enclosure is raised a few steps, and these form the basements of a row of pillars; so that, in all probability, the whole of this court was originally covered in. The scene that presented itself in this space was of most novel and exciting interest, and the motley groups of figures that thronged it gave it a very extraordinary appearance. On the upper raised steps were tables spread with coffee, sherbet, sweetmeats, and refreshments; and throughout the court were seated pedlars, and the Bethlehemite vendors of carved shells, beads, ornaments in mother of pearl, bituminous amulets, bowls made of the asphaltum of the Dead Sea, and other articles of holy merchandise, some of which each of the pilgrims purchase during their stay. Through these wares, hundreds of persons passed and repassed to the church door. Pilgrims of many nations were to be seen in their different costumes; Latin, Armenian, Russian, Greek, and Coptish friars, with Turks and Egyptian soldiers, all forming the most extraordinary scene that could be found in any spot upon the globe; and a polyglot language is heard, such as few other places in the world could exhibit.

The front of the church presents little worth describing. No architectural beauty seems to have been attempted in its erection; and it is now a poor, mean-looking building, and very much defaced, as for many years past the Turks would not permit any of the Christian edifices to be repaired.

The entrance was originally a double arch, supported by three sets of clustered pillars of grey marble and verd-antique. On the architrave above it, is represented the Messiah's triumphal entry into Jerusalem, in good basso-relievo. This is a handsome piece of sculpture, but like the others in the building, it, too, is greatly defaced. Several other scriptural devices are distinguishable round the cornices and windows. On the left stand the ancient belfry and the Greek convent, and on the right, some old walls and ruined houses. We were not a little surprised, upon entering the door of the church, to see the stiff form of an Egyptian soldier, guarding the entrance to the tomb of Christ. On the left, upon a raised platform, half a dozen turbaned Turks sat smoking and drinking coffee. These Mohammadans are necessarily placed there, for the purpose of preserving order and decorum among the devout priests and Christian pilgrims during their religious ceremonies! They keep the keys of the church and open it every morning and evening, except during passion-week, when it remains open the entire day.

One of the first objects that caught our attention on entering the sepulchre, was a large oblong slab of variegated yellow marble, raised a few inches from the floor, and having an immense candle burning at each corner. Our cicerone, Padre Benjamin, very gravely informed us, that this stone was that on which our Lord was anointed, and here, on Good Friday, the priests go through a similar ceremony with an effigy of the Saviour. At this spot the daily station of the pilgrim commences, for, on approaching it, he kneels, and not only kisses it, but touches it with his forehead, and then with both cheeks. This is the usual form of salutation at all the holy places. Whence this slab was procured, I cannot possibly discover, as it is totally different from any of the marbles found in the neighbourhood of Jerusalem; however, tradition has sanctified it, and so we pass on without questioning its antiquity. A few yards to the right of this anointing-stone, a flight of eighteen steps cut out of the solid rock, led us to a square platform, surrounded by a dome or cupola, distinct from, and of a smaller size than that covering the holy sepulchre and the rest of the church. This platform, which is mostly covered with marble and ornamented work, we are told is CALVARY. Seventeen paces from the top of the stairs brought us to a low white marble altar, towards which the pilgrims were rushing as quickly as they could on their knees. The attendant priest, perceiving that we were strangers and Europeans, very politely interfered in our behalf. He caught hold of the person who happened to delay too long under the altar, and pulling him back, procured for us an immediate entrance into the aperture. Going down upon my knees, I entered the passage to the crypt beneath. The first thing that attracted my attention on reaching this place, was a large circular plate of embossed silver, fastened on a marble flag, and containing the remains of many precious stones and gems which had been set upon it. In the centre of this plate there is an aperture, into which I sunk my arm, and at about the depth of a foot I found a square hole in the rock, where, it is said, the cross was placed on which our Lord was crucified. A few paces to the right of this spot, we were shown a silver grating which covers a cleft in the rock, which we were told was the exact spot where the rock was rent at the time of the crucifixion. We found no altars over the places where the other two crosses are said to have been placed, as was stated to have been in existence there some years ago. I anxiously inquired after the skull of Adam, said to have been found here; but that tale is now better known to the traveller and to the English reader, than to the monks of Jerusalem, and of this tradition I shall have occasion to speak in another place. This chapel is now in the hands of the Greeks, who have decorated it with their usual gaudy tinselled paintings.

A number of ornamented lamps suspended from the ceiling, shed a peculiar mellow and sombre light over the place. To the right of where the cross is said to have been fixed, the Latins have erected another altar, where, they say, he was nailed to the cross; but very few of the pilgrims seemed to pay any reverence to this altar, which, like many other places of the same kind established in the vicinity of those which have been acknowledged as possessing greater antiquity, look like so many "opposition shops." The walls of this place were adorned with some faded tapestry; and underneath the platform of rock is a small chapel belonging to the Copts, and also a place for preparing coffee. In this chapel is shown a crack or fissure in the rock, corresponding to that in the apartment above; and the examination of it, rather induces me to consider the place called Calvary, as a portion of the *original rock*, squared and hewn down to its present form; but I am at a loss to discover at what time, or under what circumstances, this place received the name of a hill or mount, as no scriptural evidence for such an appellation exists. The top of this plateau is fifteen feet above the floor of the adjoining church, and the bottom thirty-five yards from the site of the holy sepulchre. Whatever may be the diversity of opinion as to the identity of this rock, a subject which I will discuss in another place, it was not, I confess, without feelings of deep emotion, that I visited the so-called Calvary. On many of my visits to this place, particularly at an early hour in the morning, when but comparatively few pilgrims were present, I was greatly struck with the sincere and devotional feeling exhibited by many who slowly and reverently approached the altar on their knees, with tears of sorrow running down their cheeks; when sighs and stifled groans were the only sounds that broke the stillness of those moments, save the tinkle of the piaster as it fell into the moneytray of the attendant priest, who alone, among the group, remained unmoved. At these early and tranquil hours, I have watched the aged and weatherbeaten pilgrim here bowed to the earth, and mothers prostrated around the place offering up prayers, directed, I doubt not, by the promptings of their hearts, and with silent tears, presenting before the altar their lovely little ones, who gazed with mute astonishment and childish sympathy at the parent, but not venturing to break the silence or interrupt the solemnity of the scene by their innocent prattle. These were absorbing moments, and different from the scenes I witnessed during the more public and crowded hours, when hurry, bustle, and confusion, and the vast concourse of people rendered the approach to this place almost impossible. I have frequently seen, when some of the pilgrims possessed of more devotion or curiosity than the rest, remained under the altar longer than the usual time, that they were very unceremoniously reminded of their delay by the attendant priest, especially if they did not belong to his own church.

On our return from Calvary, we entered the large circular hall of the sepulchre. This part of the building is surrounded by a gallery supported on a colonnade of eighteen pillars, and surmounted by a vast dome. To the north of this hall is the Latin church, and to the east of it is the Greek chapel. A large curtain hangs before it. This chapel is, by far, the most highly decorated of any of the places of worship here. The Armenian church is situated in the gallery of the building. Beneath the centre of the dome is erected an oblong pavilion of grey and yellow marble carved in panels, which, at its southern end, is surmounted by a kind of lantern or open-work cupola, decorated with wretched looking artificial flowers made of tin, and containing lamps that are lighted only on state occasions. Attached to the western extremity of this pavilion, is a small chapel belonging to the Copts. The entrance to the pavilion is raised a little above the rest of the floor, and is covered with a carpet, on which were seated numbers of beggars and decrepit folk, demanding alms of the devout pilgrims. From the top of this pavilion, and attached to the entrance of the Greek church floated blue silk banners. This building contains the holy sepulchre, into which all the monks and pilgrims enter barefooted, but our party were not required to take off their shoes. The pavilion is divided into two apartments; the outer one was handsomely decorated with different coloured marbles and lighted by lamps suspended from the roof. This apartment, which corresponds with the usual antichamber of Eastern tombs, especially those in Judea, has oval apertures on each side opening into the church. These are for the purpose of transmitting the light during the performance of the mummery of the "holy fire." In the centre stands a square stone, said to be that on which the angel sat when Mary came to visit the tomb. It is a piece of gray compact limestone, similar to that found in the vicinity of the city, and is supported by a pedestal not unlike that of a baptismal font. Opposite to this a low narrow door leads into the sepulchre, which was then so crammed with pilgrims, that for some minutes we found it impossible and unsafe to attempt an entrance. Could mirthful feelings have been indulged in such a place as this, the scene, which was ludicrous in the extreme, was well calculated to call them forth. Two pilgrims, perhaps a Greek and an Armenian, endeavouring to pass through the door together, and neither being disposed to yield in the holy struggle, they became jammed, and thus remained till both were forcibly ejected by someone from within, who had been himself, in turn, rudely thrust out by the Padre in attendance. Seeing a group of Franks waiting for admittance, some of the other visitors made way, and our attentive friend, the curate, soon pulled away the rest from about the door-way, crying out, "*Inglese, Inglese! Milordos Inglese!*" The sepulchre within is a square chamber, six feet nine inches every way; open at the top beneath the small cupola before mentioned, which here presented an open-work of marble of the most chaste and elegant workmanship. On the right hand side, an oblong slab of bluish white marble raised two feet above the floor, is supported by another of a similar form. The upper horizontal flag was cracked across the centre in the fire of 1808, and it has been actually worn down by the kisses of the many thousands of pilgrims who have visited this place for the last fifteen centuries. Within this coating is said to be the actual soros or trough in which the body of the Saviour was laid, and to protect it from being chipped, carried off as relics, or *kissed away*, this marble was enclosed. This may, to some, appear strange and unnecessary; yet, it is related by a chronicler of the Crusades, that the Count Anjou, one of the first pilgrims who visited this shrine, while in possession of the Mooslims, bit off and carried away a mouthful of the actual tomb without the infidels being aware of it !

CHAPTER TWO

Speranza, *Poems*

Speranza's poems for Irish revolutionary magazine The Nation *were her moment of early triumph and the making of her reputation as an Irish Nationalist poet. She began publishing these influential poems from the age of twenty-five, in 1846, writing letters under the pen name John Fanshawe Ellis, sending in the poems of Speranza.* The Nation *was founded in 1843 by Irish republican activists Thomas Davis, John Dillon, and Charles Gavan Duffy: the so-called Young Irelanders. Despite her Irish Protestant heritage, Speranza was said to have been inspired by the funeral of Thomas Davis in 1845 to write for Irish freedom. The editor of* The Nation *was prosecuted in 1846 and the paper itself was closed down and prosecuted in 1848 on account of her cry for revolution.*

"To Ireland"

I.

MY COUNTRY, wounded to the heart,
    Could I but flash along thy soul
Electric power to rive apart
    The thunder-clouds that round thee roll,
And, by my burning words uplift
Thy life from out Death's icy drift,
Till the full splendours of our age
Shone round thee for thy heritage –
As Miriam's, by the Red Sea strand
Clashing proud cymbals, so my hand
      Would strike thy harp,
      Loved Ireland!

II.

She flung her triumphs to the stars
    In glorious chants for freedom won,
While over Pharaoh's gilded cars
    The fierce, death-bearing waves rolled on;
I can but look in God's great face,
And pray Him for our fated race,
To come in Sinai thunders down,
And, with His mystic radiance, crown
Some Prophet-Leader, with command
To break the strength of Egypt's band,
      And set thee free,
      Loved Ireland!

III.
New energies, from higher source,
    Must make the strong life-currents flow,
As Alpine glaciers in their course
    Stir the deep torrents 'neath the snow.
The woman's voice dies in the strife
Of Liberty's awakening life;
We wait the hero heart to lead,
The hero, who can guide at need,
And strike with bolder, stronger hand,
Though towering posts his path withstand
        Thy golden harp,
        Loved Ireland!

IV.
For I can breathe no trumpet call,
    To make the slumb'ring Soul arise;
I only lift the funeral-pall,
    That so God's light might touch thine eyes,
And ring the silver prayer-bell clear,
To rouse thee from thy trance of fear;
Yet, if thy mighty heart has stirred,
Even with one pulse-throb at my word,
Then not in vain my woman's hand
Has struck thy gold harp while I stand,
        Waiting thy rise
        Loved Ireland!

"O'Connell"

[Died March 29, 1847]

HIBERNIÆ LIBERATOR AD LIMINA APOSTOLORUM PERGENS GENOÆ
OBDORMIVIT

Crowned with a liberated people's love,
Crowned by the Nations with eternal fame,
His great heart burning still with patriot-fire,
Tho' Death's pale shadow rested on his brow,
Forth went the mighty Chief from his loved Land,
'Mid the hushed reverence paid to dying Kings,
On his last pilgrimage; yearning to find rest
For the o'erwearied hero-heart and brain,
After great trials pass'd and triumphs won,
Within the Temple-City of the World.
But, faint with combats of a glorious life,
Tho' Freedom's hymns still murmured on his lips,
And his dim eyes still tracked the western Sun
Would rise on Ireland, but no more for him,
Seeking the gates of God's great Church on earth,
He found the gates of Heaven, and entered in
There Angels met him with the conqueror's Palm,
And passing from the portal to the Throne,
Circled with golden glitter of their wings,
God crowned him Victor for his work well done!

"France in '93"

[1847]

I.

Hark! the onward heavy tread –
　　Hark! the voices rude –
'Tis the famished cry for Bread
　　From a wildered multitude.
　　　　They come! They come!
　　　　Point the cannon – roll the drum;
Thousands wail and weep with hunger –
Faster let your soldiers number.
Sword, and gun, and bayonet
A famished people's cries have met.

II.

Hark! the onwards heavy tread –
　　Hark! the voices rude –
'Tis the famished cry for Bread
　　From and armed multitude.
　　　　They come! They come!
　　　　Not with meek submissions hum.
Bloody trophy they have won,
Ghastly glares it in the sun –
Gory head on lifted pike.
Ha! they weep not now, but strike.

III.

Ye, the deaf ones to their cries –
Ye, who scorned their agonies –
'Tis no longer prayers for bread
Shriek in your ears the famished;
But wildly, fiercely, peal on peal,
Resoundeth – Down with the Bastile!
Can ye tame a people now?
Try them – flatter, promise, vow,
Swear their wrongs shall be redressed –

But patience – time will do the rest;
Swear they shall one day be fed –
Hark! the People – Dead for Dead!

IV.
Calculating statement, quail;
Proud aristocrat, grow pale;
Savage sounds that deathly song:
Down with tyrants! Down with wrong!
Blindly now they wreak revenge –
How rudely do a mob avenge!
What! coronetted Prince or Peer,
Will not the base-born slavelings fear?
Sooth, their cry is somewhat stern:
Aristocrats, à la Lanterne!
Ghastly fruit their lances bear –
Noble heads with streaming hair;
Diadem and kingly crown
Strike the famine-stricken down.
Now, the People's work is done –
On they stride o'er prostrate throne;
Royal blood of King and Queen
Streameth from the guillotine;
Wildly on the people goeth,
Reaping what the noble soweth.
Little, dreamed he, prince or peer,
Of who should be his heritor.
Hunger now, at last, is sated
In halls where once it wailed and waited;
Wild Justice fiercely rives the laws
Which failed to right a people's cause.
On that human ocean floweth,
Whither stops it no one knoweth –
Surge the wild waves in their strength
Against all chartered rights at length –
Throne, and King, and Nobel fall;
But the People – they hold Carnival!

"The Faithless Shepherds"

"Os Habent, et non loquuntur:
Oculos habent, et non vident."

DEAD! – DEAD! Ye are dead while ye live;
 Ye've a name that ye live – but are dead.
Neither counsel nor love did ye give,
 And your lips never uttered a word
While swift ruin downward sped,
 And the plague raged on undisturbed.
Not a throb of true life in your veins,
 Not a pulse in your passionate heart,
Not a thought in your dull, cold brains,
 Of how ye should bear your part,
When summoned the strife to brave,
For our Country, with Death and the Grave.

Ye have gold for the follies of fashion,
 And gold for its tinsel glare,
But none for the wild, sobbing passion
 Wrung from the lips of despair.
False Shepherds and Guides are ye,
 For the heart in each bosom is cold
As the ice on a frozen sea;
 And your trappings of velvet and gold
Lie heavy and close as a pall,
When the steps of the bearers fall
On a grave, with measured tread;
For ye seem to live – but are dead.

Ye are dead! – ye are dead! stone by stone
The temple is crumbling down;
It will fall with a crash of doom,
For the night deepens dark in its gloom.
 But ye look on with vacant stare,

Like men lying still in the tomb.
    Stand forth! face the sun, if ye dare,
With your cold eyes unwet by a tear,
For your Country laid low on your bier,
And say – have ye stretched forth a hand
To raise up our desolate Land?

She dies – but ye flourish and grow
    In the midst of the deadly maze:
Like the palm springing heavenward? – No,
    But like weeds in the churchyard fed
By the vapours of death below,
    Breathing round you a poisonous haze.
Go! – go! True life is not so –
    For decay lies beneath your tread,
And the staff in your hand is a reed –
Too weak for your Country's need;
    For you seem to live – but are dead.

Ye are dead! – ye are dead! Fling the clay
    On the noble names – noble no more;
Leave the sword in the sheath to rust;
Let the banners be trailed in the dust;
And the memory perish away
    Of the dead, who are dead evermore;
Blot them out from the book writ in gold.
    Noble neither in deed nor in soul,
    Are ye worthy to stand in the roll
Of the glorified heroes of old?

Has Ireland need of such sons?
    Floating down with a silken sail,
On the crimson tide of her life, that runs
    With a mournful, ceaseless wail,
Like rain pouring down from the eaves.
And ye laugh when the strangers deride

Her trials, the saddest and sorest,
And plunge the sword deep in her side;
   And no kindly heart sighs or grieves
For her branches, all bare as a forest,
   When the autumn wind scatters the leaves.

Laugh low with your perfumed breath,
For the air is heavy with death.
But ye hear not the gliding feet
   Of the Future, that stands at your door;
For the roses lie heavy and sweet,
   And too thick on your marble floor,
And the dead soul is dead to his call.
   And your eyes are heavy with wine;
Ye see not the letters of flame,
   Traced by a hand divine –
The writing of God on the wall –
"Ye are weighed, and found wanting" – Oh shame!
      Your life is a gilded lie;
   And the wide world that doom has read,
   With a shudder and chill of dread;
For the judgment of God is nigh,
And the universe echoes the cry –
   You've a name that ye live – but are DEAD.

"The Stricken Land"

(later republished as "The Famine Year")
[January 1847]

I.

Weary men, what reap ye? – Golden corn for the stranger.
What sow ye? – Human corpses that wait for the avenger.
Fainting forms, hunger-stricken, what see you in the offing?
Stately ships to bear our food away, amid the stranger's scoffing.
There's a proud array of soldiers – what do they need round your door?
They guard our masters' granaries from the thin hands of the poor.
Pale mothers, wherefore weeping? – Would to God that we were dead –
Our children swoon before us, and we cannot give them bread.

II.

Little children, tears are strange upon your infant faces,
God meant you but to smile within your mother's soft embraces.
Oh! we know not what is smiling, and we know not what is dying;
But we're hungry, very hungry, and we cannot stop our crying.
And some of us grow cold and white – and we know not what it means;
But, as they lie beside us, we tremble in our dreams.
There's a gaunt crowd on the highway – are ye come to pray to man,
With hollow eyes that cannot weep, and for words your faces wan?

III.

No; the blood is dead within our veins – we care not now for life;
Let us die hid in the ditches, far from children and from wife;
We cannot stay and listen to their raving, famished cries –
Bread! Bread! Bread! and none to still their agonies.
We left our infants playing with their dead mother's hand:
We left our maidens maddened by the fever's scorching brand:
Better, maiden, thou were strangled in thy own dark-twisted tresses –
Better, infant, thou wert smothered in thy mother's first caresses.

IV.

We are fainting in our misery, but God will hear our groan;
Yet, if fellow-men desert us, will He hearken from His Throne?
Accursed are we in our own land, yet toil we still and toil;
But the stranger reaps our harvest – the alien owns our soil.
O Christ! how have we sinned, that on our native plains
We perish houseless, naked, starved, with branded brow, like Cain's?
Dying, dying, wearily, with a torture sure and slow –
Dying, as a dog would die, by the wayside as we go.

V.

One by one they're falling round us, their pale faces to the sky;
We've no strength left to dig them graves – there let them lie.
The wild bird, if he's stricken, is mourned by the others,
But we – we die in Christian land – we die amid our brothers,
In the land which God has given, like a wild beast in his cave,
Without a tear, a prayer, a shroud, a coffin, or a grave.
Ha! but think ye the contortions on each livid face ye see,
Will not be read on judgment-day by eyes of Deity?

VI.

We are wretches, famished, scorned, human tools to build your pride,
But God will yet take vengeance for the souls for whom Christ died.
Now is your hour of pleasure – bask ye in the world's caress;
But our whitening bones against ye will rise as witnesses,
From the cabins and the ditches, in the charred, uncoffin'd masses,
For the Angel of the Trumpet will know them as he passes.
A ghastly, spectral army, before the great God we'll stand,
And arraign ye as our murderers, the spoilers of our land.

"The Brothers"

[March 1847]

> a scene from '98.
> _____"Oh! give me *truths*,
> For I am weary of the surfaces,
> And die of inanition." – Emerson

I.
'TIS midnight, falls the lamp-light dull and sickly,
    On a pale and anxious crowd,
Through the court, and round the judges, thronging thickly,
    With prayers none dare to speak aloud.
Two youths, two noble youths, stand prisoners at the bar –
    You can see them through the gloom –
In pride of life and manhood's beauty, there they are
    Awaiting their death doom.

II.
All eyes an earnest watch on them are keeping,
    Some, sobbing, turn away,
And the strongest men can hardly see for weeping,
    So noble and so loved were they.
Their hands are locked together, those young brothers,
    As before the judge they stand –
They feel not the deep grief that moves the others,
    For they die for Fatherland.

III.
They are pale, but it is not fear that whitens
    On each proud, high brow,
For the triumph of the martyr's glory brightens
    Around them even now.
They sought to free their land from thrall of stranger;
    Was it treason? Let them die;

But their blood will cry to Heaven – the Avenger
    Yet will hearken from on high.

IV.

Before them, shrinking, cowering, scarcely human,
    The base informer bends,
Who, Judas-like, could sell the blood of true men,
    While he clasped their hands as friends.
Aye, could fondle the young children of his victim,
    Break bread with his young wife,
At the moment that for gold his perjured dictum
    Sold the husband and the father's life.

V.

There is silence in the midnight – eyes are keeping
    Troubled watch till forth the jury come;
There is silence in the midnight – eyes are weeping –
    "Guilty!" – is the fatal uttered doom.
For a moment o'er the brothers' noble faces
    Came a shadow sad to see;
Then silently they rose up in their places,
    And embraced each other fervently.

VI.

Oh! the rudest heart might tremble at such sorrow,
    The rudest cheek might blanch at such a scene:
Twice the judge essayed to speak the word – to-morrow –
    Twice faltered, as a woman he had been.
To-morrow! – Fain the elder would have spoken,
    Prayed for respite, tho' it is not death he fears;
But thoughts of home and wife his heart hath broken,
    And his words are stopped by tears.

VII.

But the youngest – oh, he spake out bold and clearly:–
    "I have no ties of children or of wife;

Let me die – but spare the brother who more dearly
  Is loved by me than life."
Pale martyrs, ye may cease, your days are numbered;
  Next noon your sun of life goes down;
One day between the sentence and the scaffold –
  One day between the torture and the crown!

VIII.

A hymn of joy is rising from creation;
  Bright the azure of the glorious summer sky;
But human hearts weep sore in lamentation,
  For the Brothers are led forth to die.
Aye, guard them with your cannon and your lances –
  So of old came martyrs to the stake;
Aye, guard them – see the people's flashing glances,
  For those noble two are dying for their sake.

IX.

Yet none spring forth their bonds to sever
  Ah! methinks, had I been there,
I'd have dared a thousand deaths ere ever
  The sword should touch their hair.
It falls! – there is a shriek of lamentation
  From the weeping crowd around;
They're stilled – the noblest hearts within the nation –
  The noblest heads lie bleeding on the ground.

X.

Years have passed since that fatal scene of dying,
  Yet, lifelike to this day,
In their coffins still those severed heads are lying,
  Kept by angels from decay.
Oh! they preach to us, those still and pallid features –
  Those pale lips yet implore us, from their graves,
To strive for our birthright as God's creatures,
  Or die, if we can but live as slaves.

CHAPTER THREE

William Wilde, *Austria, Its Literary, Scientific and Medical Institutions*, 1843

After a six-month stay in Vienna in 1840–41 to improve his medical knowledge of ophthalmic and aural surgery, William Wilde visited Bavaria, Prague, and Berlin, with letters from the Irish novelist Maria Edgeworth opening doors for him. On his return, he wrote his second travel book, Austria, Its Literary, Scientific and Medical Institutions, *appearing in 1843 through the same publishers as his previous book: William Curry in Dublin and Longman in London. In his preface, Wilde commented that the "difficulty of obtaining accurate information on any matter connected with state policy is greater in the Austrian empire than (Russia not accepted) anywhere else in Europe." Perhaps because of these restrictions,* Austria *is a difficult read, without any of the energy of his first travel book, focusing mainly on education, science, medical practice, and the hospitals of the Austrian empire. In the following section, Wilde's enlightened view on the treatment of mental illness is evident.*

The Lunatic Asylum

Chapter X

THE IRRENTHURM – ITS SITUATION – WARDS – IMPROPER TREATMENT OF
THE INSANE – COMPARISON WITH THAT AT PRAGUE – THE LAZARETH –
ASYLUM AT YBBS – STATISTICS OF INSANE IN LOWER AUSTRIA.

The Lunatic Asylum – *Die Irrenanstalt*. This great division of the establishment is situated to the north of the *Krankenhaus*, between it and the
Military Hospital, from each of which it can be entered. It consists of
two compartments – the madhouse, where the violent and incurable are
confined; a prison, which I rejoice to say, is now scarcely known in the rest
of Europe; and the *Lazareth*, which is more of the nature of the ordinary
lunatic asylums of this country: the entire is capable of receiving as many
as three hundred and seventy patients. The former (the *Irrenthurm* or
Narrenthurm), is a huge circular tower, standing apart from the rest of the
buildings, constructed in the form of a cylinder, five stories high, with a
yard in the centre, and containing one hundred and thirty-nine wards and
cells, with beds for two hundred and fifty lunatics. The floor and ceilings
are stone-arched, and round the inner wall runs a corridor, from which
the cells radiate outward in each story; the whole is heated on the same
principle as the General Hospital.

The tower was built in 1784, at a period when the object was to secure
the greatest number of insane within the least possible space, and when
lunatic asylums were the very worst description of gaols, erected and
conducted without regard to health, cleanliness, or the hope of amending
the condition of their unhappy inmates; and, I regret to say, that as far as
my inspection of it was permitted – on two several occasions – as such it
remains to this day, a wretched, filthy prison, close and ill-ventilated, its
smell overpowering, and the sight of its unfortunate occupants, frantic,
chained, and many of them naked – disgusting to the visitor. With the
greatest care and under the kindest treatment, insanity is ever humiliating,
even to those accustomed to its horrors; but here it was, and I fear still is,
sickening to behold.

On the first morning that I visited it, a crowd of country folk, many
of whom were women, waited for admittance at the massive outer grating.

The bars and bolts having been withdrawn, they were conducted through the corridors along with me, as a mere matter of curiosity, or as one would go to see a collection of wild beasts; and wild they certainly were – the few who had by long-continued custom become thus familiar with, or indifferent to, the public gaze, had their peculiar energies soon lashed to frenzy, by the inhuman taunt of some hardened keeper, who was more than once called up by our conductor to excite the impotent rage of some particular individual, perhaps by allusion to the very cause of his or her insanity: all this was for the gratification of the rustic visitors. Further details are, I feel, superfluous; but since I visited Grand Cairo, I have not witnessed such a scene. This state of things in a city calling itself civilized, and under the very nose of monarchy, surprised me the more, for, that one of the best managed institutions of the kind I have ever seen is that at Prague, under the direction of the intelligent and philanthropic Dr. Riedel, and those of Berlin and other parts of Germany, are models for general imitation. Some years ago, Austria, impressed with the wretched condition of the Vienna lunatic asylum, sent a young physician to travel and collect information on the subject of the care of the insane of other countries. Dr. Julius, of philanthropic celebrity, has informed me that the report of this gentleman was a very good one, and ably drawn up; yet, still, this blot upon humanity is permitted to exist as an "Imperial Royal Institution."

Next is the *Lazareth*, a very old building that was formerly used as a plague hospital. It is separated from the tower by a yard and the botanic garden of the Josephinum Academy. It consists of two separate compartments, with five male and six female wards, besides twelve separate rooms for patients of a higher class – the whole number of beds being one hundred and twenty. This division of the asylum I found clean and orderly, though, as a house of recovery, the treatment still adopted there is but little conducive. The milder cases, and those still considered within the pale of hope and art, are received into this division, which has a garden attached to it for the use of the patients. Pupils are not admitted to the wards of the asylum; nor does the subject of insanity form a portion of practical medical instruction in Austria; a circumstance to be regretted in a country where so many are afflicted with that awful visitation, and the great majority of whose institutions for the insane are under such bad management.

The number of incurable lunatics having within the last few years increased so much, that they could not be provided for in the *Irrenthurm*, the extensive asylum at Ybbs has been erected. This is beautifully situated on the Danube, about two days' journey from Vienna, towards Upper Austria, and it has accommodation for from three hundred and thirty to three hundred and sixty patients. To this, the surplus of the quiet, but incurable insane, are sent yearly from the *Irrenthurm*. It is, I understand, tolerably well conducted, and its delightful and healthful situation must, no doubt, contribute much to the comfort, if not the health of its residents; that it has the latter power, we learn from the fact, that upwards of five per cent. permanently recover, of those who had been for years before confined in the tower and were pronounced incurable.

Accurate *post mortem* examinations are made of all the insane that die in the *Irrenanstalt*.

The receptions into these institutions are as follows:– There are three paying classes, and one received gratis; their *Kreis*, or the district from which they come, defraying their expenses. The first class pays forty florins monthly; or fifty florins, if they require a separate room and attendance. The second pays twenty-six, and the third, nine florins monthly.

The attendants consist of one *Primararzt*, who is over all; two secondary physicians, two secondary surgeons and two Practicants, with thirty male and twenty-eight female nurses, besides porters and other servants.

CHAPTER FOUR

Speranza, "Jacta Alea Est," *The Nation*, July 1948

On July 29, 1848, Speranza published her call to revolution, "Jacta Alea Est," the lead article for The Nation. *Partly as a result of this article, the police in Dublin closed down the journal and proceedings against the editor commenced, and this essay would earn Speranza the name of Madame Roland of the Irish Gironde. Charles Gavan Duffy was tried for treason in February 1849 and Speranza attended the trial. In later life, it was claimed that she stood up in court and said, "I am the culprit, if culprit there be," but her cries were not heeded and the charges against Duffy were eventually dropped. Below is an extract from the full text.*

The Irish Nation has at length decided. England has done us one good service at least. Her recent acts have taken away the last miserable pretext for passive submission. She has justified us before the world, and ennobled the timid, humble supplication of a degraded, insulted people, into the proud demand for independence by a resolved, prepared, and fearless Nation.

Now, indeed, were the men of Ireland *cowards* if this moment for retribution, combat, and victory, were to pass by unemployed. It finds them slaves, but it would leave them infamous.

Oh! for a hundred thousand muskets glittering brightly in the light of heaven, and the monumental barricades stretching across each of our noble streets, made desolate by England – circling around that doomed Castle [*Dublin Castle, seat of British administration in Ireland*], made infamous by England, where the foreign tyrant has held his council of treason and iniquity against our people and our country for seven hundred years.

Courage rises with danger, and heroism with resolve. Does not our breath come freer, each heart beat quicker in these rare and grand moments of human life, when all doubt and wavering, and weakness are cast to the winds, and the soul rises majestic over each petty obstacle, each low, selfish consideration, and, flinging off the fetters of prejudice, bigotry, and egotism, bounds forward into the higher, diviner life of heroism and patriotism, defiant as a conqueror, devoted as a martyr, omnipotent as a Deity!

We appeal to the whole Irish Nation – is there any man amongst us who wishes to take one further step on the base path of sufferance and slavery? Is there one man who thinks that Ireland has not been sufficiently insulted, that Ireland has not been sufficiently degraded in her honour and her rights to justify her now in fiercely turning upon her oppressor? No! a man so infamous cannot tread the earth; or, if he does, the voice of the coward is stifled in clear, wild, ringing shout that leaps from hill to hill, that echoes from sea to sea, that peals from the lips of an uprising Nation – "We must be free!"

In the name then of your trampled, insulted, degraded country; in the name of all heroic virtues, of all that makes life illustrious or death divine; in the name of your starved, your exiled, your *dead*; by your martyrs in prison cells and felon chains; in the name of God and man;

by the listening earth and the watching heaven, I call on you to make this aspiration of your souls a *deed*. Even as you read these weak words of a heart that yet palpitates with an enthusiasm as heroic as your own, and your breast heaves and your eyes grow dim with tears as the memory of Ireland's wrongs rushes upon your soul – even now lift up your right hand to swear – swear by your undying soul, by your hopes of immortality, never to lay down your arms, never to cease hostilities, till you regenerate and save this fallen land.

Gather round the standard of your chiefs. Who dares to say he will not follow, when O'Brien leads? Or who amongst you is so abject that he will grovel in the squalid misery of his hut, or be content to be flung from the ditch side into the living tomb of the poorhouse, rather than charge proudly like brave men and free men, with that glorious young Meagher at their head, upon the hired mercenaries of their enemies? One bold, one decisive move. One instant to take breath, and then a rising; a rush, a charge from north, south, east and west upon the English garrison, and *the land is ours*. Do your eyes flash, do your hearts throb at the prospect of having a *country*? For you have had no country. You have never felt the pride, the dignity, the majesty of independence. You could never lift up your head to heaven and glory in the name of Irishman, for all Europe read the brand of *slave* upon your brow.

Oh! that my words could burn like molten metal through your veins, and light up this ancient heroic darling which would make each man of you a Leonidas – each battle-field a Marathon – each pass a Thermopylae. Courage! need I preach to Irishmen of courage? Is it so hard a thing then to die? Alas! do we not all die daily of broken hearts and shattered hopes, and tortures of mind and body that make life a weariness, and of weariness worse even than the tortures; for life is one long, slow agony of death.

No! it cannot be death you fear; for you have braved the plague in the exile ship of the Atlantic, and plague in the exile's home beyond it; and famine and ruin, and a slave's life, and a dog's death; and hundreds, thousands, a *million of* you have perished thus. Courage! You will not now belie those old traditions of humanity that tell of this divine God-gift within us. I have read of a Roman wife who stabbed herself before her husband's eyes to teach him how to die. These million deaths teach us as grand a lesson. To die for Ireland! Yes; have we not sworn it in a thousand passionate words by our poets and orators – in our grave resolves of councils, leagues and confederations? Now is the moment to test whether you value most freedom or life. Now is the moment to strike, and by striking save, and the day after the victory, it will be time enough to count your dead.

But we do not provoke this war. History will write of us – that Ireland endured wrongs unexampled by any despotism – sufferings unequalled by any people – her life-blood drained by a vampire host of foreign masters and officials – her honour insulted in a paid army of spies – her cries of despair stifled by the armed hand of legalised ruffianism – that her peasants starved while they reaped the corn for their foreign lords, because no man gave them bread – that her pallid artisans pined and wasted, because no man gave them work – that her men of genius, the noblest and purest of her sons, were dragged to a felon's cell, lest the people might hear the voice of *truth*, and that in this horrible atrophy of all mental and physical powers, this stagnation of all existences, whoever dared to rise and demand wherefore it was that Ireland, made so beautiful by God, was made the plague spot of the universe by man – he was branded as a *felon* – imprisoned, robbed, tortured, chained, exiled, murdered. Thus history will write of us. And she will also write, that Ireland did not start from this horrible trance of suffering and despair until 30,000 swords were at her heart, and even then she did not rise for vengeance, only *prepared to resist*. No – we are not the aggressors – we do not provoke this terrible war – even with six million hearts to aid us, and with all the chances of success in our favour we still offer terms to England. If she capitulates even now at the eleventh hour, and grants the moderate, the just demands of Ireland, our arms shall not be raised to sever the golden link that unites the two nations. And the chances of success *are* all with us.

CHAPTER FIVE

William Wilde, *The Closing Years of the Life of Dean Swift,* 1849

William came back from Austria in 1841 and set up his own hospital in Dublin, soon becoming a successful and well-respected doctor. He was editor of the Dublin Quarterly of Medical Science *from 1845 until 1850. In that capacity, William received a letter from a Dr William Mackenzie, asking about Swift's medical history and querying the widely held belief that Swift had died insane. This readable text is the result, with William Wilde's meticulous recounting of the symptoms of Swift's life and final illness supporting a very persuasive argument that Swift was not insane but suffering from an inner ear ailment that lead to his infirmity and his disorientation. William spends a great deal of time discussing the skull and the death mask of Swift, drawing on his medical knowledge to speculate on the nature of one of Ireland's most celebrated writers. This is one of William Wilde's most enjoyable studies, particularly his musings on the triangulated relationship between Stella, Swift, and Vanessa. (In a later chapter, I include an extract from Speranza's essay on the same topic.) Below is a series of extracts from William's appendix on the question of Swift's relationship to Stella and their marriage: perhaps the most interesting part of the study.*

Swift and Stella

The accusation of the greatest heartlessness with which Swift has been ever branded, and, indeed, the story which, if true, tells most forcibly against him, is that related by Sheridan of a circumstance connected with the death of Stella. It runs thus:– when this lady saw her end approaching, she adjured Swift, in the presence of Dr. Sheridan, and in the most earnest and pathetic terms, to grant her as a dying request, "that as the ceremony of marriage had passed between them, though, for sundry reasons, they had not cohabited in that state, in order to put it out of the power of slander to be busy with her fame after death, she adjured him, by their friendship, to let her have the satisfaction of dying at least, though she had not lived, his acknowledged wife. Swift made no reply, but, turning on his heel, walked silently out of the room, *nor ever saw her afterwards during the short time she lived.* This behaviour threw Mrs. Johnson into unspeakable agonies, and for a time she sunk under the weight of so cruel a disappointment. *But soon after, roused by indignation, she inveighed against his cruelty in the bitterest terms; and, sending for a lawyer, made her will, bequeathing her fortune, by her own name, to charitable uses.* This was done in the presence of Dr. Sheridan, whom she appointed one of her executors."

This story, however, must be received with some degree of caution. The popular opinion is, that the Rev. Dr. Sheridan, the friend of Swift, is the author of the Life of that great genius, and, consequently, of this story: but this is an error. The Thomas Sheridan who wrote the Life of Swift must have been a mere child at the time when this circumstance occurred; he was only a lad when his father, of whom he is said to have received it, died; and the first edition of the work in which it was published did not appear till fifty years after the occurrence is said to have taken place. In this printed tradition it is made to appear that Stella left her fortune for charitable purposes, and, consequently, away from Swift, on account of the cruel treatment just related. That this was not the case may be learned from a letter which Swift had previously addressed to his friend Worrall upon the subject of Stella's will. During one of her severe illnesses, while Swift was in London, in 1726, he writes: "I wish it could be brought about that she might make her will. Her intentions are to leave the interest of all her fortune to her *mother and sister during their lives, afterwards to Dr.*

Steevens's Hospital, to purchase lands for such uses as she designs. Now such was not only the tenor but the very words of the will made two years afterwards, which Sheridan would have his readers believe was made in pique at the Dean's conduct.

...

From what we can glean from authentic sources, it would appear that Stella died of consumption, at the age of 47, the Dean being then aged 61, broken down in health by a most distressing malady, disappointed in his hopes, and rendered morose and discontented by those causes, physical and moral, to which we have already alluded. If Stella's death was caused by love, then indeed that affection must be of a more chronic character than poets and novelists would lead us to suppose.

We can perfectly understand how a person of Swift's peculiar temperament, and past sixty years of age, should be unwilling to witness the last moments of one so dear to him as Stella. "I would not," he writes to Mr. Worrall, in the letter already quoted from, "for the universe be present at such a trial as seeing her depart. She will be among friends that, upon her own account and great worth, will tend her with all possible care, *where I should be a trouble to her,* and the greatest torment to myself." The same expression he repeats to Dr. Sheridan: "Nay, if I were now near her I would not see her; I could not behave myself tolerably, and should redouble her sorrow." But that this was not from indifference may be gleaned from the following expressions to the same friend: "I know not whether it be an addition to my grief or not that I am now extremely ill; for it would have been a reproach to me to be in perfect health when such a friend is desperate. I do profess upon my salvation, that this distressed and desperate condition of our friend makes life so indifferent to me, who, by course of nature, have so little left, that I do not think it worth the time to struggle. Yet I should think, according to what hath been formerly, that I may happen to overcome the present disorder; and to what advantage? Why, to see the loss of that person for whose sake only life was worth preserving."

To Dr. Stopford he writes from London, in 1726, on the same subject: "I never was in so great a dejection of spirits. For I lately received a letter from Mr. Worrall, that one of the two oldest and dearest friends I have in the world is in so desperate a condition of health, as makes me expect every post to hear of her death. It is the younger of the two, with whom I have lived in the greatest friendship for thirty-three years. I know you will share in my trouble, because there were few persons whom I believe you more esteemed. For my part, as I value life very little, so the poor casual remains of it, after such a loss, would be a burden that I must heartily beg God Almighty to enable me to bear; and I think there is not a greater folly than that of entering into too strict and particular a friendship, with the loss of which a man must be absolutely miserable; but especially at an age when it is too late to engage in a new friendship. Besides, this was a person of my own rearing and instructing from childhood; who excelled in every good quality that can possibly accomplish a human creature. They have hitherto writ me deceiving letters, but Mr. Worrall has been so just and prudent as to tell me the truth, which, however racking, is better than to be struck on the sudden."

During the latter part of January, 1728, Swift was very ill and confined to the house. He received the account of Stella's death on Sunday evening, at 8 o'clock, about two hours after it occurred. She was buried by torch-light, on Tuesday, the 30th of January, in the same manner as the Dean directed himself to be buried, and nearly at the same hour. In his "Character of Mrs. Johnson," Swift thus alludes to the circumstance: "This is the night of the funeral, which my sickness will not suffer me to attend. It is now 9 at night, and I am removed into another apartment that I may not see the light in the church, which is just over against the window of my bed-chamber."

Although they never lived together as man and wife, it is generally believed that Esther Johnson and Dean Swift were married, – nay, the very date (1716) has been specified; and it is said that the ceremony was performed by Dr. St. George Ashe, Bishop of Clogher, in the garden of the Deanery, *without witnesses*; but it may be said that the evidence of this rests on questionable authority. For ourselves, we acknowledge that, notwith-standing all the powerful arguments and astute criticism of Mr. W. Monck Mason, in his learned History of the Cathedral of St. Patrick, we incline to the belief that the mere legal ceremony of marriage was absolutely performed. This persuasion is not, however, from any positive evidence of the fact, but has arisen from its being frequently repeated by Swift's biographers, inferred from collateral circumstances, and admitted by some of his personal friends. In 1752, seven years after the death of Swift, and twenty-four years after the death of Stella, Lord Orrery first promulgated the idea of this marriage. Delany tacitly acknowledges the fact in his "Observations"; the Sheridans, father and son, appeared to believe it; so did Mr. Monck Berkeley, Mr. Deane Swift, Faulkner, Dr. Hawkesworth, and others who lived nearest the Dean's time; and Sir Walter Scott, who also believed in the marriage, has collected all the information bearing upon the subject, and added some new testimony, though not of a very satisfactory description.

...

The cranium of Stella, of which the accompanying is an engraving, was exhumed from the vaults of St. Patrick's Cathedral, along with that of Swift, in 1835. "The coffin in which it lay was of the same material, and placed in the same relation to the pillar bearing the tablet to her memory, as that of the Dean; and the bones constituting the skeleton exhibited the same characters, and were in equally perfect preservation, though interred ten [seventeen] years earlier. Its exact and proper place was well known, and no other coffin lay near it from which any confusion might have arisen."

As may be seen by the foregoing representation, this skull is a perfect model of symmetry and beauty. Its outline is one of the most graceful we have ever seen; the teeth, which, for their whiteness and regularity, were, in life, the theme of general admiration, were, perhaps, the most perfect ever witnessed in a skull. On the whole, it is no great stretch of the imagination to clothe and decorate this skull again with its alabaster skin, on which the rose had slightly bloomed; to adorn it with its original luxuriant dark hair, its white, expanded forehead, its level, pencilled eye-brows, and deep, dark, lustrous eyes, its high prominent nose, its delicately chiselled mouth, and pouting upper lip, its full, rounded chin, and long but gracefully swelling neck, – when we shall find it realize all that description has handed down to us of an intellectual beauty of the style of those painted by Kneller, and with an outline and form of head accurately corresponding to the pictures of Stella which still exist.

CHAPTER SIX

Speranza, *Sidonia the Sorceress*, 1849

Speranza began her translation of the German novel, Sidonia
von Borcke, *by J. W. Meinhold, in 1847, and published her two-
volume version in 1849, although keeping her name from the title
page. The original novel was inspired by the real-life Sidonia, who
was burned in 1620 as a witch for her many crimes. Speranza's
translation is pacey and lively, a full account of the ways in which
the evil Sidonia seduces and murders to her heart's content, only
to die suitably punished. This was an influence on Dante Gabriel
Rossetti, who read her translation in 1851 and pronounced it a
masterpiece. The cultural influence of Speranza's translation was
profound: Walter Pater wrote of it, as did Swinburne; Charlotte
Brontë read it and included references to it in her novel* Villette;
*Edward Burne-Jones painted on the theme. Speranza's son Oscar
said it was his favorite book as a child!*

Chapter 1
Of the Education of Sidonia

The illustrious and high-born prince and Lord, Bogislaff, 14th Duke of Pomerania, Prince of Cassuben, Wenden, and Rugen, Count of Güzkow, Lord of the lands of Lauenburg and Butow, and my gracious feudal seigneur, having commanded me, Dr. Theodore Plönnnies, formerly bailiff at the ducal court, to make search throughout all the land for information respecting the world-famed sorceress, Sidonia von Bork, and write down the same in a book, I set out for Stargard, accompanied by a servant, early one Friday after the *Visitationis Mariæ*, 1629; for, in my opinion, in order to form a just judgment respecting the character of any one, it is necessary to make one's self acquainted with the circumstances of their early life; the future man lies enshrined in the child, and the peculiar development of each individual nature is the result of entirely of education. Sidonia's history is a remarkable proof of this. I visited first, therefore, the scenes of her early years; but almost all who had known her were long since in their graves, seeing that ninety years had passed since the time of her birth. However, the old innkeeper at Stargard, Zabel Wiese, himself very far advanced in years ... told me that the old bachelor, Claude Uckermann of Dalow, an aged man of ninety-two years old, was the only person who could give me the information I desired, as in his youth he had been one of the many followers of Sidonia. His memory was certainly well nigh gone from age, still all that had happened in the early period of his life lay as fresh as the Lord's Prayer upon his tongue. Mine host also related some important circumstances to me myself, which shall appear in their proper place.

I accordingly proceeded to Dalow, a little town half a mile from Stargard, and visited Claude Uckermann. I found him seated by the chimney corner, his hair as white as snow. "What did I want? He was too old to receive strangers; I must go on to his son Wedig's house, and leave him in quiet," &c. &c. But when I said that I brought him a greeting from his Highness, his manner changed, and he pushed the seat over for me beside the fire, and began to chat first about the fine pine-trees, from which he cut his fire-wood, they were so full of resin; and how his son, a year before, had found an iron pot in the turf moor under a tree, full of bracelets and ear-rings, which his little grand-daughter now wore.

When he had tired himself out, I communicated what his highness had so nobly commanded to be done, and prayed him to relate all he knew and could remember of this detestable sorceress, Sidonia von Bork. He sighed deeply and then went on talking for about two hours, giving me all his recollections just as they started to his memory. I have arranged what he then related, in proper order. It was to the following effect:–

Whenever his father, Philip Uckermann, attended the fair at Stramehl, a town belonging to the Bork family, he was in the habit of visiting Otto von Bork at his castle, who, being very rich, gave free quarters to all the young noblemen in the vicinity, so that from thirty to forty of them were generally assembled at his castle while the fair lasted; but after some time his father discontinued these visits, his conscience not permitting him further intercourse. The reason was this. Otto von Bork, during his residence in Poland, had joined the sect of the Enthusiasts, and had lost his faith there, as a young maiden might her honour. He made no secret of his new opinions, but openly at Martinmas fair, 1560, told the young nobles at dinner that Christ was but a man like other people, and ignorance alone had elevated him to a God; which notion had been encouraged by the greed and the avarice of the clergy. They should, therefore, not credit what the hypocritical priests chattered to them every Sunday, but believe only what reason and their five senses told them was the truth, and that, in fine, if he had his will, he would send every priest to the devil.

All the young nobles remained silent but Claude Zastrow, a feudal retainer of the Borks, who rose up (it was an evil moment to him) and ma[d]e answer – "Most powerful feudal lord, were the holy apostles then filled with greed and covetousness, who were the first to proclaim that Christ was God, and who left all for his sake? Or the early Christians who, with one accord, sold their possessions, and gave the price to the poor." Claude had before this displeased the knight, who now grew red with anger at the insolence of his vassal in thus answering him, and replied, "If they were not preachers for gain, they were at least stupid fellows." Hereupon a great murmur arose in the hall, but the aforesaid Zastrow is not silenced, and answered, "It is surprising, then, that the twelve stupid apostles performed more than twelve times twelve Greek or Roman philosophers. The knight might rage until he was black in the face, and strike the table. But, he had better hold his tongue and use his understanding; though, after all, the intellect of a man who believed nothing but what he received through his five senses was not worth much; for the brute beasts were his equals, inasmuch as they received no evidence either but from the senses."

Then Otto sprang up raging, and asked him what he meant, to which the other answered: "Nothing more than to express his opinion that man differed from the brute, not through his understanding, but by his faith, for that animals had evidently understanding, but no trace of faith had ever been discovered in them."

Otto's rage now knew no bounds, and he drew his dagger, roaring, "What! thou insolent knave, dost thou dare to compare thy feudal lord to a brute?" And before the other had time to draw his poignard to defend himself, or the guests could in any way interfere to prevent him, Otto stabbed him to the heart, as he sat there by the table. (It was a blessed death, I think, to die for his Lord Christ.)

...

After that, he fell into disrepute with the old nobility, for which he cared little, seeing that his riches and magnificence always secured him companions enough, who were willing to listen to his wisdom, and were consoled by his wine.

...

As to Otto, no one observed any sign of repentance in him. On the contrary, he seemed to glory in his crime, and the neighbouring nobles related that he frequently brought his little daughter Sidonia, whom he adored for her beauty, to the assembled guests, magnificently attired; and when she was bowing to the company, he would say, "Who art thou, my little daughter?" then she would cease the salutations which she had learned from her mother, and drawing herself up, proudly exclaim, "I am a noble maiden, dowered with towns and castles!" Then he would ask, if the conversation turned upon his enemies – and half the nobles were so – "Sidonia, how does thy father treat his enemies?" Upon which the child would straighten her finger, and running at her father, strike it into his heart, saying, "*Thus* he treats them." At which Otto would laugh loudly, and tell her to show him how the knave looked when he was dying. Then Sidonia would fall down, twist her face, and writhe her little hands and feet in horrible contortions. Upon which Otto would lift her up, and kiss her upon the mouth. But it will be seen how the just God punished him for all this, and how the words of the Scriptures were fulfilled: "Err not, God is not mocked; for what a man soweth, that shall he also reap."

The parson of Stramehl, David Dilavius, related also to old Ucker-mann another fact, which, though it hardly seems credible, the bachelor reported thus to me:–

This Dilavius was a learned man whom Otto had selected as instructor to his young daughter, "but only teach her," he said, "to read and write, and the first article of the Ten Commandments. The other Christian doctrines I can teach her myself; besides, I do not wish the child to learn so many dogmas."

Dilavius, who was a worthy matter-of-fact, good simple character, did as he was ordered, and gave himself no further trouble until he came to ask the child to recite the first article of the creed out of the catechism for him. There was nothing wrong in that; but when he came to the second article, he crossed himself, not because it concerned the Lord Christ, but her own Father, Otto von Bork, and ran somewhat thus:–

"And I believe in my earthly father, Otto von Bork, a distinguished son of God, born of Anna von Kleist, who sitteth in his castle in Stramehl, from whence he will come to help his children and friends, but to slay his enemies and tread them in the dust."

The third article was much in the same style, but he had partly forgotten it, neither could he remember if Dilavius had called the father to any account for his profanity, or taught the daughter some better Chris-tian doctrine. In fine, this was all the old bachelor could tell me of Sidonia's education. Yes – he remembered one anecdote more. Her father had asked her one day, when she was about ten or twelve years old, "What kind of a husband she would like?" and she replied, "One of equal birth." "Who is her equal in the whole of Pomerania?" "Only the Duke of Pomerania, or the Count von Ebersburg." Right! therefore she must never marry any other but one of these."

It happened soon after, old Philip Uckermann, his father, riding one day through the fields near Stramehl, saw a country-girl seated by the road-side, weeping bitterly. "Why do you weep?" he asked. "Has any one injured you?" "Sidonia has injured me," she replied. "What could she have done? Come dry your tears, and tell me." Whereupon the little girl related that Sidonia, who was then about fourteen, had besought her to tell her what marriage was, because her father was always talking to her about it. The girl told her to the best of her ability, but the young lady beat her, and said it was not so, that long Dorothy had told her quite differently about marriage, and there she went on tormenting her for several days, but upon this evening Sidonia, with long Dorothy, and some of the milk-maids of the neighbourhood, had taken away one of the fine geese which the peasants had given her in payment of her labour. They picked it alive, all except the head and neck, then built up a large fire in a circle, and put the goose and a vessel of water in the centre. So the fat dripped down from the poor creature alive, and was fried in a pan as it fell, just as the girls eat it on their bread for supper. And the goose, having no means of escape, still went on drinking the water as the fat dripped down, whilst they kept cooling its head and heart with a sponge dipped in cold water, fastened to a stick, until at last the goose fell down when quite roasted, though it still screamed, and then Sidonia and her companions cut it up for their amuse-ment, living as it was, and ate it for their supper, in proof of which, the girl showed him the bones and the remains of the fire, and the drops of fat still lying on the grass.

Then she wept afresh, for Sidonia had promised to take away a goose every day, and destroy it as she had done the first. So my father consoled her by giving her a piece of gold, and said, "If she does so again, run by night and cloud, and come to Dalow by Stargard, where I will make thee keeper of my geese." But she never came to him, and he never heard more of the maiden and her geese.

CHAPTER SEVEN

William Wilde, *The Beauties of the Boyne and the Blackwater*, 1850

William's charming account of the River Boyne, republished in the following year in an expanded edition (the edition used here), was to prove one of his most popular books and the one that stayed in print for most of his lifetime. William fished along the river and loved it, and he fills the book with legends and stories from Irish history. In this section, William discusses historical accounts of the Battle of the Boyne, a key moment in the defeat of Catholic Ireland and a founding moment for Irish Protestant Unionism. Evidence of the growing relationship between William and Speranza can be taken from the fact that Speranza had reviewed some of his essays on Irish popular superstitions published in the Dublin University Magazine. *William, in his turn, quoted a stanza of her verse in this book.*

The Battle-Field of Oldbridge – Duleek

We suppose our readers are already acquainted with the political events which led to the "Battle of the Boyne," and of the details of the campaign, from the time of the landing of King William III to the end of the month of June, 1690; and as we have neither space nor desire to discuss the various political circumstances which led to this engagement, nor at all to enter into the general history of the country prior to this event, we shall here chiefly confine ourselves to a topographical description of the battle-field and a brief narrative of the fight, not only because they are more immediately connected with the object of this work, but on account of the discrepancies which, from their want of knowledge of those subjects, appear in the writings of various authors, historians, and tourists, hereto-fore considered authorities. And now as we approach the spot on which, for the last time in Great Britain, the crown of these realms was contested by kings in person, it is our duty to present our readers with a picture of the scene, and to point out to those who may visit the place, the most memorable and best authenticated localities.

…

King James's army, having fallen back towards Leinster, passed through Drogheda, and occupied the northern face of the hill of Donore, and the sloping ground between that elevation and the fords near Oldbridge, within the sweep of the river already alluded to. The Irish cannon, then consisting of twelve field-pieces, were planted upon two elevations commanding the fords, one a little to the south of Oldbridge village, which was here inter-sected by narrow lanes; the other nearly opposite the Yellow Island, on some projecting hillocks in advance of the right of the Irish lines; the latter place is now marked by a fir plantation. According to Story's map, a third small battery was placed opposite the ford, near the Mattock river. Some temporary, and it would appear very inefficient breast-works were also thrown up in front of the village, which was chiefly occupied by the Irish soldiery under Tirconnell.

James and his staff took up a position on the summit of the elevation of Donore, in the little church on which the deposed monarch, it is said, slept the night before the battle.

Upon the left, or Louth bank of the river, a bluff hill, sloping off upon its northern face, continues on from Townley Hall towards Drogheda, intersected here and there by deep, narrow defiles, which run down toward the water's edge; behind it is the rising ground of Tullyallen, where the site of King William's camp is still pointed out. At the end of Townley Hall demesne, a deep, narrow gorge, now generally known as King William's Glen, opens out upon the river, from which it is not more than three hundred paces distant, and, owing to the circumstance of a projecting brow of the hill through which it cuts, as well as its winding direction, the view up this valley is completely obscured, so that a whole army, of many thousand men, within it, might be screened from cannon-shot, and hid from observation, even from the eminences on the opposite side. On the high bank above, and to the east of this valley, was placed King William's chief battery, consisting of about fifty heavy guns and some field mortars.

William and his army marched in two columns from Ardee, upon the 30th of June. Having arrived within view of Drogheda, the position of the Irish encampment, stretching along the slopes of Donore, was at once recognised. A person standing upon any of the elevations in that neighbourhood, could with ease recognise every tent in the Irish camp; and, looking up the charming valley of the Boyne from this spot, over the scene which the celebrated tourist, Arthur Young, said, was "one of the completest landscapes he had ever seen," William may well have given utterance to the exclamation, "Well, it is a country worth fighting for!" The English army then turned slightly westward along the northern slope of the ridge we have described, and by which it was in a great measure concealed from the Irish, and took up its position nearly parallel with the Boyne; its right descending into the hollow of the King's Glen, and its left resting in another narrow ravine, at the eastern extremity of the hill, and very similar to the former. It had thus the advantage of being able to reach the Boyne in a few minutes through either of those two deep, narrow ravines; and William not only had this advantage of position, but, while his own army was completely concealed from view, every tent in that of his opponent was plainly mapped before him, and many of them within point-blank range of his cannon. The English being encamped, and their batteries erected, the firing commenced upon both sides, and was

continued during the greater portion of the day. The old ballad says, and
perhaps truly:

> "King James he pitched his tents between
>   The lines, *for to retire*,
> But King William threw his bomb-balls in,
>   And set them all on fire,"

alluding, no doubt, to James's intention of retreating, and to the murderous
effect of the heavy English artillery, which it is stated soon dismounted
two of the enemy's guns.

It is related, that the Prince of Orange (William III) rode with his
staff along the heights which run parallel with the river. George Story, a
chaplain in the English army, and an eye-witness of the scene, relates the
following incident, which we insert, principally because we have been
enabled, from a very careful examination of the locality, to decide upon
the exact spot where it occurred.

"His majesty rid on to the pass at Oldbridge, and stood upon the side
of the bank, within musquet-shot of the ford, there to make his observations on the enemies' camp and posture; there stood a small party of the
enemies' horse, in a little island within the river; and on the other bank,
there were several hedges, and little Irish houses almost close to the river,
there was one house likewise of stone, that had a court, and some little
works about it; this, the Irish had filled with souldiers, and all the hedges
and little houses we saw, were lined and filled with musqueteers; there
were also several brest-works cast up to the right, just at the ford. However,
this was the place through which his majesty resolved to force his way;
and, therefore, he and his great officers spent some time in contriving the
methods of passing, and the places where to plant our batteries. After some
time, his majesty rid about 200 yards further up the river, nigh the west of
all the enemies' camp; and whilst his army was marching in, he alighted,
and sate him down upon a rising ground, where he refreshed himself;
whilst his majesty sate there we observed five gentlemen of the Irish army
ride softly along the other side, and make their remarks upon our men
as they marched in; those, I heard afterwards, were the Duke of Berwick,
my Lord Tyrconel, Sarcefield, Parker, and some say Lauzun. Captain

Pownel, of Colonel Levison's regiment, was sent with a party of horse and dragoons, towards the bridg[e] of Slane; and whilst his majesty sate on the grass (being about an hour) there came some of the Irish, with long guns, and shot at our dragoons, who went down to the river to drink, and some of ours went down to return the favour, then a party of about forty horse advanced very slowly, and stood upon a plowd field, over against us, for near half an hour, and so retired to their camp; this small party, as I have heard from their own officers since, brought two field-pieces amongst them, dropping them by an hedg[e] on the plowd land undiscovered; they did not offer to fire them, till his majesty was mounted; and then, he and the rest, riding softly the same way back, their gunner fires a piece, which killed us two horses and a man, about 100 yards above where the king was; but immediately comes a second, which had been almost a fatal one, for it graized upon the bank of the river, and in the rising, slanted upon the king's right shoulder, took out a piece of his coat, and tore the skin and flesh, and afterwards broke the head of a gentleman's pistol."*

William took, it seems, but little notice of the affair, but rode quietly back into the glen, merely observing to those who came to render him assistance, – "There is no necessity: the bullet should have come nearer." The enemy were, however, so far deceived, that they raised a great shout, and an express was immediately sent off to the Continent, and bonfires, it is said, actually lighted in Paris to celebrate the fall of Nassau. James says in his memoirs that he himself ordered the guns to fire on this occasion.

The place where this accident occurred was on the side of a small hillock, by the water's edge, a little below the glen, and from which the stones have been taken to build the obelisk since erected just beside it. The real object of William's near approach to the enemy at this place was not, it seems to us, to reconnoitre their position, which he could have done more effectually from the hill behind him, but for the purpose of observing the tide and noting the proper time for crossing the river next morning.

In one of the editions of the Memoirs of the Duke of Berwick (son of James II) there is related a curious account of what would appear to be the same story, of which the following is an outline. The day before the

---

* The torn buff coat William wore on this occasion was given to Colonel Thompson, and is still in the possession of the family at Ravensdale.

action a considerable number of the officers of the Prince of Orange were standing together in a group. As it appeared probable that the Prince of Orange was one of the number, the young Duke of Berwick exclaimed: "'Behold a splendid opportunity for putting an end to this war! We must attack that troop and destroy the Prince of Orange.' 'And who will dare to do it?' observed some one. 'I, myself,' said the Duke; and immediately, followed by a band of officers drawn on by his example, he attacked and defeated this very troop where he hoped to find the Prince. He looked about in search of him in defiance of every danger, but the Prince was not there." This account of a piece of heroism, however, ceases to interest us when we remember the fact that at the time alluded to the Boyne at full tide was rolling between the belligerents! Of such tales, however, is history, and the history of battles in particular, often composed.

Thus ended the 30th of June, and thus stood the hostile armies upon the eve of the engagement. We have written the foregoing description of the battle-field from a careful examination of the scene, and the perusal of the most trustworthy documents within our reach. The exact position of each general's division in either army had not been ascertained with certainty, neither has any correct or veritable military plan of the battle ever appeared. The accompanying map we have had engraved from a plan of the battle, made about sixty years ago, by a Major Brown, for the Right Hon. John Foster, Speaker of the Irish House of Commons. We present it to our readers and the tourists to the Boyne, because it conveys to our mind a much better idea of the scene than either of the two older, ill-constructed plans of Story or Richardson.

Heretofore, the descriptions of the battle of the Boyne have been almost all one-sided, being, for the most part, written by violent partisans, pandering to the vanity of one party and exciting the sensitiveness of the other. The authorities from which the historians drew were nearly all Williamite; but within the last few years the gleaners in this department of Irish history have had access to documents written by officers in the Irish army and others in every way worthy of credit, and which must now induce the calm searcher after truth to very much modify some, and altogether reject other statements put forward by the former, and which have been generally received as facts. To give these latter their fair share of merit, and to weigh and discuss the adverse statements of both parties, would not suit the intention of the present work, and would require a more critical examination of the subject than our space would warrant.

We should like, 'tis true, to fight this battle in detail, and record the gallant deeds of the O'Neals and Schombergs, – the Caillimottes and Sarsfields, – of Berwick, Sidney, Ginkle, Geraldine, Hamilton, and others who have left material for many a tribute to their fame. But this, at present, is denied us; perhaps some other day we'll try our hand at this "grievous battle," so bravely fought by a comparatively young, but experienced general, – gallant in the field and wise in council, with a highly disciplined army, a part of which had been trained in many a hard contested battle in France and Flanders, then the great battle-ground of European warfare, – against a weak and vacillating prince, advanced in years, and borne down by misfortunes, neither wise in council nor gallant in action, remaining in the rere of, but not commanding an army, which, however great its devotion, was totally unable to cope with its opponent.

The army of King William amounted, according to the most moderate calculation, to 36,000 men; some authorities make it upwards of 40,000; all well-disciplined soldiers; numbers of them tried veterans, whose prowess had been tested and their courage schooled in many a well-fought field in Europe; hardy warriors, well-appointed, and composed of the greatest number of nations that ever fought for or against the crown of England before or since – Danes, Dutch, Swedes, and Flemings, Swiss, French Huguenots, English, Scotch, Anglo-Irish, and Germans, – led by some of the most esteemed officers of the day, the two Schombergs, Douglas, Sidney, and La Mellionere, and commanded by one of the greatest generals of the age, personally brave, energetic, and well-skilled in war. The Williamite force, being chiefly composed of mercenaries, was less likely to be influenced by any feeling of loyalty towards the deposed sovereign than if it had been entirely English.

To this was opposed an army scarcely three and twenty thousand strong, a large portion of which, the French excepted, was composed of raw levies; undisciplined, and but ill supplied with arms or money; under generals no doubt brave and skilful, but whose interests were so constantly clashing that it was with great difficulty they could ever be brought to act in unison; and moreover commanded by a Prince whose weakness, imbecility, and bigotry, had already lost him a crown, who was totally unskilled in war, and whose heart was not in the country nor the cause of the men who fought for him. Either in order to secure a retreat, or fearing the issue of the engagement, James sent off all the baggage, and *six of his twelve guns,* to Dublin, the night before the battle, and dispatched a trusty messenger to the south to prepare a vessel for his departure.

In the "Irish Journal," a small quarto of thirteen pages, published in London, July 17, 1690, we find the best account of the condition of Dublin at the time of the engagement, as well as a very succinct and circumstantial recital of the battle of the Boyne. From this rare old tract we gladly present our readers with the following extracts: "On Saturday, 21st (June), we heard the Irish army retreated, and the English were come towards Droghedah. We knew King James's design was to *avoid a battle* as much as he could, and to have walked the English army along the Boyne river, and so across the country to Limerick; but this day we were told from the camp that the enemy seemed to press towards Dublin, and King James was resolved to defend it, and that therefore they thought he could not be able to keep off a battle above ten days. On Sunday the Irish army came on this side the Boyne, and King James, as it would seem, distrusting the issue, Sir Pat Trant, First Commissioner of the Revenue, and another gentleman, were ordered to go from hence on Monday morning, to Waterford, to prepare ships.

"On Monday, the last of June, the English army, having had very little rest or victuals, drew to the Boyne; Lieutenant-General Douglas's horse were ordered to post themselves at a ford near Drogheda, upon a rising ground over against a battery of the Irish, of six guns, guarded by a party of their horse. Here the English stood the shot of the enemy, every man on foot by his horse, several hours, while there passed 200 shots; the King, in the mean time, having rid between them and the ford, where he received the hurt on his shoulder by a cannon shot, which disabled him the next day from holding his sword. At last, when the King had said, "Now I see my men will stand," some guns were sent to them, upon the first discharge of which among the Irish horse, they retreated from their battery, and stood farther off."

There is one point in the battle of the Boyne (which we were the first to point out, in the earlier edition of this work), on which sufficient stress has not been laid, although it would appear to have had a greater influence on the issue of the fight than historians are aware. The right wing of the Irish army was completely protected by Drogheda, the Boyne, and the sea; its left towards Slane was unprotected; and if this was once turned or outflanked, the road to Duleek must be occupied, Dublin would be cut off, and then the temporary refuge of the fortress of Drogheda afforded the only hope for the Irish army. This could not escape the notice of a skilful opposing general, neither was it unforeseen to some of the advisers of King James, although he himself does not appear to have paid sufficient attention to it. At break of day upon the morning of Tuesday, the 1st of July, which was a remarkably clear, hot day, William despatched 10,000 men under the younger Schomberg, Generals Douglas, Overkirk, and Lord Portland, to cross the river at the fords, near Slane, of the existence and passability of which he appears to have been well informed. Proceeding behind the hill, now included in the demesne of Townley Hall, and crossing the Mattock river at Monk-Newtown, they were concealed from the Irish until they appeared on the elevated banks near Knowth, above the ford of Rossnaree, where it would appear the cavalry crossed with scarcely any opposition, except from the regiment of Sir Neal O'Neale, who himself was killed in the skirmish. The foot under Portland passed round by the bridge of Slane, two miles farther off, but joined the English cavalry near a marsh or bog which stood between them and their opponents, and before a sufficient force could have been despatched by James to oppose them. Here then was an army, nearly half the size of that of King James, advancing upon the left wing of the latter, and pressing to get between it and Duleek, and so cut off the retreat towards Dublin; and then it was (for William was informed, by express, of Douglas having made good his position) that the passage of the Boyne at Oldbridge was commenced, at half-pat ten o'clock, A.M., while this left wing of the Irish army was already engaged two miles off with the division under Douglas and Count Schomberg.

"The Irish Journal," a Williamite authority, makes the amount of the army which passed at Rossnaree much more than what Story states. It says, "General Douglas was sent with 12,000 foot and 5000 horse, to a ford further up the river by Slane, where had been a battery of the Irish, but they were drawn off, and only 800 dragoons guarded the ford. The English were to go down a steep hill to the ford, and an uneven way, yet the Irish dragoons only once fired, and retreated to the body of their army, which lay towards Duleek."

That this manœuvre of William's, which so early decided the fate of the day, was not quite unexpected by the Irish generals, we learn from the fact that Hamilton had in council, on the preceding evening, advised eight regiments to be sent up the river to defend the bridge and passage at Slane; but James in reply, merely offered to despatch fifty dragoons to defend that important position! Soon, however, the error was discovered, when, at an early hour next morning, the advancing host of Douglas was observed crowning the heights of Knowth, and stretching westward towards Slane. Then, when too late, James, in the midst of hurry and confusion, despatched his *entire left wing and some of his centre*, chiefly foot, and the chosen French troops of Louis, under Lauzun, with *all his artillery*, – at most the remaining six field-pieces, – to oppose the army of Douglas, which must by that time have made good its ground, and had also been strengthened by the infantry of Portland. This must have occurred between 9 and 10 o'clock in the morning. The sudden withdrawal of this large body of the best disciplined troops, from the centre and left wing of the Irish, not only materially weakened but confused and disheartened the army at Oldbridge, which had been until that moment drawn up in battle array in two formidable lines to defend the fords of that place. It was at this moment, with the tide at its lowest ebb, and 10,000 picked men outflanking his opponent upon the opposite bank, – a circumstance of which he was then well aware, that William saw was the most auspicious to cross the ford at Oldbridge, and lead on in person his six-and-twenty thousand men against that portion of the Irish army which remained upon the original battle-field. James himself, as we learn from his own memoirs, was not at any time of the day at the battle of Oldbridge, and did not, as popular opinion and several histories would lead us to believe, view the fight, a passive spectator, from the church of Donore. The army of Douglas extended its line to the right, to outflank the Irish, and cut off their retreat to Dublin, by getting before them to Duleek, and keeping them behind the Nanny-Water; which Lauzun observing, marched his army parallel with them, in order to prevent such a disaster. "While this was doing," say the Royal Memoirs, "the King went to the right to hasten up the troops to follow Lauzune, *believing the main body of the enemie's army was following their right, which had passed at Slane.* The King took the reserve, consisting of Purcel's hors and Brown's foot, with which he marched till he came up to the rear of the foot, that follow'd Lausune, and there ordering Sir Charles Carny, who commanded the reserve, to post himself at the right of the first line of those foot, to make a sort of left wing there, and the rid along the line, where he found Lausune and the Enemie's right drawn up in battle, within half cannon shot, faceing each other: the King did not think fit to charge just then, being in expectation of the troops he had left at Old bridg, but while he was discoursing this matter with Lausune, an Aid de Camp came to give the King an account that the enemy had forced the pass at Old bridg[e] and that the right wing was beaten; which the King wispering in Lausun's ear, tould him, there was now nothing to be done but to charge the enemie forthwith, before his troops knew what had happen'd on the right, and by that means try if they could recover the day; and accordingly sent Mons. Hoguette to the head of the French foot, made all the Dragoons to light, and placed them in the intervalls between the hors[e], and ordered Lausune to lead on: but just as they were beginning to move, Sarsfield and Maxwell, who had been to view the ground betwixt the two armys, sayd it was impossible for the hors[e] to charg[e] the enemie, by reason of two double ditches with high banks, and a little brook betwixt them, that run along the small valley that divided the two armys, and at the same time the enemie's Dragoons go on hors back, and their whole line began to march by their flank to their right, and we soon lost sight of their van by a village that interposed; only by the dust that ris behind it, they seem'd to *endeavour to gaine Dublin road*; upon which the King (since he could not attack them) thought fit to march also by his left towards Dublin road too, to pass a small brook at Dulick, which was impracticable higher up by reason of a bog. The King was no sooner on his march, but the right wing's being beaten was no longer a mistery, for severall of the scattered and wounded horsemen got in amongst them before they rought Dulick."

We have quoted this passage at length, because we believe it is the true history of the turning point of the battle. The retreat had already commenced; the best disciplined portion of the Irish were with the King himself, and also some of his most experienced officers, miles away from the field of Oldbridge, and hotly pursued by young Schomberg, thirsting to revenge his father's death, of which he was then aware. Even the repulse of the centre and left of the English army, at the ford at Oldbridge, would not then have saved the day.

Besides the authorities already quoted or referred to [above], we have become acquainted with a most interesting historic document, from which we have made the following extracts. It is a copy of the Journal of Colonel Bellingham of Gernonstown, now Castle Bellingham, "kept during the years 1688, 1689, 1690, including the whole of King William's campaigns in Ireland during the last year, when Colonel Bellingham attended the King and acted as a guide to the Army till after the battle of the Boyne."

"The 30th, very hott, I called at Mr. Townley's in our march towards Boyne. I was for some time with the King on the hill of Tullahescar, from whence he view'd Drogheda, and then went towards Oldbridge. On the south side of Boyne lay the enemy's camp, which the King going to view, he was hitt by a cannon ball on the shoulder, which putt us into the greatest consternation imaginable, but, blessed be God, it proved but a slight hurte; he went round his own camp and was received with the greatest joy and acclamations imaginable. The cannon fir'd att caste all the afternoon. We drew a great body of our horse up on the hills in sight of the enemy. We fir'd several bombs which did execution, and our cannon dismounted 2 of the enemy's batterye's.

"July the 1st, 1690, a joyfull day, excessive hott; about 6 this morning the King got on horseback and gave the necessary orders. Kirke ordered me to bring him some account from the enemy. I brought him a youth, one Fyans, who came that morning from Drogheda.* I carry'd him to the King, who was then standing att the battery, seeing his cannon play att the house of Oldbridge. He had sent early a strong detachment *of about* 15,000 men with Douglas towards Slane, who pass'd the river without any opposition, and putt the enemy to route who were on that wing."

---

* Sir Alan E. Bellingham writes to us: "The late Sir William Bellingham told me he was at a nobleman's house (I think the Duke of Portland's) who had a picture of the battle of the Boyne, in which an officer appears bringing up a young man to the King. The owner of the picture did not then know the object. The journal of Col. Bellingham explains it. The family of Fyans were at Dunleer within a few years back."

We have already remarked upon the admirable position of the English army, protected by the immense battery immediately opposite the ford, and screened by the natural lie of the ground. The tide being out, the passage of the river was attempted in four different places. The Blue Dutch guards, the Irish Enniskilleners, and the French Huguenots, led by Caillimotte and the gallant old Schomberg, passed quickly out of the little glen opposite the principal ford, with drums beating, and dashing into the water both there and over the upper end of Grove island, a little lower down, formed upon the opposite side, and carried the village and rude outworks at Oldbridge; not, however, without considerable opposition, some of the Irish soldiers rushing into the water to meet them. It was here the brave old Schomberg was killed,* and also Dr. Walker, the gallant defender of Derry, and Caillimotte received his death wound.† The third crossing was made by the Danes and Germans, at a shallow between the two principal islands, where the water must have been up to their armpits, while the left wing, entirely composed of cavalry, consisting chiefly of Danes and Dutch, passed or swam across opposite the eastern valley which intersects the hill of Tullyallen, and effected a landing, apparently with little opposition, at a very deep and dangerous part of the river, nearly opposite the spot where one of the Irish batteries stood the day before, and where the margin of the stream is wet and swampy. Here it was, however, that, accompanied by the Prince of Denmark, William himself, with his

---

* Schomberg's body was immediately carried back, across the river, to the English camp. His skull is still shown in the cathedral of St. Patrick's, where Dean Swift caused a monument to be erected to him. The family vault of the Schombergs is in the cathedral of Mayence. His sword is now the charter sword of the "Friendly Brothers".

Schomberg, it is said, was the person who advised the attack on the left wing of the Irish army. William having, in a council of war held at nine o'clock the evening before the battle, declared his intention of crossing the river next morning, "this was at first opposed by Duke Schomberg, as too dangerous an attempt; but finding His Majesty persist therein, he advised that part of the army should be sent *that night*, about twelve, to Stone Bridge (Slane) in order to pass the river thereabouts, and to get between the enemy and the pass at Duleek; but this advice was not followed, which would probably have ended the war in one campaign. It was opposed by the Dutch generals, which made the Duke retire to his tent."

† Caillimotte is buried near the gate of Mr. Coddington's demesne.

arm in a sling from the effects of his wound, plunged into the stream, with Colonel Woolstey, and passed with great difficulty, "for his horse was bogg'd on the other side, and he was forced to alight, till a gentleman help'd him to get his horse out." Colonel Bellingham's Journal thus continues: "He sent another detachment of horse to the left to goe over at the Mill-foord, but the tide coming in and the foord bad, the passage was very difficult, most of them being forced to swim, insomuch that they could not come upp time enough to assist our foot who went over the foord att Oldbridge about 11 of the clock. The enemy had laid an ambush behind the ditches and houses on the other side of the water, who fir'd incessantly att our men as they were passing the river; who, as soon as arriv'd on land, immediately putt those musqueteers to the route, and advanc'd farther into the field in battalia. Here the brave old Duke Shomberg was kill'd, and Dr. Walker and Coll. Callemott mortally wounded. The enemy advanc'd towards us and made a brisk effort upon us, but we soon repell'd them with considerable loss on theyr side. They made two other attempts on us, but were still bravely beaten back; and when our horse of the left came upp the enemy quite quitted that field, having left several dead bodyes behind them. 'Twas there we took Lieut.-General Hamilton. The enemye's horse of Tireconnell's regiment behav'd themselves well; *but our Dutch like angells.* The K. charged in person at the head of the Inniskilleners, and expos'd himself with undaunted bravery."

The royal memoirs thus confirm the view which we have taken of the admirable generalship of William in causing a diversion of the centre and left of the Irish army before he attempted to cross the Boyne. "As for what pass'd at Oldbridge it seems the enemie, perceiving the left wing and most of the foot had marched after Lauzune, attacked the regiment which was at the village of Oldbridge."

Thus, then, there were at least six and twenty thousand men, with a large battery, arrayed against fifteen or sixteen thousand, for we must subtract those already engaged, under Lauzun, Sarsfield, and James himself, towards Slane, fully three miles off, and *the Irish had not* (it would appear) *a single cannon at Oldbridge that day.** The right wing of the

---

* William had, it is said, a portion of his boot carried away by a cannonball during the action, but at what place or at what time is not specified. If the Irish had

Irish army, chiefly composed of cavalry, was commanded by the Duke of Berwick, and the centre by Tyrconnel and Hamilton. Notwithstanding the very great disparity of numbers, their want of discipline, – the newly raised levies of Irish foot being nearly all at Oldbridge and immediately opposite the principal ford, – and their being unsupported by artillery, this portion of James's army behaved with great firmness, and parts of it with signal gallantry, some of the Irish rushing into the water to meet the Dutch, and others, the Royal Guards for instance, dashing through them as they were forming on the Meath bank of the river, and being nearly all cut to pieces in their endeavour to return. Sir John Hanmer's brigade "were so valiantly attacked in front by Hamilton's horse that they were forced to retreat, and some of them to cross the river again." As the Irish fell back, retreating up the hill towards Donore, they suddenly halted, and so furiously turned upon their opponents that the vaunted courage of the Enniskilleners quailed before them, although at the moment William himself led on that body, and His Majesty, being left upwards of a hundred yards in advance of his men, was thus exposed to most imminent danger. In the subsequent charge some of Schomberg's horse took those two standards of the Irish which are still preserved among the trophies in the chapel of the Royal Hospital of Kilmainham.* At another part of the field, in the lane or small bridle road (which still exists) to the left of the ford, Ginkle met with a serious repulse, "being overpowered there and also forced to retreat," till aided by the troops of Colonel Levison and Sir Albert Cunningham, who

a park of artillery at Oldbridge, what became of it? They could not have taken it with them in the rout. If the English captured any guns, surely it would have been mentioned by some author.

*   Among the memorabilia of the Boyne may be mentioned, besides those already specified, King William's sword, which is at Townley Hall; his saddle and bridle are in the possession of Mr. Baker. His horse was brought to Connaught, and died at Mr. Mulloy's of Hewstown, near Carrick-on-Shannon. It was given to a Captain Mulloy, in return for one with which he supplied the King when his own was shot under him, at the time his pistol was broken and a portion of his boot carried away. The O'Mulloys were hereditary standard-bearers to the English Kings in Ireland. The kettle drums of one of the Irish regiments are in the Town Hall of Drogheda. The heart of James II was embalmed, and is now in a shrine in a small chapel on one side of the Champs Elysees in Paris.

lined the hedge bordering the lane, and also possessed themselves of a farm-house adjoining, when a fierce conflict for some time took place, Ginkle, it is said, continuing "in the rear of his men, *endeavouring to make them keep their ground.*"

The last rally made by the Irish on the slopes near the summit of Donore was under Hamilton, who being wounded in the head and taken prisoner immediately after, the action may be said to have ceased, and the retreat from Oldbridge then began. Upon being led up to King William, in whose very presence he was captured, and who regarded him as a renegade, and being asked whether he thought the Irish would fight any more, he pledged his honour that they would, whereupon William turned upon him, and sarcastically repeated more than once, "*your* honour."

The natural consequences followed: the Irish centre and right wing fell back upon Donore, and finally, towards the close of the day, rapidly retreated to Duleek, towards which place the left wing, already beaten above Rossnaree, had previously retired.

It was now long past mid-day, the fierce conflict at Oldbridge, generally styled the "Battle of the Boyne," had raged for several hours, the sun waned in his path, and the victory already attained, almost without a blow, by the army of Douglas, was crowned by the retreat of the entire Irish force under the Duke of Berwick and Lord Tyrconnel. From Donore Hill to Duleek, a distance of about three miles, where the first natural obstacle presents in the deep sedgy stream of the Nanny Water, a succession of hills slope from the high grounds above the right or southern bank of the Boyne in a somewhat triangular form. The base of this triangle is the Boyne, between Oldbridge and Rossnaree, from which latter the retreat under James and Lauzun first commenced, and its apex, the little bridge which spans the Nanny at the village of Duleek. The sides of the triangle mark the two lines of the retreat. The high road from Duleek to Donore by the hill of Cruzrath (from which latter a good view of the whole scene may be obtained) marks pretty accurately the eastern line of the retreat. The left wing of the Irish, having succeeded in reaching the pass of Duleek "untouched," and bringing with them five of their six guns, long before the English right had come up, here stood, first upon the common which surrounds the village upon the north, where some stand was made, and them, falling back behind the river, they defended the bridge for several hours, until the centre and left wing, which had been beaten at Donore, rushed down upon them in confusion, hotly pursued by their opponents. While the pass of Duleek was retained by the Irish and French, King James, accompanied by a troop of horse, fled to Dublin, which he reached about ten o'clock so that he must have left his army about five or six o'clock in the afternoon, probably when the retreating, or rather the flying army from Donore appeared in sight. Then, for the first time on that memorable day, the *entire* of the two armies stood opposed, but how different their situations may be gleamed from the foregoing details. Some skirmishing occurred at Duleek, but the bridge was soon gained, and William in person pressed on the victorious army in the pursuit, towards the Naul, a deep defile, at another small brook about six miles farther on. Here, night coming on, the pursuit was abandoned, and the English returned to Duleek, where they lay under arms during the night. The diary already quoted thus describes the circumstance. The King "pursued almost as far as the Naul, and left them not till near 10 o'clock at night. I was his guide back to Duleek. We killed about 2000 of their men, besides Lords Carlingford, Dangan, and several other officers of ranke killed and taken prisoners. We lost not above 200 in the whole action, many of which were killed by our own men through mistake. I returned to the camp at Oldbridge, having left the King in his coach at Duleek, where he stayed that night. I was almost faint from want of drink and meat."

All the Williamite authorities worthy of credit bear testimony to the "orderly" and "well-managed retreat" made chiefly by the Irish horse and French foot.

The "Irish Journal" thus describes the state of Dublin upon the day of the battle. "Now as to us in this place, we were waken'd very early this Tuesday morning by an alarm, and the news that there would be a battel. The gates were kept strictly guarded, and the Protestants kept their houses. The issue we expected with the greatest apprehensions. Several reports were spread abroad every hour; one while that the French fleet was in our bay; another, that a French express was come from Waterford, with the news of taking the Isle of Wight by the French, and of their being gone to Dover; then that the English right wing was quite routed; then, that the Prince of Orange was taken prisoner; but at five that afternoon, some that had made their escape on tired horses told us the Irish were much worsted; and others at six, that they were totally defeated; from hence, till one that night, all the entries of the town were filled with dusty, wounded, and tired soldiers, and carriages perpetually coming in. We see several of King James's horse guards coming in straggling, without pistols or swords, and could not tell what was become of himself. Near 10 that night be came in with about 200 horse all in disorder. We concluded now that it was a total rout, and that the enemy were just ready to come into town, but were greatly surprized when an hour or two after we heard the whole body of the Irish horse come in in very good order, with kettle-drums, haut-boys, and trumpets, and early next morning the French and a great party of the Irish foot." James departed for Waterford early the next morning, and none of the English army appeared until eight o'clock at night upon Thursday, the second day after the engagement, when an officer and one troop of dragoons arrived to take charge of the stores; the town having been previously evacuated of all the Irish force. King William arrived and encamped at Finglas, outside the city, upon Friday, the 4th.

With all their faults, the Stuarts elicited more loyalty than the world will ever witness again. We will not say that James II was a coward, – he had previously shown his bravery upon sea, – but certainly he was no general, His defeat here was, however, inevitable. The King was then the palladium of his party, and his person was therefore of great conse-quence to his adherents, who may have forced him off the field. Under the circumstances he should not have delayed not fought at the Boyne, where he had got into a most unlucky position, the apex of a triangle, one side of which was formed by the sea; and when William hemmed him round, defeating him at every point, not only by the superior discipline of his troops, which, after all, is courage, but by force of numbers and general-ship, then retreat – flight, was the inevitable, the last resource. Looking back at this distance of time, it would appear to have been safer for James to have retreated with his small army, according to his original plan, and have garrisoned the principal fortified towns, and by laying waste the country, and destroying, as was intended, the English fleet in the Channel, thus cut off William's supplies, while a guerilla warfare would have greatly harassed and considerably diminished his forces. James cared nothing for Ireland not the Irish, except so far as they could be made use of to restore to him his lost crown; he also hoped that a counter-revolution would have been got up in his favour in England, and that the King of France would have lent him further assistance. This, however, is not the place to discuss these subjects at greater length.

The numbers killed at the battle of the Boyne were not considerable, when we take into account the amount of the belligerents, and that the engagement and retreat lasted nearly twelve hours. On the Irish side it is stated to have been upwards of a thousand, and upon the English above four hundred. The orange and green have long been party words in Ireland; – are our readers aware of the fact, that while the Irish troops wore pieces of white paper in their caps, the livery of France, every English soldier was decorated with a branch of *green*? The English watchword was "Westminster."

Thus ended the battle of the 1st of July, 1690, the cause of so much subsequent party feud and so many heart-burnings in this country. To the one party it gave victory; liberty, civil and religious; broad lands, power, and dominant sway: while the other suffered not only present defeat, but subsequent confiscation, penal laws, exile, death.

CHAPTER EIGHT

William Wilde, *Irish Popular Superstitions*, 1852

William bought a fishing lodge on Lough Fee in 1853, just after he had published his Irish Popular Superstitions, *part of his commitment to the recovery and preservation of Irish native culture, as well as a record of his interest in folk culture, history, and archaeology. In many ways, this short book, much of which had been published in the* Dublin University Magazine, *was more like a memoir, and William draws on his own childhood in Castlerea. Indeed, Connaught is central to his examination and his celebration of Irish superstitions. This collection, dedicated to Speranza, would later influence her in her own collections of Irish folklore, published in London after William's death.*

The Decline of the Irish Superstition

Had not Shakespeare embalmed in the "Midsummer Night's Dream" the Popular Superstitions and Fairy lore current in England at the time of Elizabeth, the present generation could form but a very faint idea of the ancient beliefs of our forefathers in the witcheries of their sylvan deities and household gods. In this utilitarian age it would be superfluous to discuss, or even to enumerate, the causes which have combined to obliterate this poetry of the people in England; suffice it to say, that it has gradually vanished before the spread of education, and the rapid growth of towns and manufactories.

A wild and daring spirit of adventure – a love of legendary romance – a deep-rooted belief in the supernatural – an unconquerable reverence for ancient customs, and an extensive superstitious creed has, from the earliest times, belonged to the Celtic race. We cannot, therefore, wonder that among the but partially civilized, because neglected and uneducated, yet withal chivalrous inhabitants of a large portion of Ireland, a belief in the marvellous should linger even to the present day. It is … rapidly becoming obliterated; never to return. When now I enquire after the old farmer who conducted me, in former years, to the ruined Castle or Abbey, and told me the story of its early history and inhabitants, I hear that he died during the famine. On asking for the peasant who used to sit with me in the ancient Rath, and recite the Fairy legends of the locality, the answer is: "He is gone to America"; and the old woman who took me to the Blessed Well, and gave me an account of its wondrous cures and charms – "Where is she?" – "Living in the Workhouse."

These legendary tales and Popular Superstitions have now become the history of the past – a portion of the traits and characteristics of other days. Will their recital revive their practice? No! Nothing contributes more to uproot superstitious rites and forms than to print them; to make them known to the many instead of leaving them hidden among, and secretly practised by the few.

These tales form part of a large collection made for my amusement many years ago, or which were remembered since my boyhood, and they have been written as a relaxation from severer toil. Several of them have already appeared in the "Dublin University Magazine." They are now collected and presented to the public in their present form, chiefly in the hope of eliciting information from those who may be further acquainted with such matters.

Revolution in Irish Life

The great convulsion which society of all grades here has lately experienced, the failure of the potato crop, pestilence, famine, and a most unparalleled extent of emigration, together with bankrupt landlords, pauperizing poor-laws, grinding officials, and decimating workhouses have broken up the very foundations of social intercourse, have swept away the established theories of political economists, and uprooted many of our long-cherished opinions. In some places, all the domestic usages of life have been outraged; the tenderest bonds of kindred have been severed, some of the noblest and holiest feelings of human nature have been blotted from the heart, and many of the finest, yet firmest links which united the various classes in the community have been rudely burst asunder. Even the ceremonial of religion has been neglected, and the very rites of sepulture, the most sacred and enduring of all the tributes of affection or respect, have been neglected or forgotten; the dead body has rotted where it fell, or formed a scanty meal for the famished dogs of the vicinity, or has been thrown, without prayer or mourning, into the adjoining ditch, the hum of the spinning-wheel has long since ceased to form an accompaniment to the colleen's song; and that song itself, so sweet and fresh in cabin, field, or byre, has scarcely left an echo in our glens, or among the hamlets of our land. The Shannaghie and the Callegh in the chimney corner, tell no more the tales and legends of other days. Unwaked, *unkeened*, the dead are buried where Christian burial has at all been observed; and the ear no longer catches the mournful cadence of the wild Irish cry, wailing on the blast, rising up to us from the valleys, or floating along the winding river, when

> "The skies, the fountains, every region near,
> Seemed all one mutual cry."

The fire on the peasant's hearth was quenched, and its comforts banished, even before his roof-tree fell, while the remnant of the hardiest and most stalwart of the people crawl about, listless spectres, unable or unwilling to rise out of their despair. In this state of things, with depopulation the most terrific which any country ever experienced, on the one hand, and the spread of education, and the introduction of railroads, colleges, industrial and other educational schools, on the other, – together with the rapid decay of the Irish vernacular, in which most of our legends, romantic tales, ballads, and bardic annals, the vestiges of Pagan rites, and the relics of fairy charms were preserved, – can superstition, or if superstitious belief, can superstitious practices continue to exist?

But these matters of popular belief and folks'-lore, these rites and legends, and superstitions, were, after all, *the poetry of the people*, the bond that knit the peasant to the soil, and cheered and solaced many a cottier's fireside. Without these, on the one side, and without proper education and well-directed means of partaking of and enjoying its blessings, on the other, and without rational amusement besides, he will, and must, and has in many instances, already become a perfect brute. The rath which he revered has been, to our knowledge, ploughed up, the ancient thorn which he reverenced has been cut down, and the sacred well polluted, merely in order to uproot his prejudices, and efface his superstition. Has he been improved by such desecration of the landmarks of the past, objects which, independent of their natural beauty, are often the surest footprints of history? We fear not.

Medical Superstitions

Of all superstitions, the medical lingers longest, perhaps, because the incentive to its existence must remain, while disease, real or imaginary – either that capable of relief, or totally incurable – continues to afflict mankind, and, therefore, in every country, no matter how civilized, the quack, the mountebank, the charm-worker, and the medico-religious impostor and nostrum-vendor, will find a gullible, *payable* public to prey upon. The only difference between the water-doctor living in his schloss, the mesmeriser practising in the lordly hall, or the cancer and the consumption curer of the count or duchess, spending five thousand a-year in advertisements, paid into the queen's exchequer, who drives his carriage and lives in Soho-square, and the "medicine man" of the Indian, or the "knowledgeable woman" of the half-savage islander, residing in a hut cut of the side of the bog-hole, or formed in the cleft of a granite rock, is, that the former are almost invariably wilful imposters, and the latter frequently believe firmly in the efficacy of their art, and often refuse payment for its exercise.

The May-Day Festival in Ireland

Now then, fair and gentle, rude and rustic readers – country swains and city dames – boys of the Liberty, from Blackpits to Mullinahack, from the banks of the Dodder to the heights of Ballynascorney – girls of Finglas and bucks of Fingal, how have you spent your May Eve? – how did you welcome May Morning, and how do you purpose to celebrate the birth-day of summer? Have you danced to the elfin pipers that played under the thorns of the Phœnix last night? Did you leap through the bonfires that blazed upon Tallaght and Harold's-cross Green? Were you out yester-eve to welcome the "Young May Moon?" or up before sunrise this morning to gather the maiden dew from the sparkling gossamer, to keep the freckles off your pretty faces? – or have you been –

——————————— "seeking
A spell in the young year's flowers.
The magical May-dew is weeping
Its charms o'er the summer bow'rs."

Have you found the name of your true love smeared by the snail you set between the plates last evening? and have you chosen a Queen of the May, whose path you'll strew with pasture flowers, as you lead her round the garlanded pole of the Tolka? Are your doors and windows decorated with primroses and cowslips, and May-flowers gathered by the meadows and green inches of your lovely Anna Liffey? Butchers of Patrick's Market and Bull Alley, and boys of the Coombe and the Poddle, are you ready, as of yore, to "cut de bosh, spite of de Devil and de Polis?" Up, weavers of Newmarket and Meath Street, and join with the Ormond boys; will you suffer the white-coated boddaghs of Meath to carry off the prizes at Finglas, and steal the May-dew from the rosy-lipped girls of Glasnevin?

Alas! what are we dreaming about – things that were, not are – memories of other, of better and happier times – of ancient customs sneered away by modern utilitarianism – of ceremonies almost forgotten, and healthful rustic sports and pastimes, now prohibited by law, put down by force – starved out of our light-hearted people, or carried beyond the blue waves of the broad Atlantic? Politics have of late years occupied the place of pantomimes – our Finglas sports were interdicted by a special act of the Privy Council – fairy lore has given place to a newspaper political religion – the new police banished the bonfires: and where is the piper or fiddler who would enliven the gardens of the "Grinding Young" after hearing a temperance band, all dressed like Jack Puddings and drum majors coming down the road from Kimmage or Dolphin's Barn?

All gone, dead and gone, save a few dirty urchins in the suburbs, who, with the twigs of a second-hand broom, decked with stinking daffydown-dillies, annoy the passengers by asking "a hay'penny to honour the May."

The Oracle of Love

In the North, particularly in Raherty Island, several May Day superstitions, resembling those usually performed at Hollandtide, still remain. If a young woman wishes to know who is to be her future spouse, she goes, late on May Eve, to a black sally-tree, and plucks therefrom nine sprigs, the last of which she throws over her right shoulder, and puts the remaining eight into the foot of her right stocking. She then, on her knees, reads the third verse of the 17th chapter of Job; and on going to bed she places the stocking, with its contents, under her head. These rights duly performed, and her faith being strong, she will, in a dream during the night, be treated to a sight of her future husband.

Another mode of obtaining the same knowledge consists of going, after sunset on May Eve, to a bank on which the yarrow (*ahirhallune*) is growing plentifully, and gathering therefrom nine springs of the plant, while she repeats the following words:–

"Good morrow, good morrow, fair yarrow;
  And thrice good morrow to thee;
Come tell me before to-morrow
  Who my true love shall be."

The yarrow is brought home, put into the right-foot stocking, placed under the pillow, and the mystic dream is confidently expected. But if the girl opens her lips to speak after she has pulled the yarrow, the charm is broken.

II 1860–1880: Merrion Square

Settled in Merrion Square by 1855, Speranza continued her writing, with translations of Pictures of the French Revolution, *published in 1850,* The Wanderer *in 1851,* The Glacier *in 1852, and then* The First Temptation *by 1863, while William worked on the* Catalogue of the Antiquities *at the Royal Irish Academy, bringing out volumes between 1857 and 1862.*

CHAPTER NINE

William Wilde, *Ireland, Past and Present; The Land and the People*, 1864

A young woman named Mary Travers began a campaign of perse-cution against the Wildes in the aftermath of William's knighthood, which came in 1864 as a recognition of his invaluable work on the Irish census. William was invited to give a lecture entitled "Ireland, Past and Present; The Land and the People" to the Young Men's Christian Association. The lecture took place in the Metropolitan Hall in Dublin in April 1864. Later printed by McGlashan & Gill, in this lecture William provides a swift and concise overview of the history of Ireland, via the collections of the Royal Irish Academy, drawing also on the archeological work he himself had done, his folk collecting, and work on raths and crannogs. His lecture is a summation of his knowledge of early Irish history, right back to the first inhabitants. In the extract below, William gives his opinion on the Great Famine and on the economy of Ireland in the 1860s.

Outside the hall where he was speaking, Mary Travers distributed a poem entitled "On the Dubbing in Dublin Castle," a satire on William's recent knighthood, which marked the begin-ning of her campaign of agitation. On the night, Mary Travers paid young boys to carry placards with the words SIR WILLIAM WILDE AND SPERANZA and sold copies of her letters to William in an attempt to sabotage the talk. The ensuing libel case is documented below, in Chapter 10.

Despite or maybe because of this drama, the lecture was well received. The extract here is from the concluding section of William's lecture on his contemporary Ireland.

Ireland, Past and Present

Let me now turn to the *present*. Two thousand years at least have elapsed since the earlier raths, the stone circles, the great forts, and the sepulchral monuments which I have described to you, were constructed. During that long period, which dates from the early occupation of Ireland by the Celtic race until now, Firbolgs, and Tuatha de Dannans mixed with Milesians, have gradually but steadily pressed towards the setting sun, and finally accumulated in the south and west, there living for the last century at least upon potatoes and with a landholding scarcely capable of supporting human life, and paid for, not by its produce but with money continually earned in England or at public works at home, and continually crying for aid and not to be relieved from the consequences of food failure. Often magnified and sometimes unjustly denied, which though practical in extent, were almost perennial in occurrence, since the sudden potato blight, famine, and mortality of 1745, until that cycle culminated in the great calamity through which we have so recently passed. Thousands of the race remain yet in Connaught and parts of Munster, although thinned out by the famine, the pestilence and by emigration, eking out a miserable existence on one or two acres of land, and, as I have already stated, earning the price of it by annual harvest migration.

...

Twenty-two years ago there certainly were in Ireland about eight and a half million of people. Had the rate of increase continued at even the low calculation of one per cent, per annum, what, think you, would our population have been now? Upwards of ten millions – a number that England, with all of her wealth and manufactories, has occasionally found difficult to feed in times past. What would have become of them, I know not; but this I do believe, that had not events to which I have glanced in a previous part of this lecture taken place, some of us would not have had as good dinners as we seem to have enjoyed today; few would have been able to wear as fine clothes; nor should I have been addressing as happy and smiling faces as I see around me. The cry is still "Westward Ho!" The manifest destiny of the Celt is being fulfilled; and ocean steamers, each capable of holding 10,000 persons, are sending these hardy pioneers to help, by amalgamation, with other races, in founding the great empires of Australia, America and Canada; to spread the English language, and to carry Irish hardihood, bravery and poetry throughout the world.

Let us take good care of those who remain; respect their prejudices, comfort them in their afflictions; sympathize with them in their sorrows, join with them in their mirth; above all, be just with them in our dealings and teach them by example as well as precept, a love of truth, cleanliness, self-reliance, and a more perfect system of agriculture. Education they have got the offer of from the State. Let us bid God speed to those who have left, or are leaving, in this great exodus, at the rate of "a million a decade" and which has been lately well-described in the *Times* as one of "attraction and not repulsion," – and let the Celt, from whatever land he may have settled in, still look Erin-wards, not with envious and angry eyes, but with "fond affection and recollection" of the land of his birth.

CHAPTER TEN

Letters from Speranza

A scandal rocked Dublin and brought the Wildes even more national and international attention when, in 1864, Jane Wilde was sued for libel by Mary Travers, possibly William Wilde's mistress. On December 12, 1864, the case of Travers versus Wilde opened in the old Four Courts in Dublin. The case was brought before Chief Justice Monaghan and lasted five days, with a formidable legal team lined up on each side. Isaac Butt, nationalist MP, was one of the team of counsel for Mary Travers, and Edward Sullivan, later Lord Chancellor of Ireland, headed the Wildes' legal team. The Travers libel case attracted widespread public interest and amusement as the private life and letters of the Wildes became public property and fodder for newspaper articles. Below is the letter that was the main focus of attention and the cause of the charge of libel. Mary Travers won, but was awarded a derisory one farthing, for damage to her "honor." It was generally felt that Speranza had been the winner in terms of public opinion.

May 6, 1864

Sir – You may not be aware of the disreputable conduct of your daughter at Bray, where she consorts with all the low newsboys in the place, employing them to disseminate offensive placards in which she makes it appear that she has had an intrigue with Sir William Wilde. If she chooses to disgrace herself that is not my affair; but as her object in insulting me is the hope of extorting money, for which she has several times applied to Sir William Wilde, with threats of more annoyance if not given, I think it right to inform you that no threat or additional insult shall ever extort money for her from our hands. The wages of disgrace she has so loosely treated for and demanded shall never be given her.

Jane F. Wilde[1]

Speranza continued to write poetry, as well as translate, and brought out Poems by Speranza *in 1864, dedicated to her two sons. Froken Lotten von Kraemer was a Swedish friend of Speranza's, the daughter of Baron Robert von Kraemer, lieutenant of the province of Upsalla. They visited Dublin in August 1857, where they consulted William about Lotten's hearing problems. Speranza befriended the young woman Lotten and returned her visit in 1859 and again in 1961, which she mentions in* Driftwood, *teaching herself Swedish and maintaining a lively correspondence. In this letter, Speranza writes of the heartbreaking sudden death of her young daughter Isola, in 1867.*

Dearest Lotten,

I write to you in deep affliction. You will see by the paper I send that we have lost our darling only daughter … she had been a little ill with fever in the winter – but recovered – Then we sent her for a change of air to her uncle's – about 50 miles away – There she had a relapse and sudden effusion on the brain. We were summoned by telegraph and only arrived to see her die – Such sorrows are hard to bear. My heart seems broken – Still I have to live for my sons – & thank God – They are as fine a pair of boys as one would desire. But Isola was the radiant angel of our home – & so bright & strong and joyous. We never dreamed the word death was meant for her. Yet I had an uncontrollable sadness over me all last winter – a foreboding of evil – & I even delayed writing to you till I felt in my heart more of energy & life – Alas! I was then entering the shadow which now never more will be lifted.[2]

CHAPTER ELEVEN

William Wilde, *Lough Corrib and its Shores*, 1867

William had been spending a great deal of time in his house in the West of Ireland, Moytura, near Cong, where he purchased part of his mother's family lands – a place known to him since childhood. In 1867, he published his most popular book, Lough Corrib, the only one which ran to a third edition, a love letter to his native part of Ireland, opening with the refrain, "Westward Ho!" and providing an attractive account of the region for the general reader, using archaeology, history, and mythology as the basis for his travel writing. William uses a lively, amusing style of narration and says, "our object is rather to interest the reader, and the tourist in the history, antiquities and scenery of this portion of the West, than amuse him."

Cong

CONG – in Irish, *Cunga*, "a neck," so called for its situation upon the isthmus that here divides Lough Mask from Lough Corrib, and also *Conga-Fechin*, in remembrance of its patron saint – is an island formed by a number of streams that surround it on all sides. There is water everywhere – gliding by in the broad river; gushing from the surrounding rocks; boiling up in vast pools that supply several mills; oozing through the crevices of stones; rising in the interior of caverns; appearing and disappearing wherever its wayward nature wills; passing in and out everywhere, except where man tried to turn it – into the monster dry canal. The village, which is approachable by four bridges, and occupies a small hill, is T-shaped, and consisted in 1861 of 88 houses, and 469 inhabitants. It is a market town, and was formerly a great milling depot; to which latter circumstances, and the patronage of the adjoining extensive ecclesiastical establishment, it no doubt owed its origin. As the tourist approaches it, a good view of the eastern end of its old abbey is presented; and, turning up by the main street, he has before him the base of the ancient cross.

Outside the confines of this village, the scene presents a remarkable contrast – upon the south and east, all is bare, grey limestone rock; while on the west and south lies a beautiful, well-wooded, and highly cultivated demesne, through which glides the clear stream of the Cong River, up the lower portion of which we passed in the "Eglinton." The eastern roads lead to The Neale, Ballinrobe, and Kilmain, and by Headford to Galway; and its south-western to Lough Mask, and through the Joyce's Country by Maam to Connamara. The northern and western streams divide the village from the county of Galway.

The Annals of Cong, which, if all collected, would almost form a history of Ireland, might commence with the battle of Moytura, stated by the bards, and believed by the early writers (where they assign dates to events), to have been fought in the year of the world 3303. For some centuries after that period, and down to the Christian era, the great plain to the west and north immediately adjoining this village, and on which the battle took place, was thickly studded with inhabitants, whose dwellings and monuments the tourist is now about to visit, and which are certainly amongst the most remarkable in the British Isles. It does not appear, either from history or tradition, that St. Patrick or his attendants visited Cong, or that his immediate successors approached nearer to it than Inchangoill; but, in the seventh century, St. Fechin of Fore, struck, perhaps, with the extraordinary resemblance which the natural features of Cong, and its underground rivers, &c., bore to his ecclesiastical home in Westmeath, is said to have blessed this neck of land, from which the extensive parish of Cong still takes its name, and to have erected a church here; and the good man left his track, and gave his name to several holy wells and churches in the district westward of this village.

It is also said that, so early as A.D. 624, an Irish king, Domhnall Mac Aedh Mac Ainmire, founded an abbey here, and that St. Fechin was its first abbot. The hagiologists, or saints' historians, must settle this question. Colgan also states that Cong was "celebrated for diverse churches, as their walls and remains at this day testify." Such may have been the case at the beginning of the seventeenth century, but they no longer exist, and the name of only one remains, attached to the field of the *Killeen-breac*, or "little speckled church," to the south of the present abbey grounds. There is, however, a stone near the river side, in an old garden to the left of the second eastern bridge, which takes precedence of all other stones in Cong, upon which the craft of man had been exercised in Christian times, and which, as known by the Irish name of *Leach-na-poll*, or the "flagstone of the holes," is here figured. It is a large triangular red grit flag, 2 feet thick, and 8½ feet long in its greatest diameter, from under which a never-failing limpid spring issues. Its upper surface is hollowed into five basin-like smooth excavations, averaging 12 inches wide, and 4½ deep, and usually known as *Bullauns*, from the Latin *bulla*, a bowl; and which, from their being invariably found in immediate connexion with the most ancient churches, may be regarded as primitive baptismal fonts.

What description of church St. Fechin erected here and dedicated to the Virgin before his death, in 664, or where it stood, is unknown, although Colgan states, in the *Acta Sanctorum*, that it was "his own monastery." But in truth the Irish church of that period was but the daimliag, or domhnach ... and the Culdees or early ecclesiastics lived either within it, or in stone cells, or cloghaunes, or in wooden houses, in the surrounding enclosure, and occasionally in the adjoining round tower.

Cong was originally a bishopric, and with those of Tuam, Killala, Clonfert, and Ardcharne, was named among the five sees of the province of Connaught, regulated by the Synod of Rath-Breasill, in Leagh (the present Queen's County), in the year 1010; but ... the see was shortly afterwards removed to Enaghdun. Keating also styled it a bishopric.

In 1114 the Annals of the Four Masters state that Cunga, with Kilbanon and several other ecclesiastical establishments, "were all burned this year." The bishopric removed, and the cathedral burned; but the odour of sanctity still clinging to the venerable locality, hallowed by the remembrance of St. Fechin, a fine opening offered to the Augustinians to display their architectural taste, and to establish their ecclesiastical power in Connaught – so that probably between the former date and 1127–28, when the deaths of two of its Airenaghs (or conventual superiors), Gilla-Keerin O'Roda, and O'Draeda, are recorded, the abbey and monastery were founded. This magnificent establishment was erected for Canons Regular of the Order of St. Augustine, whose vast territories and rich possessions extended not merely throughout Connaught, but into several counties in the South and East of Ireland; in whose keeping were placed the great family deeds and records of the West country chieftains and landed proprietors; who constructed the grandest piece of metal work of its age now extant in Europe; whose principal was a Lord Abbot; and who left us the beautiful structure we are now hastening to examine.

To fill up, however, the middle distance, and paint the foreground of the historic picture of Cong after the erection of its abbey and monastery, without stopping to notice the accession or to record the deaths of its dignitaries, we find it the peaceful sanctuary of the last monarch of Ireland during the ruthless times which followed the English invasion, when the O'Conors and O'Donnells, sometimes joining with and sometimes fighting against, the Anglo-Normans, devastated the country, pillaging and burning the abbeys and churches, and then slaughtering one another; – down through the dark period of Saxon misrule and legalized injustice, when the white-rocheted friars formed their last long-winding procession, as, passing out of their beauteous abbey they wound their way with lingering footsteps over the adjoining bridge, and took their *Iompo-tuaghfil*, or "left-handed turn," ere they cast a final look upon its tall tower and peaked gables, cutting sharp and clear against the western sky.

The Augustinian monks have departed – the bells have tolled their last peal; the altar lights are extinguished; a few valuables, snatched in haste, have been preserved, and Cong is a ruin – whence every sculptured stone that could be removed was built into the hovels around – and which was barely held together by the fostering arms of the luxuriant ivy, until lately cleared of rubbish, and its mullioned windows and decorated doorways carefully restored.

What an eventful period has intervened, during which Cong and its environs were granted to the Kings and Binghams, or were possessed by the O'Donnells and the Brownes – when Macnamara, the freebooter, and Webb, the murderer, left tales for the guides and their gaping auditors to batten upon – when it was attempted to alter and amend religious opinion by persecution and penal enactments – when law, if at all administered without the aid of the cudgel or the horsewhip, was an injustice: and clerical magistrates (not in the days of Cromwell) could command the regular army to remove from public view a stone bearing the name of two venerable, and perhaps pious, ecclesiastics, who flourished here some eight hundred years ago!

Governmental confiscations of property there were in abundance. Debts accumulated as the result of reckless extravagance, contested elections, unsuccessful horse racing, Chancery suits transmitted for generations, bills of cost, interest on loans, and mortgages – the dowers of dowagers, and the jointures of grandmothers and aunts. All these kept the gentry poor; but they were tolerably loyal to the State, which sheltered them in a country where the king's writ did not run. The people were also poor, and likewise ignorant, improvident, and uneducated, although far superior to the same class in the sister country; but they were disloyal – not so much on account of Protestantism, tithes, Catholic disabilities, the want of educational resources, or any other real or sentimental grievance, but because they had never been conquered by either force, justice, or kindness. However, what diplomacy and the sword could not effect for so many centuries, a single night of blight, followed by a few years' failure of the tuber introduced by Raleigh, achieved. It cut off almost in a moment the food of an entire nation. The rent ceased; the mortgages were unpaid; the agents failed; the poor rates could not be collected. Pestilence followed the famine; the herds diminished; the workhouses buried such of the dead as had not fallen by the wayside; emigration helped off the remaining living; the Encumbered Estates Court sold up the bankrupt landlords, as in a sheriff's sale, and often at half the value of the land; the old properties changed hands; and, although hundreds of thousands were lost both to the owners and creditors, new blood was infused, and new life and energy thrown into the country. And now, the old Abbey of Cong, and the adjoining estates, with many a mile to westward of this famed locality, have been purchased with the produce of ability, honest industry, and successful commercial enterprise. The ruins of Cong church and monastery occupy the south-western angle of the island, but have become so mixed up with modern buildings, that it is now difficult to find a point of view from which to give a good representation of the entire. The succeeding illustration, taken upwards of forty years ago by Samuel Lover, R.H.A., from a point somewhat to the north-east of the bridge of the Killeen-breac, truthfully represents the scene.

Among the splendid ecclesiastical remains of Cong, the twelfth century advocates may revel, and defy us to prove an earlier date for their erection than that of the introduction of the Augustinian order into Ireland, even if their ornamentation and design did not afford ample data for judging of their age.

These ruins would scarcely have held together to the present day, had not Sir B. L. Guinness restored several of the dilapidations, cleared out much of the rubbish which had accumulated within and around them, and rendered the burial ground sufficiently decent for the interment of Christian people. As the following observations, made nearly thirty years ago upon this abbey by that keen observer, graphic, witty describer, and patriotic antiquary. Cæsar Otway, faithfully accord with our own early recollections of Cong, we here insert them in order that the contrast may be the more striking: – "Though the Connaught abbeys suffered less waste and demolition from those who originally suppressed them, the busy and fond superstition that turned their interior into places of much-desired sepulture, has defaced and destroyed what the avarice of Henry's court-iers and the curse of Cromwell had spared; and so there is now no one to care for and protect an Irish abbey – it, instead of being allowed to repose in the much-respected solitude of a Tintern, a Bolton, or Fountains, in England, is now anything but beautiful, it is not even decent; the *genius loci*, outraged, we might almost personify as weeping, while all around is disgraced and desecrated." And, after describing the rooting pigs and the rioting boys that he found enjoying themselves among the ruins, he adds, "Whoever enters an Irish abbey, let him be Protestant or Romanist, must sigh for some law appointing conservators able to restrain the ignorant and reckless hands that are, day after day, obliterating the religious monuments of the island. And here let me be allowed another remark respecting the, to me, evident difference that exists between the monastic remains previous and subsequent to the Anglo-Norman conquest. Of the former we find no remains that were not directly devoted to religious worship, churches, oratories, crypts, and shrines (except the round towers, which alone seem to have answered any secular purpose). The old Irish monastic, in his Culdee simplicity, was contented with his little hermitage composed of wattles, his humble cell of perishable materials; living on the milk of a few cows, and the fish that the adjoining river (as at Cong) abundantly supplied; enough for him was the conviction, that at the approach of the barbarous spoiler he could retreat, with his vestments and holy things, by means of a ladder, into the round tower, through its high-placed doors; from thence to see his humble cell committed to the flames, there to bear the privations he was so well accustomed to, until the ravagers retreated, and the tyranny was overpast." And, of Cong, he further adds, "I have seldom, indeed, seen a place so dilapidated; I was not only disappointed, but vexed, to see it so overthrown and dismantled."

We enter the abbey from the village by a very beautiful doorway, which, although it has been often figured, we would here present to our readers, but that we know it is of the "composite order," having been made up some years ago of stones taken from another arch in this northern wall. Within it, we find ourselves in the great abbey church, 140 feet long, entirely paved with tombstones; – facing the east window, with its three long, narrow lights, and having in each side wall of the chancel a slender window looking north and south. The chancel walls are perfect, but the northern wall of the nave no longer exists. Underneath the chancel window the guides and village folk maintain that Roderick O'Conor was buried, when, after fifteen years' retirement within this abbey, he died here in 1198. But this we know from history to be incorrect, for the Donegal Annals distinctly state that "Ruodri Ua Concobair, King of Connaught and of all Ireland, both the Irish and English, died among the canons at Cong, after exemplary penance, victorious over the world and the devil. His body was conveyed to Clonmacnois, and interred on the north side of the altar."

But, although Roderick himself was not buried here, others of his name and lineage were. Thus we read that, in 1224, "Maurice the Canon, son of Roderick O'Conor – the most illustrious of the Irish for learning psalm-singing and poetical compositions, died – and was interred at Cong." It is probably his tomb which is pointed out as that of the king. "A.D. 1226, Nuala, daughter of Roderick O'Conor, and Queen of Ulidia, died at Conga Fechin, and was honourably interred in the church of the canons." And, in 1247, Finola, daughter of King Roderick, died at, and was probably buried at, Cong. But, although the dust of the last monarch is not beneath our feet, that of chieftains, warriors, and prelates remains, and especially that of the abbots, down to the days of James Lynch, whose decorated tomb is dated 1703; and even later, for the Rev. Patrick Prendergast, who was always styled "The Lord Abbot," was interred here in 1829.

Several of these ecclesiastical tomb flags are decorated with crosses, fleur-de-lis, chalices, and ornate croziers, &c.; and there are a few Latin inscriptions in raised letters, but with one exception no Irish writing can be discerned anywhere within the confines of the abbey. In the south wall there is a recess, with a circular arch, and probably the tomb of the founder, or some munificent endower; there are also in the south wall piscinæ, and other minor details of church architecture, unnecessary to describe; and lower down upon the same side is the small chapel-tomb of the Berminghams, once so powerful in Ireland, and who so identified themselves with their adopted country, that they dropped the Norman name, and assumed that of Mac Feoris. They became Lords of Athenry, and acquired great possessions in Connaught.

During the clearances recently made, a few objects of interest were discovered, and among them a stone, bearing a portion of the incised cross here figured. It is too narrow to have been a monumental flag, the longest arm of the cross being but thirteen inches; it was probably one of the terminal crosses that marked the boundaries of the ancient sacred enclosure.

CHAPTER TWELVE

Jane Wilde, *William Carleton*, 1869

This poem is a tribute to Speranza's friend and correspondent from her early days, William Carleton, born 1794, an older novelist and author of the popular 1830 collection Traits and Stories of the Irish Peasantry. *When Carlton died in 1869, in Dublin, an unhappy and bitter man, she wrote this poem in his honour and published it in* The Nation.

died, January 30th, 1869

Our land has lost a glory! Never more,
    Tho' years roll on, can Ireland hope to see
Another Carleton, cradled in the lore
    Of our loved Country's rich humanity.

The weird traditions, the old, plaintive strain,
    The murmured legends of a vengeful past,
When a down-trodden people strove in vain
    To rend the fetters centuries made fast;

These, with the song and dance and tender tale,
    Linked to our ancient music, have swept on
And died in far-off echoes, like the wail
    Of Israel's broken Harps in Babylon.
No hand like his can wake them now, for he
    Sprang from amidst the people: bathed his soul
In their strong passions, stormy as the sea,
    And wild as skies before the thunder-roll.

Yet, was he gentle; with divinest art
    And tears that shook his nature over much,
He struck the key-note of a people's heart,
    And all the nations answered to his touch,
Even as he swayed them, giving smiles for gloom,
    And childlike tenderness for hate that kills –
As rain clouds threat'ning with a weight of doom
    Flash sudden, silver light upon the hills.

But, he had faults – men said. Oh, fling them back
    These cold deductions, marring praise with blame;
When earthquakes rend the rocks they leave a track
    For central fires issuing forth in flame;
And by the passionate heat of gifted minds
    The ruddest stones are crystallised to gems
Of glorious worth, such as a poet binds
    Upon his brow, right royal diadems!

Like the great image of the Monarch's dream,
  Genius lifts up on high the head of gold,
And cleaves with iron limbs Time's mighty stream,
  Tho' all too deep the feet may press earth's mould.
Yet, by his gifts made dedicate to God
  In noblest teachings of each gentle grace,
Through every land that Irishmen have trod
  We claim for him the homage of our race.

With pen of light he drew great pictures when
  Nothing but scorn was ours; and without fear
He flung them down before the face of men,
  Saying, in words the whole world paused to hear:
So brave, so pure, so noble, grand, and true
  Is this, our Irish People. Thus he gave
His fame to build our glory, and undo
  The taunts of ages, – strong to life and save

So, with a nation's gratitude we vow
  In every Irish heart a shrine shall be
To The Great Peasant, on whose deathless brow
  Rests the star-crown of immortality.
The kings of mind, unlike the kings of earth,
  Can bear their honours with them to illume
The grave's dark vault; so Carleton passes forth,
  As through triumphal arches, to the tomb!

CHAPTER THIRTEEN

Jane Wilde (with Sir William Wilde), *Memoir of Gabriel Beranger*, 1880

Before he died, William Wilde was working on a three-part life of the antiquarian and illustrator, Gabriel Berenger; Speranza completed it upon William's death. A French Huguenot, Beranger had been born in Rotterdam in 1729 and came to Dublin in 1750, where he opened a print-shop. Touring throughout Ireland, he sketched many now-vanished churches and ruins. He died in 1817. William collected his prints and volumes. The first three sections of William's book had already been published by the Royal Historical and Archaeological Association of Ireland between 1870 and 1873; Speranza wrote the fourth part, which appeared in 1876. William's project was then published as one work in 1880.

Nothing material remains now to be added to the closing words of the MS volume, except to give a list of Beranger's principal sketches, with a description of the buildings and monuments, as written by himself, and appended to the drawings in his authentic sketch-books. Sir William Wilde left a list of above 200 Irish sketches, taken about the same time by Beranger and other artists, and states that Mr. Huband Smith has in his possession a very valuable volume, dated 1782, containing 127 sketches of castles and churches in the county of Dublin, many of them being by Beranger; and he expresses a hope that this volume may be placed in the care of the Royal Irish Academy, to whose keeping Dr. Sharkey, of Ballinasloe, has already entrusted the large volume of Beranger's drawings of which he was the possessor.

The list compiled by Sir William was intended for publication, should the memoir of Beranger have appeared as a volume, to accompany a selection of specimens of his art taken from the coloured sketches. In the interests of archæology it is to be hoped that this project may yet be fulfilled, as it would be of the highest importance to have accurate drawings and descriptions of the state of the castles, abbeys, and architectural remains of Ireland a hundred years ago, made accessible to the artists and antiquaries of the present day. The whole of the list would occupy too much space in this Journal, but some of Beranger's descriptions of remarkable places and monuments will be found interesting, and may be given from his note-book.

In all cases he seems to have made his observations with the greatest care and accuracy, and simple, conscientious truth of detail. It is these qualities which give a permanent value to his sketches as works of art and of authority. The three small sketch-books, Nos. 2, 3, and 4, contain altogether seventy-two coloured drawings, including thirty castles, several cromleachs, round towers, abbeys, and mountain views. The sketch-book No. 1 is wanting. In a note on the subject Sir William says: – "The sketch-book lost by Mr. Clarke may be that to which Dr. Petrie alludes, as affording the original of the illustrations which follow on page 247 of his work. They must have been drawn with great accuracy to satisfy Petrie's fastidious taste."

The cromleachs and Druidical remains are amongst the best of Beranger's drawings. The clear, firmly defined outline of these grand old monuments suited exactly the strong precision of his artist hand. Of the Druid monument on the Three-Rock Mountain, of which there is a highly effective sketch, he says:-

"This mountain has on its summit three huge heaps of rock, piled one on another, and seen at some miles distance, from which the mountain takes its name. I take them to be altars on which sacrifices were offered. The Plate represents one of the most entire; it rises about eighteen feet above the ground, and is accessible by an easy ascent. It has several basins cut in the rock on its top of the size of the inside of a man's hat; but one more remarkable than the rest, being of an oval form, and measures 2 ft. 6 in. in length by 2 ft. broad, the depth in the centre 9 inches. Another of these, but less entire, is at some distance. I have copied every stone as they are fixed, and the regularity which is observed in piling them convinces me that they are the work of men, as they could not grow in that position. The sea is seen, though more than six miles off. The extensive summit of this mountain, the parched ground, and its solitude, made it the most awful spot I had ever seen."

The cromleach on Howth he describes as one of the grandest mausoleums, the supporters, or rough pillars, being 6½ ft. high, 6 ft. 2 in. broad, and 2 ft. 8 in. thick.

"The two pillars remaining are nearly of the same prodigious bulk, but the others lay in fragments on the ground, under and about the stone, which by some shock was thrown down. The top stone is about 14 ft. long, and from 10 to 12 ft. broad, and the supporters being so high, it must have made a noble figure standing, as the tallest man might stand and walk under it at his ease."

The sketch of this cromleach is very fine and bold, and gives one an idea of the gigantic power of the men who raised it. It is followed in the sketch-book by a calm and beautiful scene – the Round Tower at Swords, the ruined church, and the old burial ground.

"This tower," says Beranger, "is not as elegantly built as some others, and is all plastered over and yellow washed. From the continual burying in the cemetery the ground is much raised round it, so that the door of the Round Tower is accessible from the ground, which is not so in anywhere the soil has not been raised, and they required a ladder, the entrance being generally from 12 to 14 feet from the ground. Some projecting stones, like brackets, appear inside at various heights, on which, I suppose, wooden stairs were fastened."

A distant view of Croagh Patrick, with Clew Bay in the foreground, is a faithful, but inartistic drawing. Beranger says:–

"The view from the summit is most extensive and delightful, having before us Clew Bay, with its 400 islands, and for a background the mountains of Erris and Tyrawley. To the left are the islands of Achill and Clara, and in the rear the wild romantic Joyce country. It is the highest mountain in Ireland, and famous for the residence of St. Patrick there, and from whence he expelled all the venomous reptiles. The top has the form of a cone. It is generally enveloped in clouds, and through it appear points. On the summit is a stone altar, where mass is said on the Saint's day. I believe it to have been formed by a volcano, as may be seen from the drawing."

On the islands in Clew Bay he saw several "sea monsters basking in the sun." The bay and islands form a beautiful picture. The tumulus of Dowth is represented by a faithful, well-defined outline of the mound, with the little temple, or tea-house, on its summit erected by one of the Netterville family. This drawing, taken ninety years ago, is the more interesting, because, owing to the excavations made some years ago, the appearance of the mound had been greatly effaced. Beranger calls it "a sepulchral monument, composed of stones and sods," and believes it to be 60 ft. high. He adds: "There is a modern temple at the top, intended for a gala-room, with a gallery to hold an orchestra."

"About a mile distant, at New Grange, is just such another monument, of which the stones were used to pave all the neighbouring roads, and by constantly demolishing it a long gallery was discovered, leading to an octagon room, with three closets of a curious construction, being composed of rough stones without mortar, in which a corpse was found. I did not draw its view, because Governor Pownall has given so accurate a description in the *Archæologia* that I had nothing left to add."

The Moate, at Navan, Beranger considered a place of strength – a fort – and not a sepulchral monument. He described it as

"A Danish fort, defended by a high and rapid *glacis*, very difficult of ascent. The mound seems to have been divided by steps, which I did not perceive in mounting, but the sun, which was hid, emerging from a cloud whilst I was drawing, made the steps appear as represented in the drawing. It is very difficult to draw monuments of this description."

There is a very striking description of the Druid's chair, five miles from Dublin, thus described:–

"This piece of antiquity, the only one yet discovered, is situated at the foot of the Three-Rock Mountain. It is supposed to have been the seat of judgment of the Arch-Druid, from whence he delivered his oracles. It has the form of an easy chair wanting the seat, and is composed of three rough unhewn stones, about 7 feet high, all clear above ground. How deep they are in the earth remains unknown. Close to it is a sepulchral monument or cromleach, supposed to be the tomb of the Arch-Druid. It is 15 feet in girth, and stands on three supporters, about 2 feet high, and is planted round with trees. The top stone is 8½ feet long."

Of Dalkey, and the castles existing there in his time, he writes:–

"Dalkey was formerly a strong fortress, composed of high walls, defended by seven strong towers, at some distance each from the other. One of them was demolished for the sake of the stones; the others remain in ruins, inhabited in part by some poor people. The place is very rocky; many like woolsacks are scattered about close to the building."

In the view of Balymount Castle, three miles from Dublin, described as a place of considerable strength, as proved by the massive walls and towers, is appended the following adventure:–

"Hearing from some cottagers that there was at a little distance an enchanted cave, with subterranean wards extending various ways for some miles, which some men at different times had tried to explore, but never returned, I was piqued by curiosity, and begged to be shown the place.

"I found a vault of good masonry, about 8 feet high and 6 broad; descending this a few steps, I found at the end a square opening, which had to be entered on all fours. I procured two candles, and on offering a small reward, got a boy to follow me. For fear of mephitic vapours and suffocation, I fastened a solid branch of a tree to my cane, on which I stuck my candle, so that the light was about four feet before me.

"I then entered on my hands and feet, holding the light before me, followed by the boy, with a candle in his hand. I went this way some yards, and then found two shafts – one leading to the right, the other to the left. I took the first, and advanced a good way, until I met with two more shafts and a very cadaverous smell. Here my boy began to be afraid, and I thrust my candle as far as I could in the two passages, but it always burned clear. Considering, however, that the boy would not go further, and if I went alone, and my candle was to be extinguished, it would be hard to find my way back in the dark, I prudently returned the way I came, observing the construction, which was of stone, and in good preservation. It was clearly an aqueduct for supplying the fortress with water, and must have been made at a great expense by some powerful chieftain, who had his residence there."

Beranger excelled in drawing cromleachs, and the sketch of the Druidical remains at Dowth is one of his best. He thus describes it:–

"This monument was once a circle of large stones, of which four only remain erect. Two are fallen. A quarry, on which they stand, being worked, occasioned the demolition. The stones are of great size, one measuring 9 feet above ground, and 21 feet in circumference. They strike the mind with their awful appearance, and make one wonder at the immense labour it must have cost to gather and move such enormous masses, and fix them as they are. Some great chief is undeniably buried within this circle. I suppose by this time the continual quarrying has destroyed even these four stones; if so, I saved them from oblivion."

Rath Croghan, where the kings of Connaught were crowned, makes but a poor, bleak picture. The mound is, however, grand in extent, the height being 400 feet, and the circumference 1350 feet. He was conducted to it by Charles O'Connor, the celebrated historian, "which history," says Beranger, "has just gone to press. It is composed out of the Annals of Connaught, kept by the kings, the originals, in Irish, being in his possession, and form a large parcel of folio MSS on parchment, which occupied a whole side of his library."

The cromleach at Brennan's Town, seven miles from Dublin, forms an excellent picture, from its great mass and perfect preservation. He says of it:–

"Though it has stood for many ages, it is as entire as if it was lately erected. It differs from all that I have seen in this particular, that it has a large stone for a floor, on which stand six supporters, which seem to support the top stone, though it rests only on three. These supporters are half sunk in the ground, and form at present a kind of cave, of which the top stone is the roof, and I could stand easily under it erect. I drew it sitting on the ground, to show the under part of the top stone, which I could not do when standing upright."

Many of the ancient castles drawn by Beranger are extremely pictur-esque; but descriptions would be only tedious, unless the originals could be represented by a series of woodcuts, and at some future time this may be done.

The task of bringing Beranger's life and works before the public, so ably commenced, and almost completed, by Sir William Wilde, has now ended. The predecessor of Petrie (both of them of French origin) in the perfect and sympathetic rendering of Irish scenes, though lacking Petrie's exquisite and delicate artistic touch, Beranger holds a high and important place in the history of Irish art; and to Sir William is due the merit of having directed the attention of the present generation, by whom he was almost unknown, to the labours of this zealous and accomplished artist.

Beranger's admirable and accurate sketches, preserving with such fidelity for the present age the appearance and characteristics of Irish architectural remains, as seen existing a hundred years ago, have added a valuable page to our national history; and our modern artists also might be incited by the study of his works to follow in the same interesting line of artistic work. At present they are devoting themselves, perhaps too exclu-sively, to copying the aspects of a mute, unsouled nature. We all know how beautiful are the silent glories of the Irish landscape school – the sunsets – the moonlights – the glancing green and gold on forest trees – the purple haze of the mountain height; but these aspects and effects are the same all the world over, wherever light falls on tree, or rock, or river; they are linked with no human emotion, and are independent of all historic memories: they do not speak to us of men, nor of nationhood.

Beranger, on the contrary, worked systematically at the art symbols of a people's life. He tracks their history in the savage gloom of the Druid's altar – the graceful form of the mystic pillar-tower – the fierce strength of the Norman fortress, and the stately grandeur of the mediæval abbeys and castles, with their splendour of architectural symmetry and beauty, and their sacred or warlike memories and associations. While our modern artists, for the most part, lavish their genius on the ever-changing moods of Nature, he gives us the changeless work of human minds – the passions and storms of great epochs – the warfare and the piety, the culture and the progress, of a people, as expressed and symbolised by their national monuments – in a word, the whole life of the past races out of which our nation was builded, and which only can be known by the works their hands have wrought, and the beauty of the ruins they have left. And it is, truly, a nobler thing for an artist to evolve the soul of a people from its monuments, and to give as subjects for our contemplation the steadfast historic landmarks of our country, than to note the atmospheric changes of our skies. Let us have both if we can, but not neglect the higher and greater aim while perfecting the lower.

Petrie has combined both in that most wonderful of pictures, which Irish genius has given to Irish art – his "Clonmacnoise" – where all that is holy and beautiful in work, and thought, and symbol, is blended together – the sculptured cross – the ruined church – the graves of the kings – the kneeling people – history, poetry, reverence – the deepest pathos, and the sublimest hope: while the whole scene is flooded in the magic beauty, the softest atmospheric lights of an Irish sunset sky.

The great solemn Past has its claims upon our artists; the lonely island church, where a saint has prayed – the grim ruins of the castles of the Pale – our beautiful and desolated abbeys – here are subjects for the artist's hand, illustrative of the faith, the suffering, and the struggles against oppression, that have made up the history of Ireland for the last thousand years.

It was the earnest wish of Sir William Wilde that Beranger's sketches, so rich in suggestions for our living artists, and so important to the antiquary and archæologist, should be published in a volume along with the Journal. Probably more than two hundred of these interesting works of art may be still forthcoming. He would have undertaken the work himself, even at his own expense, had health and life been spared to him. But it is to be hoped that the project will not fall to the ground, and that the publication of so useful and valuable a book will be accomplished by some one with an intellect as energetic, a mind as well stored with the requisite knowledge, a heart as zealous for the advancement of Irish art and literature, as were the intellect, the mind, and the heart of Sir William Wilde.

III   1880–1893: Speranza in London

Speranza moved to London in 1879 to join her sons there and made her living by writing for the Pall Mall Gazette, *the* Burlington Magazine, *and other journals and magazines.* Driftwood from Scandinavia *was Speranza's first full-length book that was not a translation or a book of poetry and proved popular. An entertaining travel book, it drew on her contacts in Sweden and her visits there. Covering her journeys from Dublin to Denmark and Sweden and her return home via Germany, accompanied by William, Speranza includes her translations of Scandinavian poetry. It was published in 1884 by Richard Bentley, paying her 50 guineas for the first printing of 1,000 copies. Lively and polemical, the book reflects her interest in contextualizing questions of cultural importance in Ireland and England within a wider European context. In one chapter, for example, Speranza makes the point that Swedish women writers were celebrated and valued within their society, much more than was the case in Britain and Ireland. She also draws parallels between Irish nationalism and Prussian patriotism in the age of Napoleon.*

CHAPTER FOURTEEN

Jane Wilde, *Driftwood from Scandinavia*, 1884

Stockholm to Berlin

Again we are on the Baltic; the gentle summer sea of forest foliage and winding curves, and granite crags crowned with pines, and the thirteen hundred islands, each island a verdant park, lying on the calm blue water.

We see now how easily the early races in their migrations could pass from island to island, and find food and sustenance in plenty, with the great shadowy pine forests for their dwelling-place; and in their wild, joyous freedom, with nature, energy, independence, and vigorous work, lived a healthier and therefore happier life than all our vaunted civilization can now offer to poor, dyspeptic, nervous, depressed, worn-out, hypochondriacal humanity.

The black eagle of Prussia floats above us – the vulture, it should rather be called, as nothing escapes its talons nor the desolating swoop of its terrible wings – and German resounds on all sides. It seems quite easy to speak, after the obscurities of Danish; but we scarcely need to practise our lingual knowledge, for all the Prussian officers on board speak English perfectly.

The captain is monosyllabic and stern, and is quite insensible to flattery. How to reach the heart of a Prussian is as difficult a problem as to find the fourth dimension. They are a very intelligent people, but morose. They cannot help it; they are born so. Courtesy is the grace of the Gothic branch of the Teutons only.

On the third day after leaving Sweden, that land of noble hears and noble manners, we reached Stettin. It was evening. A sea of light was around us; a roseate mist filled the atmosphere, through which soft cloud-masses rose like the snow-peaks of an Alpine world, and every peak was flushed crimson in the last rays of the setting sun. Thus transfigured, even Germany looked beautiful.

At once on arrival the *Douaniers* came on board, and there was great rending and searching of bags and boxes by rude, resolute Prussian hands. Alas, for the Scandinavian homage to womanhood! It had vanished along with the mountains and the islands and the glorious pine forests of the North.

Stettin is a handsome town, the bright, gay port of the Baltic where every traveller takes the rail to Berlin. There are fine public buildings and splendid terraces and handsome private residences, every window draped as for a festival with the gayest of painted blinds and the whitest of muslin draperies. The quays are crowded with shipping. Swedish iron is unloading in quantities to send over Europe; grapes are in cart-loads; potatoes ranged in huge sacks for export, like Ali Baba's forty thieves; fish enough to feed five thousand without a miracle; and excellent peaches at a penny a dozen.

There is much vociferation in the market-place. Every one is rapid, busy, and energetic in this active population.

Rows of women were standing in tubs under the bridges at their laundry work, beating the clothes in the water with resounding vehemence; other rows of women were seated behind huge water-vats filled with live fish, which they brought up in strainers for the buyers to inspect. Altogether, after a careful study of the market prices, I came to the conclusion that in Stettin one could live comfortably, even luxuriously, for sixpence a day; and in these days of confiscation without compensation, it is well to know that such a refuge exists for the plundered victims of a paternal legislature.

The fishwomen all wore immense black bonnets, with a high top-knot, precisely like the old caricatures of Queen Caroline; but the nurses looked very coquettish and theatrical in short, full petticoats, showing the long red stocking to the knee, high lace cap, with gold back, and massive gold earrings. There was no beauty, however, amongst the women. How unlike the bright, fresh faces of Hamburg, that city of pretty maidens, are these neutral-tinted north Germans! Already we miss the oval Swedish type and dark hair, and have come suddenly upon the globular head and hay-coloured face and tresses of the original Teuton.

A wedding was going on in the fine old church of St. James, and we entered unopposed. The altar was decorated with coronals of scarlet and white roses, and large high pots of myrtle and orange trees in full bloom were placed at each side. Two chairs were set in front on a carpet for the happy pair, and a circle of chairs behind for the company. There was no emotion; every one looked sensible, stolid, and staid, and the crowd of spectators was short, square, and hay-coloured, according to the national type. But a wedding is always a pretty sight. It is so interesting to contemplate the beautiful confidence of youth and love that believes the book of fate is now closed with golden clasps, and that no word of sorrow will ever be written there again.

The bridegroom was a young Prussian officer, tall, straight, handsome, with broad shoulders and slim waist, erect and manly, the regulation moustache perfect. The bride had a pale, dreamy, Marguerite aspect, with her forget-me-not eyes and coils of fair hair, like masses of unspun silk. The upper class women have all this dreamy, mist-woven, wraith-like look; while the lower classes seem made of sandy grit, like their soil.

Scandinavia is a granite world upheaved by a volcano, veined with silver and rifted with cataracts, a land of untamed, tumultuous forces; but Germany is the sandy deposit of an ocean which once must have overflowed it, and out of the sediment the German population has evidently been formed, mere rolled-up balls of sand, heavy and colourless, without type or form or feature worth mentioning. On the railroads and at other public places where crowds gather together, I never could distinguish the back from the front of a German head, and talked to both hemispheres indiscriminately – hair, eyes, skin all being of the one colour, and the features quite unappreciable.

...

From Stettin to Berlin is a four hours' journey by rail over level land, dry, sandy, flat, and monotonous. No horizon, no outline; nothing to be seen except saw-mills, turf bogs, the quaint red Noah's ark, the waving skeletons of the tall thin poplars, potato-fields, and hay-ricks precisely similar in form to the German heads. Now the dust begins from these dry plains. Dust-coloured women look up at us from the potato-ridges; dust-coloured men, strong and stolid, are busy at work, patient industry in their faces – a people evidently made for work; to stand in the furrows to plough and sow, and never lift their eyes from the oxen they drive. Industry is the special virtue of the Saxon race. While the Celt is willing to die, perhaps uselessly, for an idea, the Saxon labours and lives for gain. It is the one sole ideal that stirs the sluggish current of his nature. Toil is his element, his destiny, and the greed of gain the one impulsive force of his life. Nature meant him for this; to stand by the wheels of commerce and civilization, and keep the machine well oiled and in order. In the workshop of the world the Saxon is master.

But now the empire city of Germany rises up from the circling, sandy desert, stately and grand in the dim, misty, uncertain twilight. The city that proceeded out of the mouth of a king: he commanded, and it was made. The capital of an empire generally expresses the life of a whole people in stone and marble, and is the product of many generations; but Berlin is the city of one man and one mind. When the father of the great Frederic chose to have a capital worthy of his name and fame, he ordered the citizens to build houses, palatial residences, with magnificent frontage. Nothing at the back, nothing inside, he cared not; nor even if the unhappy builders were ruined and made bankrupt. So Berlin arose, the daughter of kings, the Palmyra of the northern desert. The old portion of the town is narrow, poor, and mean; but the grand, world-celebrated Unter den Linden is a pathway for kings.

From the great Brandenburg gate, surmounted by the Car of Victory, to the royal palace, is an avenue of architectural splendours nearly a mile in length, unrivalled in any capital of Europe. Two rows of lime trees extend the whole way. Between them is the fashionable promenade; at each side is a broad carriage drive, and beyond are the palatial houses, palaces, hotels, gardens, and numerous statues, not of Greek gods and nymphs, but of national heroes who have lived and worked for the national glory; the colossal equestrian statue and monument to the Prussian hero, king, and chief, the great Fritz, Rauch's greatest work, towering above all. On the palace bridge that crosses the Spree are eight fine marble groups, representing Strength, Wisdom, and Victory, the fitting symbols of the Prussian people. A flight of marble steps leads up to the museum. On one side is the colossal group of the Amazon and Tiger; on the other the Lion-tamer, by Rauch. The royal palace is opposite, a vast and magnificent edifice, with its grand and stately Rittersaal, the scene of the torch-dance, and many other grand and awful ceremonials which the Prussian court hold sacred.

These Margraves of the Marshes have been a wonderful race, and bravely fought their way, by intellect, courage, and hard work, from obscurity to empire, making of this poor sandy desert of Prussia, for which Nature has done so little, one of the foremost nations and powers of the world – a power, indeed, that could crush all Europe with its immense military strength, if it were so minded, and not restrained by family ties and diplomatic motives.

Some parties in Germany dread the chances of Russian supremacy, but there is no fear. The Slav will never conquer the Teuton. So it is written in the book of fate. Neither will the French ever succeed in a war of reprisal or revenge. They need not attempt it; for still, as of old, the two races, Celt and Teuton, have their destiny marked out distinct and separate. The Celt is the head of gold, but the Teuton is the hand of iron to bind and hold and rule. To the Celt is given the empire over ideas, to the Teuton the empire over men. One is the brain of the world, the other the strong arm and dauntless will. In 1806 France stood with her foot upon the neck of prostrate Germany; but destiny is irresistible, and in 1870 we saw the vengeance of Nemesis, and beheld Germany with her sword at the heart of fallen France. Napoleon the Great, having resolved to make the Rhine the boundary of France, and France the head of all Europe, declared war against the whole Teutonic race. At Jena the power of Prussia was annihilated, and twenty days after, the conqueror entered Berlin in triumph, from which the King of Prussia, and his sad, beautiful queen, Louise, fled in terror and dismay, to undergo a series of the most mournful humiliations, which resulted finally in the death of the broken-hearted queen. But her wonderful beauty and tragic fate has made her memory undying in the hearts of the people, and endeared her race to the nation.

Meanwhile, Napoleon enthroned himself in the royal palace at Berlin, drank from the king's golden cups, drove in the king's chariot, and packed up and sent off to Paris all the royal, national, and artistic treasures that struck his fancy; amongst others, the magnificent bronze Car of Victory from the Brandenburg gate. But here, again, Nemesis displayed her fatal and unerring justice; for the French, too busy for a long time afterwards with wars and changing dynasties to arrange their spoils, never had time to unpack the case containing the Car of Victory; and after the entry of the allies into Paris, it was found exactly as it had been removed, and, being brought back to Berlin in triumph by the Prussians, was replaced in its old position over the splendid portal to the Unter den Linden, where it still remains.

But in 1806 Prussia had no thought of triumph; for, devastated and prostrate, she was forced to accept peace at the sacrifice of half her territory and five millions of her subjects, and for seven long years afterwards Germany was but the vassal of France, too humbled to remonstrate, too weak to strike. Prussia had been wholly crushed at Jena; Austria at Austerlitz; after which the Emperor Franz laid down the imperial crown of Germany at the feet of Napoleon, and the thousand-year-old German Empire ceased to exist. But throughout these weary years of servitude and weakness a new spirit was awakening in Germany. Above all, in Prussia arose a fierce hatred of oppression and a resolute determination to regain independence. Cities, fortresses, and armies were, indeed, fallen and lost; but the king, wise beyond his time, saw that a country can still be regenerated by the will and energy of the people, and he set himself the task of arousing and stimulating the slumbering soul of the nation to a sense of its rights and duties by education and organization, by civil and intellectual freedom.

The old feudal bondage, with all its pompous pretensions of caste and class, was swept away. King, nobles, and peasants became united in the one common bond of nationality, and the sacred and indivisible formula, "For God and our Country," was accepted as the national creed. This reaction from oppression, this recognition of the eternal rights of man, in opposition to the claims of an oppressive, exclusive aristocracy, created a nation of heroes. The sublime truth at last was seen and acknowledged, that above all defences for a nation the spirit of patriotism in the breast of a people is the most powerful and invincible.

With the overthrow of feudalism and the spread of education, all barriers were removed from progress, and the people sprang to their full stature when they obtained the consciousness of their full powers.

Bondage to another nation was resented as a wrong done to human freedom, and indignation against this long vassalage to France raged in every heart, and soon found utterance in the words of earnest men, of the patriots, orators, and poets, which were heard above the thunders of the French cannon.

A great writer has said, "Beware of cadenced words; they make revolutions." And it was the poets of Germany, above all, that aroused the patriotism in the heart of the German people that rushed like a tempest over the armies of France. Poets like Arndt, Follen, and Theodore Koerner, who chanted "The Holy War of Liberation" – for by that name the national movement took its place in history – led the youth of the generation in a fever of excitement that dared all hazards and chances to death or glory. Then it was also that Fichte, the sublime philosopher of the eternal laws of right and duty, "who would have made of humanity a republic of gods," poured forth those eloquent addresses to the German people, which ran like liquid fire in their veins; and Heinrich Steffens, professor of philosophy, in place of a prelection to his class, uttered *ex cathedrâ* a fiery appeal to the students to join the holy war. "I could not rest," he said, "till I spoke out the feelings of my heart. Tears were in my eyes, and at last I fell on my knees, and the appeal became a prayer." Goethe alone of all the leaders of intellect stood silent and apart. "How," he said, "can I sing without hatred, and how can I hate without youth?" Besides, he told the nation, "The man is too strong for you; you will never break his chains."

But the youth of Germany were lifted by enthusiasm above all fear, and they at once established the celebrated Tugendbund, in which they bound themselves by solemn oaths to freedom or death. Destiny also came to their aid, for the strength of "the man" had already begun to melt away in the snows of Russia. This was in 1812, and the next year, 1813, Prussia boldly took the field against Napoleon, and all Germany raged with the inspiration and the hopes of freedom. Thus, on one side was Napoleon, with his dazzling glory, his iron will, and his colossal armies; the man who had shed more blood to give crowns to his brothers than the great Revolution to gain the rights of man. On the other side were arrayed youth, courage, great eternal principles, all that lift life above egotism, and makes one sacrifice it without regret. Ideas against force; justice against oppression; the people against an insulting foreign government; and to break this foreign yoke the nation was ready for any sacrifice. Every one brought in their gifts to the national treasury to defray the expenses of the war. The ladies of the highest rank gave their costly jewels, and were proud to wear ornaments of iron in place of circlets of diamonds. A nobleman who had entertained the king one day with splendid magnificence, as soon as the banquet was over, sent the whole service of silver, and heirlooms of centuries, to the mint to be melted down for the national fund; and the young girls, who had nothing else to offer, cut off their long golden tresses and laid them as an offering on the altars of their country. Thus all classes were united in one great brotherhood of nationality – kings, nobles, philosophers, the fiery youths of the universities, the peasants in their devastated homes, all had but one object – to free their country from the power and presence of their French masters. "The War of Liberation" had then all the intoxication of a holy crusade. "One fortress of ours at least has never been prostrated," exclaimed one of the leaders – "the national hatred of foreign oppression." But the glowing aspirations of the country thus arrayed against France was represented, above all, by the two poets, Arndt and Theodore Koerner, whose words were as a living flame that kindled the hearts of all the youth of Germany to the wildest enthusiasm.

With the opening of the year 1813 both Russia and Prussia declared war against Napoleon, and "The War of Liberation" began in earnest. Then it was that Koerner, with all the most daring spirits of the time, joined Lutzow's celebrated band, called "The Black Band of Vengeance." This name sufficiently expressed their purpose. Even their dress had a sombre significance. It was black, with red-and-gold facings. These were the colours of Germany, but also the emblem of their resolve – victory or death.

The brilliant heroism of "Lutzow's Wild Huntsmen" has made the corps illustrious in German history. For them Koerner write his most passionate songs of freedom, and chanted them to the music of clashing swords. In his first engagement against the French he was severely wounded, but immediately on his recovery rejoined the band, having taken an affecting leave of his family and of his affianced bride, never to behold them more.

On the last night of his fated young life, when an engagement on the morrow seemed imminent, as the French army, under Davoust, were hovering near, the excitement of his feelings denied him either sleep or rest. His soul, like a burning altar-brand, sheathed in the frailest clay, could not choose but reveal itself in flame; and as he paced up and down in the early dawn, he wrote down, on a leaf torn from his pocket-book, that wild, wonderful song, destined to be so famous from the tragic circumstances of the composition, in which the fire of his nature has become, as it were, fixed and enduring for all ages, as the fiery spark prisoned within the opal gem.

In the following translation I have endeavoured to give some idea of the fierce power of this bridal hymn of battle.

The Sword Song

> Sword in my right hand gleaming,
> Where Freedom's flag is streaming,
>> I grasp thee in pride,
>> My love, my bride,
>>> Hurrah!

> Fierce in thy glorious beauty,
> I'll guard thee with lover's duty,
>> Unsheathed in the fight,
>> For God and the right.
>>> Hurrah!

> "Where the blood-red rain is falling,
> I'll answer my lover's calling;
>> For the sword by thy side
>> Is a patriot's bride.
>>> Hurrah!

> "And so thou art crowned victorious,
> With the palm or the laurel glorious;
>> Let the battle's breath
>> Bring life – bring death.
>>> Hurrah!"

Ha, sword, in thy scabbard clashing,
Dost thirst for the wild war flashing,
 Round the flag of the free,
 When thou'rt wed with me?
  Hurrah!

Our vows be the swift balls bounding,
Our hymns be the trumpet's sounding,
 Let the earth flush red
 For our bridal bed.
  Hurrah!

"Where Freedom's flag is leading,
Where tyrant foes lie bleeding,
 I pant and pine
 For the crimson wine.
  Hurrah!

"The sheath may no longer cover
My lips from the lips of my lover.
 As the lightning bright,
 I leap to the fight.
  Hurrah!"

Then, forward! all dangers braving,
As a flame in my right hand waving,
 Whether crowned or dead,
 Ere the day has fled.
  Hurrah!

Forward! where glory is calling –
Forward! where tyrants are falling –
 Where the red ranks ride
 I shall bear my bride.
  Hurrah!

As a lover her bright form pressing
To my heart in a mad caressing,
   With a wild delight,
   As a bridegroom might.
     Hurrah!

Thunder with thunder meeting,
Be the chant of our bridal greeting;
   At the altar stand
   Freedom's sacred band.
     Hurrah!

Curse on the coward would falter
By such a bride at the altar!
   Be her kiss rose red,
   On the dying or dead.
     Hurrah!

Now the bridal morn is breaking,
The trumpets peal the awaking,
   With my iron bride
   Death and fate are defied.
   Hurrah for the bride –
     Hurrah!

As Theodore read aloud this song to his comrades, he struck his sword against the scabbard at the end of each verse. At the same instant every sword was unsheathed, and the clash and clang of the sabres of Lutzow's Wild Huntsmen responded in magnificent music to the poet's "hurrah!" Ere the mighty echo had died away, the French were seen approaching through the grey mist in overwhelming numbers; but the Black Band of Vengeance never retreated before a foe, and in vain Lutzow sounded the *rappel*.

Theodore, foremost and bravest, the boldest of the bold, dashed forward amidst a shower of bullets, performing prodigies of valour as he cut his way through the enemy's ranks with his sword, his iron bride. At length his horse was shot under him, and he fell. In an instant he was surrounded, for the young poet of freedom was the most dangerous enemy which tyranny had evoked in Germany. For him, whose genius had inspired a nation to vengeance, there was no quarter. A bullet passed through the young hero's body as he lay prostrate, shattering his spine, and Theodore lay dead with the music of his own wild death-song still vibrating on his lips.

The eldest son of the beautiful Queen Louise was the late Frederick William King of Prussia. Her second son reigns now as Emperor of Germany, and three prospective emperors of her line are already existing. When she received the conquering Napoleon at Berlin, after the humiliation of Prussia, it was observed that at dinner the queen could neither eat nor speak for tears. The great master of Europe could then scarcely have imagined that the fragile, helpless victim of his ambition was destined to found a great and enduring empire in Europe, while his own race and dynasty were fated to fall from every throne he had erected, and to lose all he had gained through countless victories and millions of dead.

In 1848 the Berliners again grew mad with a dream of freedom; this time, however, not against France, but, inspired by French ideas, they denounced kings, priests, churches, and all authority, and demanded the establishment of a European republic, and the universal brotherhood of nations. One pities the poor king at this crisis, for everything that is told of him shows his goodness of heart and inspires interest. He was full of talent and noble impulses; true and honest, self-sacrificing and devoted to the nation, yet fated for a life of much trial and sorrow, and a weary, lingering death. The ingratitude of the people must, above all, have been bitter to him. He devoted all his energies and his income to beautifying the capital, and making it a city worthy of a great nation. At one time, it is said, he gave away a whole year's income to expend on the decoration of the museum; and the rumour went that he lived upon nothing, half-starved himself, to save money for artists' paintings and statues to glorify Berlin. And what splendid workers he gathered round him! Rauch, and Schwanthaler, and Danneker, and Kaulbach, and Cornelius, names unsurpassed in any age or country. Berlin is so grand and regal, and has been made so beautiful by the kings and the artists, that one wonders how the people who threw up the barricades, and fought the troops in '48, were not too much awed to pass along this magnificent Unter den Linden, the Via Sacra of great memories and the works of transcendent genius, to lay their dead before the windows of the palace, and to call upon the king to come forth on the balcony and remove his hat to salute them.

The poor, humiliated king! In the face of old Blucher on his marble pedestal! Even the queen had to appear, and the palace servants were ordered to serve out costly wines to the Berlin mob, whose hands were red with blood, and who had just defied and insulted the king.

Herwegh was the favourite poet of that era, and his spirited songs served to keep the revolutionary tendency at fever heat. They were chanted in chorus in the *cafés*; in the streets, the barricades, and wherever the young generation gathered in the wild tumult of their reckless daring. I have translated one of his songs here as a specimen. It is comparatively mild, but was a great favourite with the heroes of the barricades; and still, even during the late Franco-Prussian War, it was the favourite of the people, and was constantly sung by the ardent and fiery young students at their assemblies and suppers while waiting to be summoned to fight for Fatherland against the invading French foe.

The Knight's Pledge

> The tedious night at length hath passed;
> To horse! to horse! we'll ride as fast
>   As ever bird did fly.
> Ha! but the morning air is chill;
> Mine hostess, one last goblet fill;
>   We'll drain it ere we die!

> Thou summer grass, why look'st so green?
> Soon dyed in blood of mine, I ween,
>   With damask rose thou'lt vie.
> The goblet here! with sword in hand
> I pledge thee first, my Fatherland,
>   Oh, blessed for thee to die!

Again our mailed hands raise the cup:
Freedom, to thee we drink it up.
　　Low may that coward lie
Who fails to pledge, with heart and hand,
The freedom of our glorious land –
　　Her freedom, ere we die!

Our loved ones! – ah! the glass is clear;
The cannon thunders – grasp the spear;
　　We'll pledge them in a sigh.
Now, on the foe like thunder crash!
We'll scathe them as a lightning flash,
　　And conquer, though we die!

As we are discussing the revolutionary poets of Germany, I must add here one specimen also from *Rueckart*, yet of a gentler and tenderer beauty than can be found in Herwegh's "Songs of Hatred," or the war-chants of the period – a poem by a true poet, in which the human pathos is deeper, and the subject-motive diviner than even the wrongs of a nation, or a victory gained in the strife of contending armies, can evolve from the heart.

The Poet's Destiny

The Priest of Beauty, the Anointed One,
Through the wide world passes the poet on.
All that is noble by his word is crowned,
But on his brow th'acanthus wreath is bound.
Eternal temples rise beneath his hand,
While his own griefs are written in the sand;
He plants the blooming gardens, trails the vine –
But others wear the flowers, drink the wine;
He plunges in the depths of life to seek
Rich joys for other hearts – his own may break.
Like the poor diver beneath Indian skies,
He flings the pearl upon the shore – and dies.

A fine park lies outside the great Brandenburg Thor; but beyond that all is bleak and barren – a vast, colourless sandy desert.

For about two miles or so round the city Berlin is magnificent. Trees are cultivated in profusion – the sombre pine, the shadowy linden, the feathery acacia – for without this forest shadow the glare and heat in summer would be intolerable from the sand-plains; and the effect of trees along the roads and through the streets of a great city is in the highest degree beautiful and refreshing.

We put up at one of the great hotels Unter den Linden, where the full stream of life was for ever passing before the windows; and the first visit we received was from the police, for the law requires that directly on arriving at Berlin you must state your name, business, object in travelling, whence you come and whither you go. I confess that I like this solemn intensity of espionage as a contrast after the unfettered independence of the North. You feel you are becoming of importance to Europe, and taken up once more, like a lost stitch that was running to perdition, and woven again into the vast mesh of European diplomacy.

Hotels, *cafés*, and the *table d'hôte* of civilization are the same all over the world – a composition of glare, gilding, mirrors, and marble tables. Berlin has perhaps more gilding than usual; but the Berliners thoroughly understand room-decoration and cookery. Our private apartments were panelled in white and gold; the ceiling papered in white satin; cornice of white and gold; a broad border of crimson flock below the cornice, another above, placed flat on the ceiling, both sides edged with gilt moulding; – the effect, with the crimson velvet chairs and sofas, being altogether pleasant and bright. Ceilings painted with wreaths of foliage are very general in Germany, as in Scandinavia, and nothing can be more refreshing to the eye.

It is wonderful that some of our home artists do not make ceiling-painting a speciality, and save us from the dull depression of a great square of whitewash over the head; a surface actually ready for the artist's work and hand, but which is never utilized in our ordinary houses.

As there is no stone near Berlin, brick is universally used for building purposes, and much stucco is employed. Mr. Ruskin abhors stucco as a sin against truth; yet without its aid Berlin would look very sombre in its sandy plain, with the atmosphere of bleak grey vapour overhead. Even the great Brandenburg gate is of brick made to simulate stone. Now, with the adventitious adornment of stucco, the city has an affluent, festive, well-kept, well-cared-for aspect, to which the bright window-decorations greatly contribute.

Flowers and gay, painted blinds are the peculiarity of all continental towns; the windows always seem draped fresh and garnished as if for a festival or a wedding, and never have the dull and dingy look of ordinary London windows.

Berlin is determined to look beautiful before the world, in spite of all natural disadvantages and deficiencies; and successive kings have vied with each other in glorifying the city and making it worthy to be the capital of the great Prussian nation. True, there is no grand Gothic pile like Westminster Abbey, no ancient feudal fortress like Windsor, for Berlin is but little more than a century old. All that is beautiful is quite modern, and truly it was no easy task to fight against soil and climate, and to surround the mere creations of yesterday with a noble historic interest by uniting them with the eternal sympathies and associations of a great people. The idea in all the great buildings is always palatial and superb. A whole parish might live in one of those great edifices, Unter den Linden, and there is quite a reckless expenditure in Berlin on everything intended for the public eye and the public pleasure.

The Zoological Gardens happen to be located in damp, dreary grounds – probably no other site could be had – where the animals die off rapidly of malaria. "But what matter?" said our *insouciant* Berlin friend; "we are rich enough to buy others." A thousand pounds was paid for an elephant; it died soon after, and then they bought another. There is neither sun nor air in the gardens, for the place is crowded with trees, so the extent of animal mortality is not surprising; and there is no view save from pond to pond. But the Berliners require shadow, and will not allow the trees to be cut down. The animals may suffer, but they are of no more consequence to the citizens than the little states and the little kingdoms the empire swallowed up in its path to glory. Yet whatever inspires respect for the great Prussian monarchy is treated with dignified reverence. The reviews, the pageants, birthday ceremonies, and royal processions are arranged with the most splendid scenic effect; always stately, impressive, and organized with dramatic precision, even to the number of captive kings and worshipping satellites that attend the triumph of the imperial victor. London never accomplishes anything so gorgeous in the way of a pictorial effect; a London pageant, indeed, seldom goes beyond a few soldiers, an unpicturesque crowd, and a huge mass of stolid police in frightful uniforms, who are in everybody's way, and add nothing to the beauty of the scene.

But we must now ascend the great white marble stairs of the museum. The central hall is supported on gilt pillars; colossal marble groups are at each side; and the walls are painted in fresco by Kaulbach and Cornelius, illustrating the history of humanity from the dispersion at Babel to the present time. Every great nation of the world is represented by a separate room: Egypt, Etruria, Greece, Rome, the Celt, and the Goth; and the religion, life, habits, dress, and arms of each people are illustrated by colossal mural paintings; while the cases are filled with actual specimens of their life and works. The temples of Attica are painted with all the splendour of sea, sky, and light. Rome is there, with its Forum, columns, and palaces, from the Tiber to the Capitol. The rude early races of the Stone Age and the fierce Turanian nomads are all represented with living power: the Huns of Attica; the Goths, with their warrior strength and weird, mystic mythology; the priests and temples of Odin; the Valkyrias in their white robes, with bare arms and long floating hair; Germania in her youthful prime as she trod the primal forests of Europe; – nothing has been omitted that could illustrate the races of the earth for six thousand years.

The Egyptian, Etruscan, and Byzantine cases are the most interesting. Some of the ornaments are beautiful and highly artistic. In the Etruscan collection were several small bronze figures wearing a diadem precisely similar in form to the antique gold Irish crown, with circular ornaments at the ears, now in the museum of the Royal Irish Academy. The crown on the statuettes was placed far back on the middle of the head, and the hair waved beneath. Many Etruscan Celts were also there, precisely similar to the Irish, an evidence of relation between the two races that would have delighted the author of "The Etruria Celtica."

Miscellaneous galleries of art are necessary, but they do not inspire like paintings, such as those of the Berlin museum, which are placed for a definite purpose, to illustrate an epoch, an idea, a great race, or a great history. German artists, above all, deal with the real life of humanity, or of their own people. All the great monuments of Berlin have the inspiration of nationality, from the kings and heroes of the Linden to the colossal

Germania that was unveiled but recently with such national fervour by the aged warrior-emperor in the presence of his people.

Christian Rauch is to Berlin what Thorwaldsen is to Copenhagen – the chief and head of sculptural art, the crowning glory of the capitol. But while Thorwaldsen's inspiration was wholly pagan and Greek, that of Rauch was wholly national and German. His life and career are interesting. As he himself said, he worked for sixty years unceasingly for the German people, for he was eighty years of age at the time of his death, in 1857. He began life as a mere youth in the service of the king – a kind of lackey in the palace. There he had ample opportunities of observing the beautiful queen, Louise, in all moods and attitudes, and by chance she discovered his singular genius, by coming one day suddenly into the room where he was at work upon a bust of herself. From that time she became his patron, and by her interest he was sent to Italy to study. There he became the pupil of the great Canova, and speedily made his mark amongst the best artists of Rome. Shortly after this period of his career Berlin fell under the power of Napoleon, and the unhappy Queen Louise, humbled and miserable, died of a broken heart at the early age of thirty-five. Inspired by gratitude, homage, and admiration for his beautiful patroness, Ruach, by order of the king, designed and executed the exquisite recumbent statue of the queen, in the purest white marble, now in the royal chapel at Charlottenburg. The young sculptor adored her memory, and, in the fervour of his faith and genius, resolved to make her beauty and his own name immortal. She wears the crown upon her head, and the features are chiselled with the utmost delicacy and grace.

On the king's death some years after, his statue, by Rauch also, was placed beside that of the queen. A soft rich light from the stained-glass windows falls on the two white marble figures placed side by side, and on a marble Christ upon the Cross that stands upon the altar. On the king's sarcophagus is written –

> "Meine Zeit in Unruhe,
> Meine Hoffnung in Gott."

He had need of the hope, in compensation for the bitterness of his trials and sufferings.

The Teuton gods of old were voracity and fighting; now they are smoking and philosophy. Since the end of all the excitement of the Franco-Prussian war, and the establishment of the dull routine of a universal police, a *blasé* air has become fashionable amongst the young men of society; a cavalier contempt for everything; a wearied look as if indeed life were not worth living for; and it is evident that Schopenhauer and pessimism have replaced the transcendental categories of Kant.

"The sons of the Spree," as Heine calls the Berliners, now pride themselves on being sceptical and sarcastic. A Voltairean irony is the proper thing, the *vrai chic*, when dealing with the most solemn subjects. Sentiment and sensibility have quite gone out of fashion, and no Werther is any longer possible amongst the men, nor a Bettina von Arnim amongst the women: even a Goethe may never again be evolved from the depths of the Teutonic soul.

There is no animosity whatever in their hearts against France, which is noteworthy. On the contrary, they pine to be restored to the favour of the siren nation of the world, and to drink of the cup of her enchantments. Yet there is one thing they are determined on, that Alsace and Lorraine shall never be given back. So Strasbourg may still wear her mournful veil of black crape amidst the circle of her marble sisters at Paris.

Speech has also undergone a remarkable change. The present race of fashionable Berliners only pronounce half the words in a sentence, as if accuracy and clearness were altogether too much trouble. The letter "r" is not pronounced at all. As a vocable it has entirely been extinguished in good society. The clear vocalization we noticed in Swedish pronunciation is wholly wanting. The nonchalant Berliner would look on it as an unnecessary waste of vital energy. Yet they all speak French, though with an ineffaceable German accent, and English perfectly, as if born to the manner, and they are very proud of this proficiency. It is only the native speech that they slur over and swallow and mutilate, as if, like a base-born relation, they were utterly ashamed of it.

Yet the Berliners have one excitement left that makes existence endurable. The theatres are crowded nightly. Every one finishes off the weariness or the turmoil of the day by a quiet rest, to witness simulated suffering which they are not called upon to share, or a pleasant series of complicated adventure which they can enjoy without the trouble of action.

All civilization is perhaps going the same path, for the whole science of happiness now is to forget, and at the theatres alone can weary humanity hope to find "the waters of forgetfulness." Life is becoming such a tangled mass of claims and duties, such a feverish flush of evanescent excitement, such a desolating flood of small observances that kill all great thoughts, such a poisonous undergrowth of weeds that choke the good seed till no soil is left for a serious purpose, or a deep passion to take root in, that we all long to fling off the whole burden at times; to forget the weary treadmill of social custom and usages; to end the vain strivings between desires high as heaven and the iron limitations of a cruel fate strong as the gates of hell; and peace comes best to us at the theatre. We are interested, and yet we are allowed to be passive; no false phrases are necessary, no grimace of simulated pleasure; we enjoy or disapprove inwardly, calmly, rationally; given up wholly to the idea, to the charm of fine elocution and gorgeous scenery, and the interest of a three-volume novel without the trouble of reading it. Therefore the weary, overworked, exhausted slaves of society throng the theatres everywhere, seeking rest without dullness and excitement without effort. The Berliners above all, the most exhausted apparently of all humanity, find their only solace within the enchanted circle of their magnificent opera-house.

There we had the supreme delight of seeing and hearing *Faust*, Goethe's tremendous drama of sin and doom, *acted* in his own grand words, not sung in the inane distortion of an Italian libretto.

...

The German stage has many great and gifted actors. Intense power, force, and truth, with a full resonant voice, are their leading characteristics. Above all, they act with intellect, as if entirely one with the author whose words they utter, and whose spirit they interpret.

In all these qualities, so essentially belonging to the highest dramatic genius, Mr. Irving approaches the German style more nearly than any other English actor. And the part of Mephistopheles, with all the intellect and irony, the versatility and supreme mastery over the minds of others, seems created for his weird and powerful genius.

The house was crowded from floor to ceiling, as Goethe is still a name to conjure with. He is the Shakespeare of Germany, sacred, canonical, believed in; his verbal inspiration not even questioned. Sceptics in all else, the creed of a true German still begins with the first article of faith – "I believe in Goethe."

There was little beauty or style to be seen in the crowd; only a sea of maize-coloured heads and faces, where we miss the rose tint upon snow of Danish beauty.

During the intervals every one promenades in the corridor, and takes ices or coffee. And when the play is over, there are delightful opportunities in the saloon for friendly meetings and greetings, and acute criticism and renovating refreshment.

The gas is not abruptly turned off with cruel celerity, as in our theatres, when the play ends, but ample time and space is given for social unbending and recreation after the strong intellectual strain on the nerves and feelings.

The theatres, also, are luxurious in comfort. Nothing is *gênant*; plenty of space and freedom is allowed. We are not cramped and stiffened in a stifling box, nor bound hand and foot in a narrow stall, without the power of movement or the privilege of locomotion, for three or four hours of more than mortal endurance.

We need much greater consideration for poor humanity in our insular social usages, and should take a lesson from the Continent, where they have solved the mystery of how to enjoy without weariness.

Germany, however, fails in one point: German women do not ornament a pageant or a spectacle. At theatre, opera, at the promenade or in the street, they have all the same middle-class look, without even a picturesque ugliness; for what can be hoped for pictorially from a people with pale eyes, white eyelashes, and dust-coloured complexions? In fact, the German head, face, and figure are only suited for homely life, not for the light elegancies of fashion or the majesty of queens; neither the diadem nor the laurel wreath would suit them. An imperial coiffure would be quite disproportioned to a short, square figure, and a coquettish flower at the ear would only make the broad head look still broader.

German men are better-looking than the women, for the globular head denotes strength and intellect and suits the ideal man; but for grace and beauty a woman should have the ophidian head – the head of the Venus de Medici, not of the Capitoline Jove.

It may, indeed, be accepted as a law that a woman with a globular head must be homely and undecorated; for, by the inexorable fatality of cranial formation, she is doomed to wear huge, ungainly bonnets as her only head-covering.

In Denmark, from the delicacy of colouring and feature, they all look like ladies and gentlemen, the effect being aided by their well-bred ease of manner; in Norway they have the proud bearing of Arabs in the desert; and in Sweden they have the dignity of kings. But in Germany a bourgeois air is universal. They seem a people made for the common, work-day life. And the manner suits the figure and dress: it is hard and undecorated; wants trimming and garniture. German women are an excellent working, knitting, housekeeping race; this is their mission: and they like homely virtues in others, especially in the royal family.

The Crown Princess became exceedingly popular when they heard that she looked after her purchases and her marketing. "Ach, Himmel, it is beautiful!" they exclaimed. But the Crown Princess has higher claims to national appreciation. She is the head and leader of intellect in Berlin. Artist, reader, thinker, and doer, she unites all the culture of her father, the Prince Consort, with the sterling qualities of her mother, Queen Victoria. Her palace is a small court of the Medici, where every one of note in art, science, and literature is received and entertained warmly and graciously; and the princess on these occasions shows herself quite equal to converse with the most distinguished men, not only with ease and grace, but with singular and profound insight. And still she is a diligent student, even as she has been from the first days of her married life as the youthful bride of seventeen. Every day several hours are devoted to mental work, and the princess may now fairly claim her place as the most learned and intellectual of all the royal ladies of Europe, while at the same time she is equally distinguished for her zeal in all good and charitable works – a leader of intellect in the saloon, and a sister of mercy in the hospitals.

It is surprising how she finds time for her many and various avocations, for she is never absent from any of the Court functions, but always in her place to offer her homage to the aged emperor, and set the example of affectionate reverence which is due to the founder of the empire. They rise early, however, in Berlin – perhaps this is the secret why they can cram so much work into a day; and the ordinary Court life is very simple. They all seem to get up about six in the morning; dinner at one, supper at nine, and very little toilette, except on grand occasions. Social intercourse, also, is widely extended without much formality or trouble. The emperor is the father of his people, and acts as such, with kindly, personal interest. He knows every one, what they have done for Prussia or humanity, and no one is neglected who, by word written or deed done, is entitled to recognition and honour.

The empress was a beauty in her youth, and is content to live still on memories when she had no rival in good looks. Yet, if the Berlin ladies are not handsome, they have often a mystic, dreamy, prophetic, Ossianic look, which is interesting, suggestive of mystery and strength; a Lurley of the Rhine, or a resolute Brunhilda, who would hang up her lover by his belt on a nail in her dressing-room until he grew repentant for his sins. And certainly German women can inspire a grand passion. Men have died for love of them, though English Rosalinds may doubt the fact; and the women in return are capable of the most sacrificial acts of devotion and heroism for a husband or a lover. For earnestness is a true characteristic of the Teuton feminine nature. In addition, they have all the homely virtues, and are content with simple pleasures; a little music and dancing and a love affair fill their lives. They seem wholly without vanity or love of display, even to a fault. This remark, however, applies only to North Germany. Southwards, in the vine lands, the soul expands into more passionate warmth, the eyes grow lustrous, and the pale tints deepen in colour in the rich glow of the sunlit air.

The military have more pretension and style than any other class of the people. The young officers are a fine race, but whether their breadth of shoulder, convexity of chest, and tenuity of waist, is due to Nature or the tailor I cannot determine. The erect, military bearing and firm step of the Prussian contrasts wonderfully with the shambling, shuffling gait of the French soldier, who has no more form or firmness than the knapsack he carries. And, looking at the fighting elements of the two nations, one ceases to wonder over the surrender at Sedan, or the imperial crowning at Versailles. The lower classes are heavy and sensuous, dogged and obstinate, like their Saxon brethren of England; in both the love of gain is stronger than the love of glory, therefore they are patiently industrious.

Nature created them for toil; for the material, not the spiritual progress of society.

Goethe remarked this national sluggishness of mind and body, and lamented the inert nature of the German soul. The food and stimulants of a nation may have great effect upon the nerve system. If too heavy, they deaden energy; if too fiery, they impair judgment. The French achieve revolutions upon wine, but ruin them by absinthe. The Irish dream of revolutions upon *poteen*, but it is evident that the excitement is only transient. The Germans, who live on beer and cheese, are not, and never can be, politically dangerous. On the contrary, they are quiet and apathetic, subsiding into a lazy sensuousness when work is over. Music is their chief mental gift; this results from the form of their head. The Saxon English are also fond of music, but their voices are harsh and discordant, dulled with carbon, perhaps; whereas the Germans have a full resonant tone in singing, like the peal of an organ. The chest is large and capacious, the jaws strong and firm, the teeth are fine; and they all hold themselves better than the English – straighter and firmer, from being accustomed to drill and the use of arms; and they make excellent soldiers, working like machines with unquestioning obedience. There is no ambition to lead or to excel: the Saxon is meant simply as an instrument for higher natures to work with, but he never rises beyond the level of the useful working tool. Individuality, romance, poetry, philosophy, love of art and beauty, belong to a higher Teutonic development, and also to the Celtic race in an especial degree. Therefore the Celt is eloquent, reckless, ambitious, fond of glory above all things, and the praise and recognition of an admiring world.

These radical differences of race should be kept in mind by legislators, for they are eternal and unchangeable; and if the physiology of nations were more studied by Government, there would not be so many disastrous mistakes made in the laws framed for the people governed.

Everyone goes to Potsdam from Berlin. It is but an hour's journey, and trains are incessant. Potsdam is a town of palaces, the pleasure-house of kings; made beautiful by trees and water, and art that triumphs over nature. But there is no view: windmills, of course, in profusion; sand plains, turf bogs; a river in the distance; a flock of sheep following a shepherd through a grove of pines; red-tiled houses; rows of poplars – this is all I saw. It is the unseen that interests.

The palace is a stately shrine of great memories and great names, and the mind is drawn back to the past from the present. We think of Carlyle, who passed through all these rooms, and whose visit is as memorable as that of Voltaire; and of the careworn face of the much-tried Fritz, the meteor light that flashed up out of the Brandenburg marshes; of the mad tyrant of a father, the patient mother, the little sister who watched everything and kept notes for posterity, and the strange, mad doings of the whole family. And in the bleak, cold air, under the grey sky, we muse with wonder over the iron will that created Prussia out of a sandpit, and of the mighty Teutonic prince that went on adding land to land and crown to crown, all Europe looking on helpless, till the last great closing scene at Versailles, where Celt and Teuton stood face to face in the presence of Destiny, and the triumphant Teuton founded an empire on the ruins of French glory and the scattered wreck of French power.

Voltaire's rooms are still sacredly preserved in the palace, though the walls are scribbled over with caricatures and epigrams; and there are many relics of the great Fritz – not that he cared for luxuries. He built palaces for the world to see, and for the glory of Prussia; but for himself the plainest surroundings sufficed. A deal table, much stained with ink, old clothes, and philosophy, these were all he required at the close of life. The very name of his palace, *Sans Souci*, is an epitome of the eighteenth-century philosophy.

When Napoleon was at Berlin, he paid all honour to the memory of the great Fritz, and visited Potsdam in full dress, as if going to a king's reception, standing bareheaded in the rooms with reverential formality; but he also carried off the hero's sword, which Prussia bitterly resents; for, unlike the Car of Victory, the sword was never restored, and no one knows what has become of it. But it brought no luck to France; the destiny of conquest is with Prussia.

Yet a great empire does not of necessity mean progress. Personal ambition incites kings to conquest, not love of humanity. As Victor Hugo says,

"They climb on piled-up dead to clutch at crowns."

The world gains nothing by the fall and humiliation of any centre of civilization, nor by the annihilation of small states through the dominant force of an alien power. Individuality is the source of all intellect in a nation; freedom guided by love between the governing and the governed, not tyrannous coercion under the name of law. The soul dies under an autocratic rule of blood and iron, and a vast empire becomes at last but a vast barrack-yard, where the highest ideal of life is seven o'clock drill, the regulation step, and the strangulation stock; and there is no god left to civilization except the police.

Greece, in her glory, was the smallest of nations; and Italy, at the Renaissance, when she gave immortal names and immortal works to the world, was but an aggregate of petty states. Yet all and each were emulous of glory under their own banner and chief; pride in their own people, and reverence for their own traditions, keeping the sacred fire of intellect for ever burning, with the national ambition that achieves success. It is cultivation, not vastness, that makes the glory of an empire or of a country. Texas, for instance, is as large as all England and France put together, yet it has given to the world – as yet – nothing more than a generation of Cowherds.

The Celt always resisted dominant empires and bondage to routine, according to the instinct of all passionate, impulsive natures; for individuality in a human soul, and distinct nationality in a people, must be cherished to produce the fruits of genius, otherwise life becomes the mere mechanical work of a machine, not the spiritual work of the spirit.

The Teuton instinct of law and organization has now reached its extreme expression in the Prussian military empire; but the people submit very apathetically, according to their nature, to the iron hand of the autocrat, and console themselves with beer and philosophy – a dreamy philosophy, vague and colourless as their plains, no landmarks for the eye or the soul, only infinite monotony of sand-drift and grey mist, in which all enthusiasm seems to have died out or become unfashionable. "What matter?" is the outcome of all their speculations. "We only know the present; let us make the most of it, and live as best we can."

The Berliners even find their own language now a trouble to be evaded if possible. They look on German as a heavy and ponderous relic of the Middle Ages, and chiefly affect French talk and French literature.

Indeed, a Berliner assured me that he never read a work by a German author till it was translated into French. Then he got through it in half the time, for one can glance in a moment over a whole French page. But there is no skipping over German. One must read deliberately to "the bitter end" from the torturing habit, invented by the malice of grammarians, of placing the verb at the close of a phrase, so that we never know what we have to be, to do, or to suffer till we come to the very last word in a sentence of the usual inordinate and excruciating German length.

These were the views of my Berlin friend, a very learned and able man, but who had no pride in the language of Vaterland, and glided into French or English as often as he could; or, whenever he condescended to use the native idiom, only pronounced half the words in a sentence, or half the syllables in a word, according to the usage of the best society.

Our way home from Berlin lay through Hanover, where one could mourn over the iron rule and the extinction of independent states by seeing the result in the dull stagnation of all national progress.

Hanover was once the happiest of little kingdoms, with its beautiful parks, gardens, palaces, galleries, and theatres, and a royal family, in addition, that was beloved by all classes, and the head of a bright, pleasant, friendly Court, where everyone was received with kindly grace and urbanity, as a happy father might receive his numerous family.

But the whirlwind came, called the Empire, and the royal family were driven from their palace. The queen was insulted; the king was sent forth, a broken-hearted exile, to seek a home in a foreign land; and the royal treasury of the nation was seized and plundered by the alien robber-hands of Prussia. The Court was broken up; there was no longer any bright social centre to radiate joy and hope through the land by the encouragement of the head of the State, and the presence amongst the people of their own native king, whose interest in the welfare of the nation was as warm as their own. Silence and humiliation covered Hanover with gloom, and the pleasant little kingdom became a mere outlying police station for Prussia. And how was Hanover the better for the change? The revenue that used to be spent for the good of the country and people was carried off to Berlin to pay for the pomp and pageants of the empire, and in place of the refined and intellectual influence of a Court ruled over, as it ought to be now, by a native prince, with his charming wife, the Princess Thyra, sister of our Princess of Wales, Hanover has been given over to the callous insolence of glum-faced

Prussian officials and the stern rule of the stolid Prussian police. Victor Hugo exclaims with truth –

> "Oh, workers of the world, true splendour rests
> Not on great empires built on dead men's bones,
> Where all divinest things lie slain and buried;
> But in the holy strength of noble deeds,
> The holy words, Truth, Freedom, Sacrifice,
> That light earth's gloom as heaven is lit by stars!"

After leaving Hanover, the route homeward become too familiar for a record of impressions; but whoever desires fresh impulses, renewed vitality, increased nerve power, and to find the means of sending a new spring of life rushing up through the wearied heart, let them sail away to the beautiful islands of the Baltic, plunge into the glorious pine forests of Sweden, and look on the magnificent splendours of a northern night from the sublime solitudes of the Norway mountains.

CHAPTER FIFTEEN

Jane Wilde, *Ancient Legends, Mystic Charms, and Superstitions of Ireland*, 1887

Speranza published her two folklore collections, both in London, in 1887 and 1890, and she drew on William's research from many years previously to create popular, accessible, and well-structured tales that remained in print after her death and proved enduring and influential in twentieth-century Ireland. W. B. Yeats was the first of many admirers of this work and wrote of the first collection, "We have here the innermost heart of the Celts in the moments he has grown to love through the years of persecution when, cushioning himself about with dreams and hearing fairy-songs, in the twilight, he ponders on the soul and on the dead. Here is the Celt, only it is the Celt dreaming."[1] Included in the selection from her second collection, Ancient Cures, Charms and Usages of Ireland, *are some of her materials on the medical superstitions from folklore, clearly of interest both to her and to William.*

The Horned Women

A rich woman sat up late one night carding and preparing wool, while all the family and servants were asleep. Suddenly a knock was given to the door, and a voice called – "Open! open!"

"Who is there?" said the woman of the house.

"I am the witch of the One Horn," was answered.

The mistress, supposing that one of her neighbours had called and required assistance, opened the door, and a woman entered, having in her hand a pair of wool carders, and bearing a horn on her forehead, as if growing there. She sat down by the fire in silence, and began to card the wool with violent haste. Suddenly she paused and said aloud: "Where are the women? They delay too long."

Then a second knock same to the door, and a voice called as before – "Open! open!"

The mistress felt herself constrained to rise and open to the call, and immediately a second witch entered, having two horns on her forehead, and in her hand a wheel for spinning the wool.

"Give me place," she said; "I am the Witch of the Two Horns," and she began to spin as quick as lightning.

And so the knocks went on, and the call was heard, and the witches entered, until at last twelve women sat round the fire – the first with one horn, the last with twelve horns. And they carded the thread, and turned their spinning wheels, and wound and wove, all singing together an ancient rhyme, but no word did they speak to the mistress of the house. Strange to hear, and frightful to look upon were these twelve women, with their horns and their wheels; and the mistress felt near to death, and she tried to rise that she might call for help, but she could not move, not could she utter a word or a cry, for the spell of the witches was upon her.

The one of them called to her in Irish and said –

"Rise, woman, and make us a cake."

Then the mistress searched for a vessel to bring water from the well that she might mix the meal and make the cake, but she could find none. And they said to her –

"Take a sieve and bring water in it."

And she took the sieve and went to the well; but the water poured from it, and she could fetch none for the cake, and she sat down by the well and wept. Then a voice came by her and said –

"Take yellow clay and moss and bind them together and plaster the sieve so that it will hold."

This she did, and the sieve held the water for the cake. And the voice said again –

"Return, and when thou comest to the north angle of the house, cry aloud three times and say, 'The mountain of the Fenian women and the sky over it is all on fire.'"

And she did so.

When the witches inside heard the call, a great and terrible cry broke from their lips, and they rushed forth with wild lamentations and shrieks, and fled away to Slievenamon, where was their chief abode. But the Spirit of the Well bade the mistress of the house to enter and prepare her home against the enchantments of the witches if they returned again.

And first, to break their spells, she sprinkled the water in which she had washed her child's feet (the feet-water) outside the door on the threshold; secondly, she took the cake which the witches had made in her absence, of meal mixed with the blood drawn from the sleeping family. And she broke the cake in bits, and placed a bit in the mouth of each sleeper, and they were restored; and she took the cloth they had woven and placed it half in and half out of the chest with the padlock; and lastly, she secured the door with a great cross-beam fastened in the jambs, so that they could not enter. And having done these things she waited.

Not long were the witches in coming back, and they raged and called for vengeance.

"Open! Open!" they screamed. "Open, feet-water!"

"I cannot," said the feet-water, "I am scattered on the ground and my path is down to the Lough."

"Open, open, wood and tree and beam!" they cried to the door.

"I cannot," said the door, "for the beam is fixed in the jambs and I have no power to move."

"Open, open, cake that we have made and mingled with blood," they cried again.

"I cannot," said the cake, "for I am broken and bruised, and the blood is on the lips of the sleeping children."

Then the witches rushed through the air with great cries, and fled back to Slievenamon, uttering strange curses on the Spirit of the Well, who had wished their ruin; but the woman and the house were left in peace, and a mantle dropped by one of the witches in her flight was kept hung up by the mistress as a sign of the night's awful contest; and this mantle was in possession of the same family from generation to generation for five hundred years after.

The Stolen Bride

About the year 1670 there was a fine young fellow living at a place called Querin, in the County Clare. He was brave and strong and rich, for he had his own land and his own house, and not one to lord it over him. He was called the Kern of Querin. And many a time he would go out alone to shoot the wild fowl at night along the lonely strand and sometimes cross over northward to the broad east strand, about two miles away, to find the wild geese.

One cold frosty November Eve he was watching for them, crouched down behind the ruins of an old hut, when a loud splashing noise attracted his attention. "It is the wild geese," he thought, and raising his gun waited in deathlike silence the approach of his victims.

But presently he saw a dark mass moving along the edge of the strand. And he knew there were no wild geese near him. So he watched and waited till the black mass came closer, and then he distinctly perceived four stout men carrying a bier on their shoulders, on which lay a corpse covered with a white cloth. For a few moments they laid it down, apparently to rest themselves, and the Kern instantly fired; on which the four men ran away shrieking, and the corpse was left alone on the bier. Kern of Querin immediately sprang to the place, and lifting the cloth from the face of the corpse, beheld by the freezing starlight, the form of a beautiful young girl, apparently not dead but in a deep sleep.

Gently he passed his hand over her face and raised her up, when she opened her eyes and looked around with wild wonder but spoke never a word, though he tried to soothe and encourage her. Then, thinking it was dangerous for them to remain in that place, he raised her from the bier, and taking her hand led her away to his own house. They arrived safely, but in silence. And for twelve months did she remain with the Kern, never tasting food or speaking word for all that time.

When the next November Eve came round, he resolved to visit the east strand again, and watch from the same place, in the hope of meeting with some adventure that might throw light on the history of the beautiful girl. His way lay beside the old ruined fort called *Lios-na-fallainge* (the Fort of the Mantle), and as he passed, the sound of music and mirth fell on his ear. He stopped to catch the words of the voices, and had not waited long when he heard a man say in a low whisper –

"Where shall we go to-night to carry off a bride?"

And a second voice answered –

"Wherever we go, I hope better luck will be ours than we had this day twelvemonths."

"Yes," said a third; "on that night, we carried off a rich prize, the fair daughter of O'Connor; but that clown, the Kern of Querin, broke our spell and took her from us. Yet little pleasure has he had of his bride, for she has neither eaten nor drank nor uttered a word since she entered his house."

"And so she will remain," said a fourth, "until he makes her eat off her father's table-cloth, which covered her as she lay on the bier, and which is now thrown up over the top of her bed."

On hearing all this the Kern rushed home, and without waiting even for the morning, entered the young girl's room, took down the table-cloth, spread it on the table, laid meat and drink thereon, and led her to it. "Drink," he said, "that speech may come to you." And she drank, and eat of the food, and then speech came. And she told the Kern her story – how she was to have been married to a young lord of her own country, and the wedding guests had all assembled, when she felt herself suddenly ill and swooned away, and never knew more of what had happened to her until the Kern had passed his hand over her face, by which she recovered consciousness, but could neither eat nor speak, for a spell was on her and she was helpless.

Then the Kern prepared a chariot, and carried home the young girl to her father, who was like to die for joy when he beheld her. And the Kern grew mightily in O'Connor's favour, so that at last he gave him his fair young daughter to wife; and the wedded pair lived together happily for many long years after, and no evil befell them, but good followed all the work of their hands.

This story of Kern of Querin still lingers in the faithful, vivid Irish memory, and is often told by the peasants of Clare when they gather round the fire on the awful festival of *Samhain*, or November Eve, when the dead walk, and the spirits of earth and air have power over mortals, whether for good or evil.

The Priest's Soul

An ethical purpose is not often to be detected in the Irish legends; but the following tale combines an inner meaning with the incidents in a profound and remarkable manner. The idea that underlies the story is very subtle and tragic; Calderon or Goethe might have founded a drama on it; and Browning's genius would have found a fitting subject in this contrast between the audacious, self-reliant sceptic in the hour of his triumph and the moral agony that precedes his punishment and death.

In former days there were great schools in Ireland where every sort of learning was taught to the people, and even the poorest had more knowledge at that time than many a gentleman has now. But as to the priests, their learning was above all, so that the fame of Ireland went over the whole world, and many kings from foreign lands used to send their sons all the way to Ireland to be brought up in the Irish schools.

Now, at this time there was a little boy learning at one of them who was a wonder to everyone for his cleverness. His parents were only labouring people, and of course very poor; but young as he was, and poor as he was, no king's or lord's son could come up to him in learning. Even the masters were put to shame; for when they were trying to teach him he would tell them something they never heard of before, and show them their ignorance. One of his great triumphs was in argument; and he would go on till he proved to you that black was white, and then when you gave in, for no one could beat him in talk, he would turn round and show you that white was black, or may be that there was no colour at all in the world. When he grew up, his poor father and mother were so proud of him that they resolved to make him a priest, which they did at last, though they nearly starved themselves to get the money. Well, such another learned man was not in Ireland, and he was as great in argument as ever, so that no one could stand before him. Even the Bishops tried to talk to him, but he showed them at once they knew nothing at all.

Now there were no schoolmasters in those times but it was the priests taught the people; and as this man was the cleverest in Ireland all the foreign kings sent their sons to him as long as he had house-room to give them. So he grew very proud, and began to forget how low he had been, and worst of all, even to forget God, who had made him what he was. And the pride of arguing got hold of him, so that from one thing to another he went on to prove that there was no Purgatory, and then no Hell, and then no Heaven, and then no God; and at last that men had no souls, but were no more than a dog or a cow, and when they died there was an end of them. "Who ever saw a soul ?" he would say. "If you can show me one, I will believe." No one could make any answer to this; and at last they all came to believe that as there was no other world, every one might do what they liked in this; the priest setting the example, for he took a beautiful young girl to wife. But as no priest or bishop in the whole land could be got to marry them, he was obliged to read the service over for himself. It was a great scandal, yet no one dared to say a word, for all the kings' sons were on his side, and would have slaughtered any one who tried to prevent his wicked goings-on. Poor boys! they all believed in him, and thought every word he said was the truth. In this way, his notions began to spread about, and the whole world was going to the bad, when one night an angel came down from Heaven, and told him the priest he had but twenty-four hours to live. He began to tremble, and asked for a little more time.

But the angel was stiff and told him that could not be.

"What do you want time for, you sinner?" he asked.

"Oh, Sir, have pity on my poor soul!" urged the priest.

"Oh, ho! You have a soul, then," said the angel. "Pray, how did you find that out?"

"It has been fluttering in me ever since you appeared," answered the priest. "What a fool I was not to think of it before."

"A fool indeed," said the angel. "What good was all your learning, when it could not tell you that you had a soul?"

"Ah, my lord," said the priest, "if I am to die, tell me how soon I may be in Heaven?"

"Never," replied the angel. "You denied there was a Heaven."

"Then, my lord, may I go to Purgatory?"

"You denied Purgatory also; you must go straight to Hell," said the angel.

"But, my lord, I denied Hell also," answered the priest, "so you can't send me there either."

The angel was a little puzzled.

"Well," said he, "I'll tell you what I can do for you. You may either live now on earth for a hundred years enjoying every pleasure, and then be cast into Hell for ever; or you may die in twenty-four hours in the most horrible torments, and pass through Purgatory, there to remain till the Day of Judgment, if only you can find some one person that believes, and through his belief mercy will be vouchsafed to you and your soul will be saved."

The priest did not take five minutes to make up his mind.

"I will have death in the twenty-four hours," he said, "so that my soul may be saved at last."

On this, the angel gave him directions as to what he was to do, and left him.

Then, immediately, the priest entered the large room where all his scholars and the kings' sons were seated, and called out to them –

"Now, tell me the truth and let none fear to contradict me. Tell me what is your belief. Have men souls?"

"Master," they answered, "once we believed that men had souls; but, thanks to your teaching, we believe so no longer. There is no Hell, and no Heaven, and no God. This is our belief, for it is thus you taught us."

Then the priest grew pale with fear and cried out – "Listen! I taught you a lie. There is a God, and man has an immortal soul. I believe now all I denied before."

But the shouts of laughter that rose up drowned the priest's voice, for they thought he was only trying them for argument.

"Prove it, master," they cried, "prove it. Who has ever seen God? Who has ever seen the soul?"

And the room was stirred with their laughter.

The priest stood up to answer them, but no word could he utter; all his eloquence, all his powers of argument had gone from him, and he could do nothing but wring his hands and cry out –

"There is a God! There is a God! Lord, have mercy on my soul!"

And they began to mock him, and repeat his own words that he had taught them –

"Show him to us; show us your God."

And he fled from them groaning with agony, for he saw that none believed, and how then could his soul be saved?

But he thought next of his wife.

"She will believe, "he said to himself. " Women never give up God."

And he went to her; but she told him that she believed only what he taught her, and that a good wife should believe in her husband first, and before and above all things in heaven and earth.

Then despair came on him, and he rushed from the house and began to ask every one he met if they believed. But the same answer came from one and all – "We believe only what you have taught us," for his doctrines had spread far and wide through the country.

Then he grew half mad with fear, for the hours were passing. And he flung himself down on the ground in a lonesome spot, and wept and groaned in terror, for the time was coming fast when he must die.

Just then a little child came by.

"God save you kindly," said the child to him.

The priest started up.

"Child, do you believe in God?" he asked.

"I have come from a far country to learn about Him," said the child. "Will your honour direct me to the best school that they have in these parts?"

"The best school and the best teacher is close by," said the priest, and he named himself.

"Oh, not to that man," answered the child, "for I am told he denies God, and Heaven, and Hell, and even that man has a soul, because we can't see it; but I would soon put him down."

The priest looked at him earnestly. "How?" he inquired.

"Why," said the child, "I would ask him if he believed he had life to show me his life."

"But he could not do that, my child," said the priest. "Life cannot be seen; we have it, but it is invisible."

"Then if we have life, though we cannot see it, we may also have a soul, though it is invisible," answered the child.

When the priest heard him speak these words he fell down on his knees before him, weeping for joy, for now he knew his soul was safe; he had met at last one that believed. And he told the child his whole story: all his wickedness, and pride, and blasphemy against the great God; and how the angel had come to him and told him of the only way in which he could be saved, through the faith and prayers of some one that believed.

"Now then," he said to the child, "take this penknife and strike it into my breast, and go on stabbing the flesh until you see the paleness of death on my face. Then watch – for a living thing will soar up from my body as I die, and you will then know that my soul has ascended to the presence of God. And when you see this thing, make haste and run to my school and call on all my scholars to come and see the soul of their master has left the body, and that all he taught them was a lie, for that there is a God who punishes sin, and a Heaven and a Hell, and that man has an immortal soul, destined for eternal happiness or misery."

"I will pray," said the child, "to have courage to do this work."

And he kneeled down and prayed. Then when he rose up he took the penknife and struck it into the priest's heart, and struck and struck again till all the flesh was lacerated; but still the priest lived though the agony was horrible, for he could not die until the twenty-four hours had expired. At last the agony seemed to cease, and the stillness of death settled on his face. Then the child, who was watching, saw a beautiful living creature, with four snow white wings, mount from the dead man's body into the air and go fluttering round his head.

So he ran to bring the scholars; and when they saw it, they all knew it was the soul of their master, and they watched with wonder and awe until it passed from sight into the clouds.

And this was the first butterfly that was ever seen in Ireland: and now all men know that the butterflies are the souls of the dead waiting for the moment when they may enter Purgatory, and so pass through torture to purification and peace.

But the schools of Ireland were quite deserted after that time, for people said, What is the use of going so far to learn when the wisest man in all Ireland did not know if he had a soul till he was near losing it; and was only saved at last through the simple belief of a little child?

CHAPTER SIXTEEN

Jane Wilde, *Ancient Cures, Charms and Usages of Ireland*, 1890

Ancient Cures, Charms, and Usages of Ireland

The Irish, however, have retained more of the ancient superstitions than any other European people, and hold to them with a reverential belief that cannot be shaken by any amount of modern philosophic teaching. They are also, perhaps, indebted to Egypt for the wonderful knowledge of the power of herbs, which has always characterised the Irish, both amongst the adepts and the peasants.

The Irish Doctors

From the most ancient pagan times, the Irish doctors were renowned for their skill in the treatment of disease, and the professors of medicine held a high and influential position in the Druid order. They were allowed a distinguished place at the royal table, next to the nobles, and above the armourers, smiths, and workers in metals; they were also entitled to wear a special robe of honour when at the courts of the kings, and were always attended by a large staff of pupils, who assisted the master in the diagnosis and treatment of disease, and the preparations necessary for the curative potions.

The skill of the Irish physicians was based chiefly upon a profound knowledge of the healing nature and properties of herbs; and they were also well acquainted with the most deadly and concentrated poisons that can be found in the common field plant. But, in addition to the aid given by science and observation, they also practised magic with great effect, knowing well how strongly charms, incantations, and fairy cures can act on the nerves and impress the mind of a patient. Consequently their treatment of disease was of a medico-religious character, in which various magical ceremonials largely helped the curative process.

The Tuatha-de-Danan

The oldest record of physicians in Ireland dates from the battle of Maghtura (Moytura, the plain of the Towers) fought about three thousand years ago between the Firbolgs, the primitive, unlettered dwellers in Erin, and the Tuatha-de-Danans, a new set of invaders from the Isles of the Sea, more learned and powerful than the Firbolgs, skilled as metal workers, and famous as warriors and physicians.

At this great historic battle of Moytura, Dianecht, the chief physician of the Tuatha, had a bath of herbs prepared, at the rear of the army, of singular efficiency, into which the wounded were plunged, and from which they emerged healed and whole. During the fierce combat, Nuada, the King of the Tuatha, lost his hand; but it is recorded that Dianacht made for him a silver hand, fashioned with the most perfect mechanical and artistic skill; and henceforth the King was known as *Nuada Airgeat-lamh* (Nuad of the silver hand), and by this name he lives in history. Owing to their great knowledge and skill in metallurgy, the Firbolgs looked on the powerful invaders as necromancers and enchanters, and fled before them to the extreme limit of the western coast, even out to the remote Arran Isles, where they built, for shelter and protection from the enemy, those marvellous Cyclopean forts, whose stupendous ruins, with the causeway leading to them, formed of enormous masses of stone, can be seen to this day. After this, until the final conquest of Ireland by the Milesians from Spain, the Tuatha long remained masters of Ireland, and learning and art flourished under their rule. An ancient poet thus describes their great medical power:

> The Tuatha by force of potent spells,
> Could raise a slaughtered army from the earth,
> And make the live, and breathe, and fight again.

Adjoining the royal palace or "Tara of the Kings," they erected a hospital called the "House of Sorrow," where the wounded knights and chiefs were carried after the battles and forays to be healed of their wounds, and were attended there by the doctor and his staff of pupils until quite restored.

But if the *liaigh*, or leech, took up his abode at the house of the patient, he was entitled to his diet, along with four of his pupils, in addition to his fees, during the healing of the wound. If the cure, however, did not make satisfactory progress, the *liaigh* was obliged to pay for the food already consumed, and to refund the fees, which were handed over to a better *liaigh*.

Ancient Doctors of Ireland

The practice of physic was hereditary in certain families, and each of the nobles had a special physician attached to his service. In the more ancient times, medical knowledge was handed down by oral tradition from father to son; then, as learning advanced, by written books, carefully preserved in each family. The sons were generally educated by their fathers in the practice of physic, but it is said that Dainecht, being jealous of the superior skill of his son, caused him to be slain, when from the grave of the youth sprang a number of herbs, all efficacious in curing disease; and, thus, though dead, he carried on his work.

After the introduction of Christianity by St. Patrick, schools were established both for law and physic, where Latin was sedulously taught and freely spoken. Camden describes these schools, and says of them: "They speak Latin there like the vulgar tongue, conning by rote the aphorisms of Hippocrates, Galen, Avicenna, and others amongst the great masters of surgery."

Ancient Medical Manuscripts

Numerous copies of these ancient writers were made by the learned doctors and freely distributed among the profession, so that many of the manuscripts can still be found in the chief libraries of Europe. They are written on vellum, and are beautiful specimens of penmanship. A commentary in Irish was sometimes added, besides which, several translations into Irish of the chief medical works, whole and entire, are in existence.

In proof of the great and accurate knowledge of these Irish physicians, it is stated by Sir William Wilde, that when preparing "The Status of Disease from the Earliest Times," for the Irish census, he was able to tabulate seventy-five fatal diseases accurately described by the native doctors, with many that were not fatal; and he asserts that the Irish terms for the principal diseases were of far more appropriate significance than those at present employed in English, or derived from the Latin and Greek.

. . .

Ancient Charms

A few examples of these ancient cures and charms may be given to show their simple, half-religious character, so well calculated to impress a people like the Irish, of intense faith and a strong instinct for the mystic and the supernatural.

For the Falling Sickness

"By the wood of the Cross, by the Man that overcame death, be thou healed." These words are to be said in the left ear while the fit is on the patient, and he is to be signed three times with the sign of the Cross, in the name of God and the blessed Lord, when by virtue of the charm he will be cured.

A Charm against Accidents, Fire, Tempests, Water, Knife, or Lance

"Jesus, Saviour of men. In Jesus trust, and in Mary trust truly for all grace.

"This is the measure of the wounds of Christ upon the Cross, which was brought to Constantinople to the Emperor as a most precious relic, so that no evil enemy might have power over him. And whoever reads it, or hears it, cannot be hurt by fire or tempest, or the knife, or the lance; neither can the devil have power over him, nor will he die an untimely death, but safety from all dangers will be his to the end.

For A Sprain

As St Agnes went over the moor to the mountain of Moses, she fell with her foot turned. But sinew to sinew, and bone to bone, God makes all right to him who has faith: and be thou healed, O man, in Jesu's name. Amen.

CHAPTER SEVENTEEN

Jane Wilde, *Notes on Men, Women, and Books*, 1891

This volume, in which Speranza collects her reviews and essays, including those on Tennyson, Swift, George Eliot, Thomas Moore, Calderon, Wordsworth, Disraeli, Harriet Martineau, and the Countess of Blessington, demonstrates her intellectual range. Her essay on The Girondins *is, in many ways, an autobiographical one, where she expresses her admiration for the key role played by French women within the political movements of the French Revolution: "French ladies are wiser." In many ways, her portrait of Madame Roland is a self-portrait and worth noting. She writes, "[H]er country became the object that filled the infinite necessity of love in her heart." This section includes an extract from Speranza's essay on Swift, linking with William's work on the same subject. Included also is her trenchant and polemical essay on George Eliot, where she praises some of the leading Victorian writer's qualities as a novelist and attacks others, making the sweeping statement that "Men are perpetually adding names to literature that will last for all time – women never."*

Stella and Vanessa

The English writers of the eighteenth century are rapidly vanishing from our hearts and libraries; even the best of them are only tradition-ally venerated, seldom read. The new generation never dreams of taking its inspiration from Pope, nor its philosophy from Paley, and even the great Dr. Johnson himself is mainly kept alive by the faithful love of poor Boswell. The mission of the eighteenth century was, in fact, action, not literature. It came into the world, as a French writer observes, to destroy, not to build up; to clear away the old rags and cobwebs of prejudice and cant, and the last remnants of serfdom and feudalism, by such great deeds as American independence and French revolution. It was an age of questionings and doubt; when men mocked at everything they had once venerated, and denied everything, even God. "A torch and crowbar period," Carlyle calls it, "of quick rushing doom and conflagration, when, the whole social system having fallen into rottenness, the natives took the questionable step of setting the whole thing on fire."

The literature of such a period was, of necessity, sensuous and mate-rial, or vapidly didactic, for without earnest religious faith there can be neither sublimity nor elevation of sentiment; yet even this eighteenth century, so shallow, false, and feeble in literature, produced, amidst "the men of the time," some representatives of the men of all time, destined to hold permanent rank in the grand federation of human intellect. Of these most were Irish. Swift, Goldsmith, and Burke still live and seem endowed with an irrepressible vitality, while nearly all their fellow-workers are passing, or have passed, into chaos and oblivion. Yet Swift's individuality interests even more than his works: that wonderful career of a self-made man, who by the mere force of his intellect, wit, and irony made ministries tremble, as he hurled his terrible pamphlets like thunderbolts upon his scared and startled opponents, crushing them as much by the bitterness of his sarcasm as by the remorseless logic of truth, fact, and sound sense.

It is remarkable that Swift's genius was by no means developed early. His career in Trinity College was unmarked save by some records of his unruly and insubordinate temper. On his twenty-first birthday he had to beg pardon on bended knees of the outraged college authorities, a circum-stance which made him hate his birthdays ever after, and even record them bitterly. When he went to London he was glad to earn a poor 20*l*. a year as literary drudge to Sir William Temple; but here, in the great focus of ideas, a sense of his own deficiencies dawned upon him, and he began to study assiduously for eight hours a day. Still at twenty-seven he had produced nothing beyond a few translations from the classics, and had attained nothing beyond an Irish living of 100*l*. a year. Ten years more passed away, and though his great learning, his extraordinary wit, his conversation, and his sarcasms had gained him an immense social reputation, the slumbering giant within him had not fully awoke. In fact, Swift was nearly forty years of age before he blazed upon the world with all his tremendous powers, and England knew that she possessed one great writer more. For the ten subsequent years he reigned in London the autocrat of the ministry – the undisputed master of the political world – hated, feared, and caressed by the trembling slaves who, notwithstanding his arrogance, yet knew that without him they could have no existence whatever. This man, without rank or fortune or office, ruled them all by the terrible force of his mighty intellect; yet he had in him also great and noble instincts, for without them no man can rule his fellow-men – a scorn of gain, an indomitable pride, and an invincible love of truth, right, and justice.

It was in Ireland, after he became Dean of St. Patrick's, that he wrote the famous satire, "Gulliver's Travels" – the sharp sword of his wit never keener, though he was then near sixty years of age – this wonderful tale, that, in its literal meaning, has delighted the children of every generation for the last hundred and fifty years, and whose hidden wisdom will delight all sages, politicians, and thinkers to the end of time. Who knows what hints for this grand satire of political and official weakness and absurdities Swift may not have received from his residence in Ireland? and even the land where Gulliver reports he passed some time during his travels may still exist – a land where "the bulk of the people consist, in a manner, wholly of discoverers, witnesses, informers, accusers, prosecutors, evidences, swearers, together with their several subservient and subaltern instruments, all under the colours, the conduct, and the pay of Ministers of State and their deputies; the plots in that kingdom being usually the work of those persons who desire to raise their own characters of profound politicians, to restore new vigour to a crazy administration, or to stifle or divert general discontents."

But what need to localise his pictures? The vices, frauds, follies, and meannesses he satirises are to be found everywhere and in all times. Were there not something common to all human nature in them, these profound satiric sketches would not have existed so long. He does more, however, than paint the degradation of man. He enforces the eternal principles of truth and justice, which formed the basis of his own mind, by the very poignancy of his satire against their opposites. In this strange book, indeed – this child's book, yet filled with the deepest philosophy – we seem, more than in any other of Swift's works, to stand face to face with the heart of the man – its tragic gloom and grotesque irony. Through the sarcasm of the fable we trace his noble love of freedom, his strong sense of human rights, and the dignity of intellect; his savage independence of spirit, his scorn and hatred of systems which left genius and true merit crushed under the fee of a corrupt oligarchy, and the indignant pride that made him recoil from all wrong and injustice. He not only weighed his own age in the balance and fathomed its hollowness, but he looked before and after, and sat in judgment upon the whole life of humanity. A great prophet of our own day has said: "Whoso belongs only to his own age, and reverences only its gilded popinjays or mumbo-jumbos, must needs die with it, though he were crowned seven times at the Capitol. The great man does in truth belong to his own age, but he belongs likewise to all ages, otherwise he is not great. What was transitory in him passes away, but the immortal part remains, the significance of which is inexhaustible." It is this "inexhaustible significance" of Swift's best thoughts that make them for ever worth re-interpreting in the new forms of a new age.

But, above all, the love-drama of Swift's life has helped to make his name immortal; and it is singular that a subject so full of romantic passion has never been selected as a theme by any of our native novelists. What tears would have fallen by Stella's monument in St. Patrick's aisle, or by the laurels which Vanessa planted, if some Shakespeare of our age had filled up the shadowy outline of this tragedy of fatality and despair, of which tradition only recites the fragments!

A Frenchman – M. de Wailly – attempted such a work in his romance entitled "Stella and Vanessa," but he failed to unravel the mystery of those suffering hearts, whose felicity and misery are so fatally intertwined that union or separation alike brings doom. The portraits also are coarse and distorted, drawn without any true spiritual insight. For instance, the handsome Swift – the poet, patriot, wit, statesman, the profound and subtle thinker, the brilliant, dazzling conversationist, the leading genius of his country, and the most powerfully effective writer of the age – is presented to the reader's mind as only a coarse, selfish, somewhat brutal, thoroughly uninteresting, unlikable compound of egoism and morosity, blended with a few traits of surly benevolence, springing from the promptings of conscience more than the impulses of the heart. That Swift possessed a nature shadowed by some of this dark colouring, is true, certainly; but M. de Wailly's portrait has no claim to be considered a likeness, when he has copied only the coarsest features, the harshest lines, the superficial roughness of the epidermis, and omitted all the glory that genius radiated over the faults and defects of Swift's singular and complex moral organisation.

In his sketches of the two heroines, destined to celebrity throughout all time, for their beauty, misfortunes, fatal rivalry, and mournful destiny, the author has been equally unfortunate. Vanessa, with her passionate devotion, and Stella, with her meek, sacrificing love, are drawn with as coarse a pencil and coloured with false tints. Stella, whom Swift pronounced "the most accomplished conversationist of either sex" he had ever met with, appears through the distorting prism of M. de Wailley's imagination as scarcely better than a silly, childish hoyden, without acquirements to adorn or intellect to acquire; while the proud, gifted, high-bred, poet-souled, beautiful Vanessa changes beneath his touch into a vulgar, provincial third-rate virago; not a Medea, that she might have been, but a Madge Wildfire, whose love is half fury, half madness; but M. de Wailly at least deserves some commendation for the industry with which he has accumulated materials and inwoven truth with fiction.

The incidents of the tale are all historical, but the synchronous grouping, though adapted to render the dramatic effect more striking, is too far opposed to our consciousness of the truth to make us victims of the illusion. From Swift's arrival at Laracor, to take possession of the vicarage, up to the death of Stella, the time occupied in the action of the novel exceeds scarcely a few months, and all the intermediate events of his life, with Vanessa's love and Stella's death, are crowded into that space, though they really extended over a period of thirty years.

Yet even the simple historic incidents have a power to arouse our sympathies and to lead us dreaming into the past, where those pale mute statues stand out in sad beauty by the grave of him they died for, like sculptured caryatides supporting his tomb.

Let us breathe life upon the still lips for a few moments, and, uncoiling the roll of years, stand face to face with them, as Dante by the wailing spirits of Hades, while they tell their tale.

It was in the year 1688, the year of the great Revolution, when he was just twenty-one years of age, that the gifted young Irishman, in whom a conscious genius lay struggling to be freed from the bonds of poverty and obscurity, went to England to seek his fortune, a pedestal, a position – for what is genius without one? By his mother's influence, he was received into Sir William Temple's house as tutor, clerk, secretary – in fact, general assistant to all the working brains of the establishment, from the learned baronet's down to those of little Esther Johnson, the housekeeper's daughter – then a pretty, delicate, bright-eyed child of six years old, and afterwards the "Star" of his life, the world-renowned *Stella*. After a few years residence there, Swift took orders and a vicarage in Ireland. A fit of romantic generosity, however, made him resign this living of Kilroot, after having held it only a year, in favour of a poor curate, struggling against starvation, with a wife and children, on 40*l.* a year; and at eight-and-twenty Swift found himself once more trusting to the drifting current of chances for means and a position. Yet Sir William gladly received his brilliant secretary again, and Swift resumed his position at Moor Park, as chaplain, literary assistant to Sir William, and preceptor to Stella – now a gay, gifted, beautiful girl of fourteen. But the young clergyman was no Abelard or St. Preux; Ambition was his only idol then, and his feelings towards his fair pupil never seem to have warmed, at any period of his existence, beyond the tenderest paternal regard. He continued this life for four years, until Sir William's death, reading eight hours a day, studying classics, philosophy, and politics with his all-wise, all-accomplished host; and penning pamphlets, satires, poems, and sketches of future works, that gained present celebrity and the earnest of approaching fame.

Then a change came. His patron died.

Lord Berkeley held out hopes of patronage, which were fulfilled by presenting him with the miserable little living of Laracor, in the county

Meath, with only 100*l*. a year; and Swift settled down in his obscure glebe. But a light was wanting to his drear solitude, and he writes to his friend Stella to come and settle in Ireland likewise. She obeys. Was it love led her? We know not; but before the year is out, Stella and her companion, Mrs. Dingley, are fixed in lodgings at Trim, close to their brilliant, cynical, selfish friend. How beautiful was Stella then! just eighteen, a lovely, fascinating being (as he himself described her, years long after, writing on the midnight of the day she died), with hair blacker than a raven, every feature of her face perfection, and a gracefulness more than human in every movement, word, and action. Add to this external beauty an intellect of a high order, most rich cultivated.

Swift says of her, that he had never met any of her sex gifted with a better mind, or who had improved it more by reading and cultivation. She was versed in Greek and Latin story, spoke French perfectly, understood the Platonic and Epicurean philosophies, the nature of government, somewhat of physics and anatomy, was a perfect critic both in prose and verse, whose opinion any author might rely on, always the most brilliant in conversation, no matter who was by – combining judgment, good sense, vivacity, courage, and discretion in a most extraordinary degree.

Her mind was like a temple dedicated to the Muses; wit, poetry, learning, philosophy had each an altar there. No conversation more brilliant, no face more lovely, could be found in the London circles where she moved; and yet she leaves all – the homage and the splendours of the great capital – to bury herself in the central solitudes of Ireland with one whom she could not even call a lover.

Years pass thus. Stella receives an offer of marriage from a Dr. Tisdall. She thinks of accepting it, perhaps to shield her name from the censure which Swift acknowledges shadowed it for some time, in consequence of her undefined position; or did she wish to test the affection of him whom she now felt she loved? This, too, is a mystery for us; but Tisdall was discouraged in all possible ways by Swift, and finally rejected. Years still pass on. Stella has no more offers of marriage, for her friend is henceforth considered as her lover. Perhaps Swift felt a compensation was necessary for having selfishly used the light of her young life to illuminate his otherwise cheerless, solitary existence. She had become necessary to his happiness, though assuredly he never loved her with the love that Stella's dark eyes would have desired to read in his; and there is every reason for believing that he at last entered into a vague engagement to make her his wife when his fortune was bettered and he obtained preferment.

Ten years passed thus, and Stella's youth was fading and her health failing; but still she loved and hoped and trusted. Had Swift any real intention of keeping the terms of his engagement? If he had, there is not a single line from is pen extant to prove it.

In the year 1710 his political friends came into power, and Swift hastened to England to assist them, and further his own advancement. During his three years' absence from Ireland he wrote the well-known "Journal to Stella," a record of each day of his life transmitted to her by post each night. For the first few months there is intense fondness displayed, but no word of love – not an allusion to their probable marriage throughout the whole three years' correspondence. He calls her "dearest beloved," tells her that "her felicity is the great end of all the aims at," with other generalisms, evidently in answer to some gentle pleading of hers for a definite hope or an assured promise.

Then the change comes. Poor Stella!

The words of love, faint as they were, grow fainter. She thinks, perhaps, it is from the whirl of political excitement in which he lives; and truly there is nothing stranger in the history of that era than Swift's sudden elevation to importance as a political power. An obscure Irish clergyman, without wealth, rank, or station, becomes at once the grand object which all parties are eager to secure upon their side; but he has splendid talents, they know that; also a tremendous power of satire and an unscrupulous energy in using it, they know that too; and that no opponent can stand before the fierce, scathing, terrible shafts of his ridicule. Harley and Bolingbroke declare he is the only man in England they fear, and they succeed in winning him to their side. Harley, the Prime Minister, absolutely grovels to him for his support, and Bolingbroke, the Secretary, flatters and adulates with all his own exquisite eloquence. His poor lodgings at eight shillings a week, in London, are besieged by courtly visitants and invitation to the courtly set; all the wits of London adore him or envy him; all the duchesses are emulous of his notice; he guides the councils at the palace and troubles the cabals of the courtiers. Talent, for once, has its triumphs: Genius tramples upon coronets; and one exults to see how

Swift's proud soul recoiled from yielding homage to mere rank, when God and nature had denied nobler gifts. He stood by his order, and made the haughty lords of Court sue to him for his notice, but never advanced a step to solicit theirs.

"I treat them like dogs," he says, with that contemptuous scorn which had measured their feebleness by his own colossal strength.

He refused to become chaplain to Lord Oxford, then Prime Minister, and in a letter to Bolingbroke writes: "I would have you to know, Sir, that if the Queen gave you a dukedom and the Garter to-morrow, with the Treasury staff at the end of it, I'd regard you no more than if you were not worth a groat."

This is the true Republican spirit that actuates Genius in all ages. Swift would not allow intellect even in another to descend a step from the height where God had placed it. When Lord Oxford desired that Parnell might be brought to him, as he wished his acquaintance, Swift replied: "A man of genius was above a lord; therefore the Ministry must seek Parnell, not Parnell the Ministry." His arrogance even sometimes became insolence: he bids Harley take a message to the Secretary that he cannot dine with him unless he dine early; and the Prime Minister of England takes the message.

Yet, with all this cold, cynical contempt for the men who feared and flattered him, and used his brains as the lever to lift them to power, he was capable of the warmest feelings of kindness and generosity, as a thousand anecdotes evince. Lord Peterborough tells of him "he wanted to frame a new system, to govern the world by love." Pope, whose melancholy, tender letters display an affection based upon the highest esteem, testifies warmly to "humanity, candour, charity, and sincerity." He tried to secure a place for Steele, his political opponent; and advanced Berkeley, Parnell, and Gay. For him, Genius was of no party. Almost all the great men of the day were indebted to him in some way or other; while, at the same time, singularly enough, the position his own talents and services entitled him to expect was not conceded to him. Perhaps the Ministry thought that hope would retain his services to their cause better than success; of the Queen's ear was assailed by the calumnies of the Whigs, who called him libeller and atheist; bishoprics became vacant, and dull plodders were adorned with the mitre, but Swift's brow still remained uncrowned. No wonder the bitterness of disappointed ambition displays itself openly in his treatment of Ministers. Still his war of words continues unabated on their behalf. Pamphlets, satires, poems, shake the power of the enemy, and peace or war in Europe depends upon a few strokes of his pen. He edited a paper called "The Examiner," assisted by Bolingbroke, Atterbury, and Prior. Opposed to them were Addison, Burnet, Steele, Congreve, and others – men worth breaking a lance with – who, though political opponents, were yet on terms of social intimacy with Swift.

No age can show a more numerous list of distinguished names than were Swift's contemporaries, though none amongst them, perhaps, are worthy to be ranked with the high pontiffs of literature that graced an earlier century. His was a brilliant life then. The flattered idol of the highest society in London; the companion of the gay, dazzling wits, philosophers, essayists, poets, dramatists, and prosists, that were headed by Pope, Addison, Steele, Berkeley, Bolingbroke, Congreve, Gay, Parnell, Prior, and others, whose fame illumined the century. But the brightest amongst them all has offended the Queen, it seems, by a satire on her favourite Duchess of Somerset, and is condemned to banishment in Ireland as Dean of St. Patrick's. Swift felt infinitely mortified that ministerial patronage conferred no more. All the fine ladies were in tears at his departure; all his friends mourned. Leaving London seemed to them like quitting sunlight for a cavern. How would he live without its glories and its splendour? An amusing letter from one of them, addressed to him in Ireland, shows the feeling with which they contemplated his exile: "And now, methinks, I look down into that bog of usquebaugh, and hear you gnashing your teeth, and crying: "Oh, what would I give now for a glass of that small beer I used to call sour, or a pinch of that snuff I used to say was the worst snuff in the world! Oh, what would I give to have had a monitor warning me of the sword hanging by a packthread over my head, and crying, in a voice as loud as Southwell's, '*Memento, doctor, quia Hibernus es, et in Hiberniam reverteris!*'"

"You are now cast upon an inhospitable island; no mathematical figures on the sand; no *vestigia hominum* to be seen; perhaps, at this very time, reduced to one single barrel of damaged biscuit and short allowance even of salt water. What's to be done? Another in your condition would look about; perhaps he might find some potatoes, or yet an old piece of iron, and make a harpoon, and, if he found Higgon sleeping near the shore, strike him, and eat him.

"But this, I know, is too gross a pabulum for one who hitherto has lived on wit, and whose friends, God be thanked, design he should continue to do so, and on nothing else. Therefore, I would advise you to fall upon old Joan. Eat: do I live to bid thee? Eat Addison; and when you have eat everybody else, eat my Lord-Lieutenant; he is something lean – God help the while; and though it will, for aught I know, be treason, there will be nobody left to hang you, unless you think fit to do yourself that favour; which, if you should, pray don't write me a word of it, because I should be very sorry to hear of any ill that should happen to you."

But what was poor Stella doing during these long three years, while Swift's wit was blazing brighter than the diamonds of admiring duchesses and flashing recklessly through the ice of Court formalities and startling the soul of the poor dull Queen?

Was she weeping in loneliness by the willows of Laracor while her lover was basking in the eyes of a rival? And such a rival! Alas! Poor Stella, thou hast cause to weep!

But Stella did not even know she had a rival. The daily journal from Swift had certainly become colder and chiller, and it is evident that she had even complained a little of his protracted absence and evident disinclination to return to Ireland; while, all the time, no professions of affection came to calm her solicitude. If want of fortune had prevented their marriage, Swift was now rich. The deanery was worth 700*l.* a year; but no allusion is made to such a result – no expression of joy uttered at the prospect of their meeting; on the contrary, a scarcely concealed chagrin is visible in every line, though without apparent cause; and, as if to chill any rising hope within her bosom, repeated hints are given that he will be no richer for his preferment. Stella, however, never dreams of a rival. What woman ever thinks it possible that her lover can forget her? If he is less ardent than her heart could wish, she blames ambition, not love, as the enchantress that detains him from her side. How could she be suspicious of brighter influences than her own retaining him, or that hers had ceased to attract? for, though Swift had been on terms of the greatest intimacy with the Vanhomrigh family from the time of his arrival in London, yet no mention whatever is made in the journal of the all too fascinating Esther Vanhomrigh. His conscience told him how quickly and truly Stella's instincts, if he had but trusted himself to speak of her, would have recognised a rival in the superb "Vanessa." Let us, then, wake her from the marble where she sleeps, and sketch her portrait in all the fascination of youth and beauty.

Esther Vanhomrigh was scarcely more than twenty when Swift first met her moving, a radiant star, in the brilliant London circles. Rich, beautiful, and gifted with the fatal dower of genius – that acanthus-wreath for the brow of a woman which so often leaves it bleeding – was it wonderful that she dazzled and bewildered a man of intellect and ambition, who found himself the selected object of her love? Younger, too, by eight or ten years, than Stella – a Venus Victrix – equalling in beauty, and triumphing by rank and fortune over the low-born girl, whose station in society was acquired by chance, and retained only by those transcendent merits which could compensate for the obscurity of her birth, and the dubious nature of her position; yet Swift, whether from a principle of honour, or a deficiency of passion in his nature, seems long to have struggled against Vanessa's fatal fascination. A proud, scornful, sarcastic spirit like his is rarely a loving sprit. Ambition was the ruling passion of his life – not from selfism or vanity, but from the strong consciousness of power within fitted to rule and reign amongst those who surrounded him. He loved appreciation. He rejoiced at being the centre and object of all homage; but he himself gave back no sympathies. His aim was to be a potent spirit, guiding men and ministers, and the love of woman was only a graceful luxury for his idle hours, delightful to enjoy so long as he was not called upon to make any sacrifice to retain it. It is a truth, however, of all natures gifted with genius, that they are the least capable of constant, concentrated love. They live in the Infinite; in lofty purposes and grand deeds, of which humanity at large is the object. They can throw their hearts into a cause, but not yield it to an individual. What isolated human heart is vast enough to absorb their affections or satisfy their aspirations?

Souls like theirs cannot have free action within so limited an horizon. What they call love is a sublime adoration for an idol robed in the fleeting colours of the imagination; but the delusion cannot last, and the society of minds inferior to their own often becomes in the end either wearisome or disgusting.

Fits of passion they may have, but enduring love seems almost an impossibility to genius – unless, indeed, Plato's dream were realised, and each great soul met and blended with its eternal antitype here on earth, as they may in heaven. But Swift must have been singularly passionless if a being gifted like Vanessa failed to draw down his soul from abstractions and shrine it in a human heart. In her he may have recognised at last the one that could inspire as well as sympathise – the full completion of his own nature – the ideal of his aspirations, though between them there was a great gulf fixed; for, since the gates closed of Paradise, when did Fate ever permit the union of these eternally related souls? Never. If each found it correlative on earth, Paradise would be no longer barred.

Between Swift and Vanessa rose up a separating form, strong in the sanctity of promises, beautiful, too, and gifted and loving, clinging to her cold, incomprehensible lover, as the ivy to the oak, with such helpless confidence that he knew if he rent away the tendrils she must die; but tenderness only, not the excitement of love, was in his heart. This is evident from his verses years long after: –

> Thou, Stella, wert no longer young
> When first for thee my harp was strung,
> Without one wound of Cupid's darts,
> Of killing eyes, or bleeding hearts;
> With friendship and esteem possessed,
> I ne'er admitted love a guest.

She had grown up with him, like a daughter, from her very childhood, and feelings that have once crystallised into fondness in the days of "long ago" seldom change afterwards into love. Ten years of her beautiful womanhood had bloomed and faded away beside him without exciting a glow beyond the mild Platonism of tender interest; and if he ever formed an engagement of marriage with her it was merely because he could not otherwise have felt secure of preserving her society – a charm that had now become indispensable to his lonely Irish residence. But it was an engagement he might protract indefinitely; for Stella had no means of resistance by complaints – the worst exorcism for a love. Yet the happiness of all her life was staked on this marriage. Without it she had neither name nor rank nor honourable station. She had given up country and home and relatives to accept him for her destiny, and a woman can be place in no falser position than when she has thus yielded up her independence, and claims the hand of her lover as a compensation for sacrifices, in place of conferring her love freely as a favour long sought, eagerly coveted, to be recompensed by the devotion of his life. "Keep free as an Arab of thy beloved" is the truest counsel to a woman. Men – indeed, all mortals – have a tendency to value only what seems the unattainable; but calmness, security, custom, above all, a conscientious sense of duty mingling with the feelings, are all fatal to love.

It was an influence more serene and lasting than love that attracted Swift towards his gentle companion. Accustomed to the turbid commotion of party politics, half a misanthrope from disappointed ambition, Stella, in the midst of his unquiet life, was the one pure feeling, the one untroubled holy thought where he found calm and repose. Her transparent soul mirrored his own, and blended in harmonic sympathy with all he hoped and suffered. She soothed his vexed, perturbed mind, like the inspired music that quelled the evil spirit in the breast of Saul, though, like the frantic monarch of Israel, he himself flung the javelin to pierce the heart of the player. Stella's love for him, too, was the result of circumstance rather than the sudden up-springing impulse of ecstasy and adoration when the heart recognises "the ever longer for." It was only when the dream of years was troubled by a rival that she felt the whole happiness of life, her very life itself, was staked upon its continuance.

Vanessa's, on the contrary, was a voluntary consecration; the willing immolation of her youth, fame and fortune at the shrine of her lover; a feeling raging with the tumultuary fever of passion; a worship that, in a nature so impassioned as hers, became idolatry. It was the love of a woman of genius for her equal, and no passion equals it in intensity – none have proved so fatal in the consequences. Swift would have been more or less than man could he have been insensible to the glorious gifts she flung so lavishly before him or the passionate fire that burned in her words. True, he tried to reason with her – to calm her; but the very consciousness that he *dare* not trust himself to love her was an excitement to fan the flame. "They never loved who never have loved wrongly." There was danger in his intercourse with Vanessa, but the danger made it delirium. He was her companion and instructor. They read and wrote together, dreaming away the hours in a Paradise-world of intellectual communion. The teacher was forty-four, the pupil but half his age; yet the first betrayal of love fell from her lips. Swift's surprise and emotion at the confession are portrayed in his poem of "Cadenus and Vanessa," where he relates the rise and progress of her fatal love – not with any expressions of corresponding fervour certainly, but with an evident pride and pleasure that showed how he loved to linger over the seductive picture.

In the paganised cant of the day, he commences by describing how Venus conferred all beauty and Pallas all wisdom on the maiden; how the latter gift made the follies of society intolerable to her; till at length, yielding herself up to the attractions of mind, she turns from them all to enjoy the converse of her tutor, Cadenus; but love mingles with the literature. Vanessa "owns the wandering of her thoughts," and tells him: –

> "I knew by what you said and writ
> How dangerous were men of wit;
> You cautioned me against their charms,
> But never gave me equal arms.
> Your lessons found the weakest part–
> Aim'd at the head, but reach'd the heart."
>   "Cadenus felt within him rise
> Shame, disappointment, guilt, surprise,
> Hardly, at length, he silence broke,
> And faltered every word he spoke."

But Vanessa refutes all his objections, and claims the right to love him, even from his own teachings: –

> "How was her tutor wont to praise
> The geniuses of ancient days;
> Suppose Cadenus flourished then,
> He must adore such godlike men."
>   "And this she takes to be her case;
> Cadenus answers every end–
> The book, the author, and the friend.

The utmost her desires can reach,
Is but to learn what he can teach,
While every passion of her mind
In him is centred and confined."
    "Cadenus, to his grief and shame,
Could scarce oppose Vanessa's flame,
And, though her arguments were strong,
At least could hardly wish them wrong."

The concluding verses leave the world in doubt as to whether the pleading maiden subdued the scruples of her lover, who hitherto had offered to her only friendship in return for so much love: –

But what success Vanessa met,
Is to the world a secret yet –
Whether he at last descends
To act with less scraphic ends,
Or, to compound the business, whether
They temper books and love together,
Must never to the world be told,
Nor shall the conscious muse unfold.

Notwithstanding the frigid, artificial framework of this poem, there is love evident in it; as genuine love, probably, as Swift could feel; flattered vanity at least, which forms half the love of all men. But, whatever were the elements, there is more of the sentiment – a thousand times more – than can be found in all the odes addressed to Stella.

In Vanessa's lines to him, however, there is no mistaking the deep earnestness of true passion. How beautiful are these, after contrasting the brightness of spring with the gloom of the heart when he had left her! –

Yet why should I they presence hail,
As when Cadenus blest the scene,
And shared with me those joys serene?
When, unperceived, the lambent fire
Of Friendship kindled new desire;

> Still listening to his tuneful tongue,
> The truths which Angels might have sung
> Divine imprest their gentle sway,
> And sweetly stole my soul away.
> My guide, instructor, lover, friend –
> Dear names! in one Idea blend.
> Oh! still conjoined, your incense rise,
> And waft sweet odours to the skies.

But now he is returning to the patient, weary-waiting Stella with love on his lip and treason in his heart. Vanessa, no doubt, expects him back to claim her hand when his Irish affairs are settled, and Stella is lingering for the fulfillment of the promises of thirteen years.

Hoping hearts, could ye but look into futurity!

Swift's first letter to Vanessa on his return to Ireland is steeped in melancholy. "I thought I should have died of discontent (he says) at my first coming. I hate the thought of Dublin." Alas for Stella!

A few weeks found him in London once more. Ministers could not exist without him, and he remained there till the following year (1714), when the Queen died. This event, which marred all his hopes of preferment, affected him deeply. He returned to Dublin, and never visited England again for twelve years.

At this very time Vanessa, by the death of her father and brother, succeeded to a small estate in Ireland. She was now independent in fortune, uncontrolled in action, and she resolved to follow her lover to Ireland and take up her residence beside him. Swift's alarm at such a measure was expressed in a letter warning her to be cautious. He says: "I can see you very seldom in Ireland – it is not a place for freedom – leave all to fate – perhaps we may meet in London in the winter."

But Vanessa knows no necessity for caution. She was proud of her lover – proud to confess her love. "By all the holy angels," exclaims Goethe, "by all the images of blessedness which a pure and kindly heart creates, there is not anything more heavenly than the soul of a woman that gives herself to the man she loves!'

She had no reason to blush for her devotion. But the triumph of conquest was enough for him. He fears the clashing claims of Cleopatra and Octavia; the terrible strife of loving, jealous, breaking hearts. Men have no objection to be loved, but they dread a scene. If women will break their hearts, let it at least be in silence; that is all they demand from the victims in return for the passing dream of love with which they may have favoured them.

Undismayed, however, and undeterred by her lover's objections, Vanessa arrives in Dublin, and the dread shadow falls at last upon Stella's destiny which Swift had so long vainly tried to avert. Rumours reach her of love in which she has no part. Jealousies and agonies rend her soul. How touching are these plaintive lines of hers on "Jealousy," every word of which seems written with tears:–

> Shield me from his rage, celestial Powers!
> This Tyrant who embitters all my hours.
> Ah, love! you've poorly played the hero's part!
> You conquered, but you can't defend, my heart.
> When first I bent beneath your gentle reign,
> I thought this monster banished from your train;
> But you would raise him to support your throne,
> And now he claims your empire as his own;
> Or – tell me, tyrants – have you both agreed
> That where one reigns, the other shall succeed?

And what tender devotion in the verses on Swift's birthday, where she addresses him as her "early and her only guide," and concludes: –

> Late dying, may you cast a shred
> Of your rich mantel o'er my head;
> To bear with dignity my sorrow,
> One day alone – then die the morrow.

Meanwhile, Vanessa, unconscious that a breaking heart lay between her and happiness, mourns over the reserve of her lover, which he calls "discretion," and writes to him after her arrival in Dublin: –

"Pray what can be wrong in seeing and advising an unhappy young woman? – you cannot but know that your frowns make my life insupportable. You have taught me to distinguish, and then you leave me miserable."

And in another letter suspense seems rising to torture; a thick, stifling darkness of suspicion and despair is gathering round her life like a pall, and these are not words but cries of agony wrung from a crushed heart:–

"It is impossible to describe what I have suffered since I saw you last. I could have borne the rack better than those killing, killing words of ours. Sometimes I have resolved to die without seeing your more, but the resolves, to your misfortune, did not last long. – I must beg you to see me, and speak kindly to me, for I am sure you would not condemn any one to suffer what I have done, could you but know it. – When I complain, then you are angry; and there is something awful in your looks that strikes me dumb. Oh! that you may have so much regard left that this complaint may touch your soul with pity. Did you but know what I thought, I am sure it would move you to forgive me. I cannot help telling you this, and live."

Was misery ever more eloquent? Could the deep prostration of love be more complete? No heart could have remained insensible to such passionate pleadings. Swift must have loved her; and love, fatal love, alone could have prevented him from following the course which honour dictated – that of revealing to her the bonds which bound him to another, the bar which separated their destinies for ever.

Still in the bright, dazzling prime of youth, Vanessa might have found another kindred spirit on whom to lavish all the glowing love of her nature; but Swift had not courage to utter the word that parted; nor yet could he resolve to break utterly that patient, trusting, long-suffering heart which had gently twined itself with every fibre of his being. The pale, fading form of Stella was there beside him, clinging by one frail cord of love to the wreck of her existence; could he snap it asunder, and let her die? Death was already hovering around her; there was but one word could rescue her from the grave, and Swift at last pronounced it. In 1716, two years after Vanessa's arrival in Ireland, at midnight, in the garden of the Deanery, that strange marriage ceremony was performed which made the misery of two persons irreparable, without insuring the happiness even of one. Swift bound himself by law to one woman, while he was bound by love to another; Stella's position in society was not ameliorated, as her marriage with the Dean was to be kept a profound secret. She had the name of wife without the honours or the happiness, for she returned to her lodgings after the ceremony, and lived apart from her nominal husband the same as before; but poor Vanessa's fate was sealed. Stella no longer could fear her rival, and it was to procure her this satisfaction that Swift had consented to their joyless and ill-omened marriage.

He evidently grew tenderer to Stella as her health declined, and it was about this time he began to address those birthday odes to her which have made her name illustrious, but through which no trace of passion is discoverable. Praise, esteem, friendship, gratitude, appreciation of her talents are all warmly expressed – everything, in short, that a woman cares least to hear from the man whom she adores when her heart is pining for the one word – love.

Meanwhile, Vanessa had retired to Marley Abbey, her residence, near Celbridge. There Swift visited her.

...

Two years more pass in this terrible conflict between hope, fear, love, jealousy and suspicion. Swift tries to prevail on her to leave Ireland, to seek distraction in company and exercise. "Get yourself a horse," he says, "and have always two servants to attend you, and visit your neighbours. There is a pleasure in being reverenced, and that is always in your power, for your superiority of sense and easy fortune. I long to see you in figure and equipage." There are some traces of melancholy, if not misery, too, in his letters now. One is glad of it. That he suffered was at least some compensation to Vanessa; but the catastrophe is approaching. Twelve years had passed since her first meeting with Swift – a twelve years' feverish dream of love. From the grave of buried youth and hope comes up at last the supreme cry of an agonised soul, seeking certainty in some shape – death or happiness. Holiest martyrs at the stake with heaven sustaining might have endured equal tortures, but could not have endured them longer.

She writes to Stella, and asks her fatal question:

Was she indeed married to Swift?

Stella answers in the affirmative.

No hope now – no more sunlight on her life. Nothing but a black fatality of doom. The saddest, gloomiest bar that God ever placed between a heart and happiness rose before her, beyond which no hope gleams but from across the grave of another.

Married! That word killed her.

The following day Swift rode down to Vanessa's residence, entered the room where she was seated, mourning her fate, flung her letter to Stella upon the table without a word, then quitted the house in a tempest of rage, and never again beheld Vanessa in life. A violent fever that followed this scene soon put a period to the sad existence of the unhappy Vanessa; the troubled dream of life was over – the beautiful form laid within the grave; the noble heart stilled for ever, and the passionate soul gone forth to mingle with the harmonies of the universe and with the seraphs before the Throne. Yet, better so to die than to have lived unloving and unloved.

But misery came to other hearts also, though it did not kill so speedily.

Stella's suspicions were confirmed. What was the name of wife to her without the love that makes it blessed, and a rival had claimed her holiest right! Filled with indignation and overwhelmed by grief, she quitted Dublin without seeing Swift, and they did not meet again for months; while upon him whose love had been so fatal fell a gloom which twenty succeeding years of a life brightened by as much glory, homage, worship and adoration as ever fell to the lot of an Irishman in Ireland could not dissipate; and thereof "came in the end despondency and madness."

Stella's health and heart were broken, but she lingered on for five years. Her whole life had been one of patient suffering. She was accustomed to it; still her spirit yearned for one consolation before she died – the public acknowledgment of her marriage. This was denied her. Swift was in London at the beginning of her last illness, and, from his letters, seemed anxious to remain there till all was over; but business obliged him to return, and, as he stood by Stella's deathbed, she made a last earnest appeal to his justice, adjuring him by their friendship to acknowledge her as his wife. Swift made no reply, but, turning on his heel, walked out of the room, nor ever saw her afterwards during the few days she lived. The veracity of this account has been impugned; but, in any case, who can doubt the agonies of Stella, for she died without the request being granted!

A hundred years and more have passed since death stilled the hearts of the rivals and the victims. The triumphs of Marlborough are forgotten; the pedants of the age have disappeared from our memories and our libraries;

the great statesmen who fretted their busy hour upon the stage of life have sunk into the gulf of nothingness – but the pale, beautiful, shadowy forms of Stella and Vanessa are still beside us, even as they passed from this life weeping. Over the records of true feeling time has no influence; hearts of the present and future still vibrate with the hearts of the past, and the love that kills can at least rear an enduring cenotaph. So they stand for ever in the halls of humanity, with Eloise and Juliet, crowned with the immortality of genius, love, and suffering; imploring sympathy with their soft mute eyes, and waking fresh tears from each successive generation as their sad, passion-inspired words glide across the centuries like the low tones of distant music; for the tragedies that make us weep are not of fallen empires, but of the workings of human passion in a wrecked human heart. In such alone we feel the kinship of all natures; the mournful history seems a page torn from our own heart; the woe, the agonies, the doom that ever follow true love as certainly as death follows life are phases of emotion and suffering we, too, have passed through, and our tears fall from pity for ourselves as much as for the sorrows of another.

What a tragedy, if one but thinks of it, and what a mystery! Why were these three hearts led to love, and then love made their misery? Was Swift in fault if, seeing Vanessa, he should adore her? or what law of God or man did she violate by giving her heart to him? Yet she is unconsciously made the cloud to shadow the pure and perfect life of Stella – the cruel instrument to rob her of her only blessing. Love is involuntary, yet Swift must expiate it, as if it were a crime, by sacrificing himself and Vanessa to a marriage without love. Two hearts, two lives were in his keeping; happiness for one was death to the other. Was it his fault? He tried to preserve both, and the end is despair and madness. Yet one cannot stop in any portion of the story and say, "Here there is sin." It is like one of the old Greek tragedies, in which the Fates and Furies guide the threads of life, and mortals, feeble mortals, strive in vain against an iron-handed destiny, and yet it is no more than a drama of daily life. Two more female hearts are added to the pile laid upon the altar of unhappy love. Is it so strange a fate? Is not love ever the sole tragedy of a woman's destiny? Are there not other women who have passed from amongst us, with the crowned brow of genius, who, Sappho-like, freed themselves at once from life and a fatal love by a voluntary death – women who have made the worship of genius their religion and expiated the idolatory ? Stella and Vanessa at least have won a glory to gild the gloom of fate denied to many; for the name of their lover is a catafalque whereon they lie in state for the tender sorrow of all ages, with the asbestos torch of his genius illuminating the bier.

At last Swift's proud spirit seems to have been broken by sorrow and remorse, and a gloom fell upon his life that never more was lifted.

His health declined, his intellect became clouded, the power of writing went from him, but the bitterest pang of all was his own consciousness that madness was approaching, and that all the fine chords of his brain were jangled and out of tune. For three years he never spoke though he still seemed conscious of passing events, even down to the time of his death, which took place in 1745, just fifteen years after Stella had been laid in her grave.

Thomas Moore

Strong nations fight, oppressed nations sing; and thus, not with armies and fleets, but with the passionate storm of lyric words have the Irish people kept up for centuries their ceaseless war against alien rule. For words have a mystic power over men, and with the word Liberty on their lips, and the ideal of Nationhood in their hearts, the Irish have been preserved by their poets and orators from degenerating into the coarse vulgarisms of music and song so popular amongst a people who have no aspirations, no ideal beyond the greed of gain and the plenitude of all the sensuous enjoyments of life.

It is Ruskin who says "all that is best in a nation comes from the spirit of revolt," and it is this spirit, transmitted through successive generations, that has kept Ireland from much that is debasing and degrading in the ordinary life and amusements of more prosperous nations. All honour, then, to the chief of Irish poets, "the sweetest lyrist of her saddest wrong," as Shelley has so beautifully designated Moore. Love of country was the source of all his highest utterances, the divine fire that kindled his genius, and has given enduring vitality to his words; for the Irish melodies will live for ever in the heart of the Irish race, though everything else he wrote may be forgotten. Through Moore's lyrics, set to the pathetic Irish music, the wrongs of Ireland were first made known to Europe, and the sympathy excited by them for a people so gifted and so unfortunate materially helped to break the terrible and insulting bondage of the penal laws.

Moore was born in 1780, the same year as Béranger, the national poet of France, and both sprang from the people. But while Béranger's genius was nourished by the revolution that established the rights of man, the young Irish poet found himself a degraded serf in his own land, the crushed and helpless victim of a foreign tyranny. All progress, all distinctions, all means of educations were forbidden to Catholics. They were not allowed the common rights of citizens, and were even denied the exercise of the franchise. It was not till 1793, when Moore was old enough to be conscious of the degradation of his race and creed, that Catholics were allowed to enter Trinity College, though all university honours and emoluments were still withheld from them. Moore was one of the first of the young helots who accepted the privilege of entering the university, and in time he stood for a scholarship, to which he was entitled by his answering, but was refused on account of his religion.

What wonder if he felt bitterly, and expressed openly his detestation of English rule? The college authorities grew alarmed; a spirit of nationality, which in Ireland is supposed to mean rebellion, was suspected amongst the students, and the most daring and fiery and gifted of the young alumni were arraigned before the Board, and subjected to the ordeal of a trial for sedition and sympathy with revolution. Moore behaved nobly on this occasion, denying nothing he had said or done, but refusing by a word to implicate others with his own expressed opinions. The authorities were awed, and he was permitted to continue his college course without further molestation. His time then was devoted to literature and study. Buried amongst the old books of Marsh's Library, the Psyche wings began to unfold themselves, and before he was twenty the "Anacreon," which first made him celebrated, was finished.

He went to London with the manuscript, and fortune and fame quickly followed on its publication. The first red-rose dawn of a new and true poet-soul appearing above the literary horizon was at once recognised and welcomed. From the Regent down, society seized on the young poet, and nearly strangled all that was good in him, Armida-like, with chains and roses. The "Anacreon" suited the taste of the luxurious sensualised age, and in his next work, "Little's Poems," Moore unhappily degraded his genius to the level of the society that worshipped him. The "Anacreon" had not the immortal element in it, still it lives, and is sometimes read; but "Little's Poems" had the seeds of death in them, and they died. The true fount of eternal song had not yet opened in Moore's soul. He was himself unconscious where his great strength lay, and wasted in the sentimentalities of frivolous and affected feeling the power that was made to move the world's great heart.

The magic influence that at last unsealed the fount, and revealed to the poet the riches of his genius, came from the divinely beautiful spirit of Irish music. At once, when it touched his soul, the hidden stream of inspiration rushed up to heaven, clear and pure and sparkling, and fell to earth again in showers of many coloured splendours, strengthening and refreshing not only his own loved land, but stimulating amongst the far-off nations the growth of Freedom's goodly tree.

Moore himself describes the effect which Irish music had on him when he first began to study it for the purpose of writing words suitable to the airs – this mournful music, so sad and so expressive, that made Beethoven exclaim, when he first heard it, "That must be the music of an oppressed and suffering people." The whole history and genius and temperament of the nation can be traced in its fluctuations of mirth and sadness, its transient discords, and triumphant marches mingled with wailing, pathetic minors, the alternate languor and turbulence, the despondency and defiance, so characteristic of the vain but ceaseless efforts of a nation to throw off an intolerable yoke.

All this Moore found in our national music, whose origin is lost in the night of time, but whose sweetest and saddest airs date from the cruel era of the Tudors; and his genius flowed rapidly in a divine harmony with its blended gaiety and gloom. It was not effort to him to write then; the thoughts came with tears, and crystallised into imperishable gems of song. He had felt and he had suffered, that was sufficient; he was one of the helots, with the penal brand on him, and he appealed to a whole people who burned with the same indignant sense of wrong. It was not the voice of one heart, but the cry of a nation that went up from his verses, and startled the world into sympathy and pity for Ireland.

Translations of the "Melodies" were rapidly made into all the tongues of Europe. Wherever oppression existed, they helped to give resistance utterance. They passed from nation to nation, as a burning torch passes from hand to hand, the signal of the uprising of a people against tyranny; and so they exist an enduring portion of the world's heritage, graven with a diamond pen upon the rocks for ever.

The enthusiasm kindled by them in Ireland alarmed the Government. Their tendency was pronounced "mischievous," and the idea was entertained of forcibly suppressing their publication. Moore had to defend himself against the charge of "stirring up the passions of a turbulent mob." "To those," he says, "who can identify nationality with treason, I shall not deign to offer an apology for the political sentiments expressed"; "besides," he adds sarcastically, "this volume is for the pianofortes of the rich, for those who can afford to have their national zeal a little stimulated, without exciting much dread of the excesses into which it may lead them; and whose nerves may be alarmed with advantage, since more may be expected from their fears than could be gained from their justice."

Moore was then twenty-seven, in the full flush of youth and genius, and that inspiration which fame gives to the poet while she crowns him. Whatever was best and truest in his nature he enshrined in these national songs, and by them he lives; all else he has written, rich as they are in fancy, beauty, and exquisite diction, are almost unheeded by the people; the "Melodies" form the true pedestal of his glory. He has been made immortal by a hundred songs. His principles, also triumphed at last over the petty factions of the hour, and what was pronounced "sedition" when he wrote, soon, by the overwhelming power of public opinion, was forced to become law. The strong arm of O'Connell guided the passions, and directed those mighty energies evoked by the divine gift of song, and the fetters lifted from a nation by the Act of Emancipation fell as a trophy at the poet's feet. Moore's verses were the inspiration of "the Liberator," and even Wellington may have been touched by this noble appeal:-

> Yet, still the last crown of thy toils is remaining,
>   The grandest, the purest even thou hast yet known,
> Tho' proud was they task other nations unchaining,
>   Far prouder to heal the deep wounds of they own.
> At the foot of that throne for whose weal thou hast stood,
>   Go! plead for the Land that first cradled they fame,

And bright o'er the flood of her tears and her blood
Let the rainbow of hope be her Wellington's name.

The history of Ireland repeats itself from age to age with such a mournful rhythm, that Moore's poems find as quick a response in the hearts of the people now as when first published. Each generation goes through the same phases – resistance, defeat, despair. The new generation follows with hopes as brilliant and resolves as bold, again to try, again to fail. And so the sad trilogy is acted from age to age, while the nation can only helplessly mourn, as victim after victim falls dead in the dust of the arena.

Moore was the truest interpreter of these successive moods of aspiration and gloom; and his verse so simple, yet so passionate and powerful, has become almost the national idiom for the expression of national feeling. No poet is so often quoted. His lyrics are in the hearts and on the lips of our people, and our orators still wing their arrows against oppression with a line from Moore to make the aim more fatal.

A very perfect and beautiful translation of the "Melodies" into Irish was made by Dr. McHale, the learned and patriotic Archbishop of Tuam; and as the impetuous peasantry of the West listen with tears, or wild applause to Moore's verses, sung to their national music in their native tongue, one feels that love of freedom and dreams of independence can never die out amongst a people so sensitive to all that is noble, tender, and heroic. Moore knew that his glory was linked with these songs: for all poets that have once touched the nation's heart live evermore with the nation's life [...] It was the cry of humanity against wrong, and found a universal echo. The prophetic words have been fulfilled which he wrote with prescience of his own world-wide fame –

The stranger shall hear they lament on his plains.
The sigh of thy harp shall be sent o'er the deep,
Till thy masters themselves as they rivet our chains,
Shall pause at the song of their captives and weep.

When the "Melodies" were completed, Moore was at the summit of his glory. The world and its publishers were at his feet. At once he received an offer of 3,000*l.* for any poem he would choose to write on an Eastern subject. Moore describes his own anxieties after the acceptance of this splendid offer. No inspiration came; for he had none, he says, unconnected with country; no strength unless he lay on the breast of his mother earth; and the very magnitude of the offer seemed to weigh down and deaden all thought and fancy in him. "At length," he adds, "the thought occurred to me of founding a story on the fierce struggle between the Ghebers, the ancient fire-worshippers of Persia, and their haughty Moslem masters. From this moment a new and deep interest took possession of me, and the spirit that had spoken in the 'Melodies' of Ireland soon found itself a home in the East."

Thus, the true inspiration came, and the poem flowed on rapidly.

"The Fire Worshippers," though the scene is laid in Persia, is, in fact, an episode of '98, and the portrait of Hafed, the young dauntless hero, is drawn from Lord Edward Fitzgerald. Though Moore sang of Iran, his thoughts were of Erin; and underlying every page of the poem is an allusion to the wrongs which Ireland has suffered from her conquerors; while all the smouldering indignation of his own feelings is expressed in the lines: –

> Yes, *I* am of that outcast few,
> To Iran and to vengeance true;
> Who curse the hour your Arabs came
> To desolate our shrines of flame:
> And swear, before God's burning eye,
> To break our country's chains, or die.

While the passionate but vain efforts of the Ghebers to throw off the yoke of the intolerant invader recall the story of the fated Geraldine, who is described as

> One of the ancient hero line,
> Along whose glorious currents shine
> Names that have sanctified their blood,
> As Lebanon's small mountain flood
> Is rendered holy by the ranks
> Of sainted cedars on its banks.

And our own people may find their likeness drawn in –

> Iran's sons that never, never
> Will stoop to be the victor's slaves,
> While heaven has light or earth has graves!
> Spirits of fire, that brood not long,
> But flash resentment back for wrong;
> And hearts where slow, but deep, the seeds
> Of vengeance ripen into deeds.
> Who tho' they know the riven chain
> Snaps but to enter in the heart
> Of him who rends its links apart,
> Yet dare the issue, blest to be,
> Even for one bleeding moment free,
> And die in pangs of liberty!

The allusions, also, to the desecrated altars of the people are numerous: –

> The fierce invaders pluck the gem
> From Iran's broken diadem,
>   And bind her ancient faith in chains.

In the fall of the young chief, who fought for freedom "on the green sea brink," we recognise the fate of Lord Edward: –

> 'Tis come, his hour of martyrdom
> In Iran's sacred cause, is come;
> And tho' his life hath passed away,
> Like lightening on a stormy day,
> Yet, shall his death-hour leave a track
>   Of glory, permanent and bright,
> To which the brave shall long look back
>   With fond regret, and by its light
>   Watch through the hours of slavery's night.

So does the Gheber chief:

> His glories lost, his cause betrayed,
> Iran, his own loved country, made
> A land of carcases and slaves;
> One dreary waste of chains and graves!

But he and his band meet death heroically, as many an Irish patriot had done, and call

> For God and Iran! as they fall.

Then the informers are denounced, as they might often be in Irish history before and since:

> Oh! For a tongue to curse the slave
>   Whose treason, like a deadly blight,
> Comes o'er the councils of the brave,
>   And blasts them in their hour of might.
> His country's curse, his children's shame,
> Outcast of virtue, peace, and fame.

Even the captor of Lord Edward, the exceedingly unpopular gentleman who was generally believed to be both sanctimonious and cruel, is drawn with the characteristics attributed to him by the Irish people, who detested his name: –

> He sleeps
> Calm while a nation round him weeps;
> While curses load the air he breathes,
> And falchions from unnumbered sheaths
> Are starting to avenge the shame
> His race hath brought on Iran's name,
> Hard, heartless chief, unmoved alike
> Mid eyes that weep and swords that strike,
> One of that saintly murderous brood,

Who think through unbeliever's blood,
Lies their directest path to heaven –
One who will pause, and kneel unshod
In the warm blood his hand hath pour'd,
To mutter o'er some text of God,
Engraven on his reeking sword.

The perfect and beautiful poem of "Lalla Rookh" was received by the public with the most intense enthusiasm, and "The Fire Worshippers" was pronounced the best of all the tales, probably because it was vital with true feeling. Lord Jeffrey, in the "Edinburgh," gave it the palm for excellence, though he entirely overlooked its cryptic political signification. Moore was engaged for two years on this work; for he says of himself that he worked slowly, and was a far more *painstaking workman* than people imagined.

For his next poem, "The Loves of the Angels," he received 1,000*l*. And his charming prose tale followed, "The Epicurean," which, though closely imitated from the French romance of "Sethos," is yet full of Moore's peculiar beauties. Then he worked for years at his history of Ireland, which, if somewhat imperfect for want of adequate knowledge, is yet a model of style in eloquence and diction. When the first glow of youth was over, Moore led a retired life in his English home, far from the brilliant world, in the soul's quiet that genius loves. Sometimes he visited his native country, and was always received with triumphs and ovations. When he entered the theatre at Dublin the whole audience rose up to welcome him as if he were a king; and he was a king over the hearts of the nation, and this spontaneous homage was the sacred symbol of the poet's coronation.

His last years were made sad and desolate by home sorrows; all his children died before him. His family became extinct; the race culminated and ended with him. But that which is best in the utterance of a great human soul can never die; the children of the poet's brain immortal –

And the hearts and the voices of Erin prolong
Through the answering future his name and his song.

His library and his harp, that Irish harp which gave him inspiration, have been placed in the keeping of the Royal Irish Academy, as heirlooms of the nation, and a room has been set apart for their reception, which is now called "The Moore Library"; while his statue, the first every publicly erected in Ireland to an Irishman, has, by a kind of poetical justice, been placed in sight of the college that tried to have him expelled for his nationality; and was inaugurated by the Viceroy of the Government that would willingly have stopped the publication of the "Irish Melodies" and had the poet prosecuted for sedition.

But Moore lies in his death-sleep in English earth. Is this right? Should not the poet's sacred dust be laid in holy Ireland, amidst the people to whom his genius was consecrated? Let us hope that a day will come when his mortal remains will be brought back to the land he loved so well, with the reverent homage of a nation, and then a fitting monument will be raised in the Irish capital to the great national poet of Ireland, and the most perfect lyrist of the age.

George Eliot

George Eliot was decidedly the most popular of all the female novelists of recent times; and is still adored, as without rival or equal, by a vast world of fanatical worshippers. Her reputation was world-wide; and she exacted homage from all the leading men of the day, more, however, by her conversation, which was singularly profound and interesting, than even by her works. She achieved also an unexampled financial success. No other woman, perhaps, of her generation realised forty thousand pounds by writing. And she deserved it, for she strove earnestly to perfect her work, though often in the effort to seem wise she attained only to being dull. Yet "Romola" is a great book to add to literature; sufficient to ensure lasting fame to the author, even had she written nothing else; but in "Daniel Deronda" and several of her later works she enforces her views with rather too much wearisome prolixity and assertive dogmatism. She is determined on teaching, and will interrupt a love-scene with a disquisition on the return of the Jews or the appearance of infusoria under the microscope.

She also abounds in commonplaces, delivered in language of oracular obscurity, as if they were deep truths brought to the surface for the first time, and given to us covered with the hard grit of primitive formations.

"Middlemarch" especially exhausts our patience by page after page of pretentious commonplace; and probably no amount of bribery would induce anyone to read it through a second time.

Middlemarch is a small provincial place, within and around which are located the persons introduced to our notice. Chief of those is the heroine, Miss Brooke – a young lady of birth and fortune, whose head is filled with schemes of social regeneration, to be worked out mainly by improved labourers' dwellings, for which she is always drawing new plans, while teasing her friends incessantly on the subject. A young lady of birth, beauty, and fortune devoting herself to social regeneration might be made a very splendid central figure of a drama; and we are led to expect great things from the preface, where Santa Theresa – the most gifted of female writers, as well as the holiest of women, whose words glowed with a lofty and spiritual eloquence seldom equalled, and whose life was an incessant manifestation of angelic zeal in the cause of God and for the good of humanity – is presented to us as the type from which Miss Brooke is drawn, but with what miserable result all readers can judge for themselves. The lofty, ideal woman, with the "soul-hunger" for some great purpose, "enamoured of intensity and greatness," "yearning to sway the destinies of mankind," which the author tells us she is going to describe, is never manifested by word or deed. Dorothea Brooke is simply a foolish young person, with a brain full of crotchets, but utterly devoid of common sense; and with her prosy sayings and stupid projects is about the most wearisome creation ever introduced into a novel. Before the volume is half ended she marries an old philosopher, equally prosy, described by a lady friend, with a coarseness not unusual to George Eliot, as "bad as the wrong physic; nasty to take, and sure to disagree."

About this period of the story we get a glimpse of a cousin of the ancient bridegroom, a young man of Polish blood, an artist – poor, clever, and evidently unscrupulous; and we feel that something may be worked out of him. He may fall in love with the young woman who "yearns," or poison the ancient philosopher, who already fears that his young wife may be troublesome while he is writing his great history of the Aryan Myths. But for this faint hope of a passion and a tragedy no one would have courage to cut the leaves of the second volume. Of the bridegroom, we are told that "his blood under a microscope was found to be all semicolons and parentheses," and of the young cousin, that he laughed derisively to himself when he beheld the ill-assorted pair.

The philosophic husband, in fact, only wants a steady good young person to look after his house and comforts and read aloud to him, as his eyes are failing. Yet, even though his blood did run into punctuation, George Eliot need not have made him write love-letters of such ponderous obscurity as the one where he tells Miss Dorothea Brooke of his desire to marry her in adverbs of extraordinary length. "A consciousness," he says, "of need in my own life arose contemporaneously with the possibility of my becoming acquainted with you! and I find in you an eminent fitness to supply that need, connected, I may say, with such activity of the affections as even the preoccupation of a work too special to be abandoned would not uninterruptedly dissimulate." "And," he adds, "I now felt convinced emphatically of the feelings I had preconceived, this evoking more decidedly those affections which I have referred."

No man of ordinary human nature, and more than average intellect, could indite such jargon, and the author has failed completely in her endeavour to sketch either the man of letters and learning or the woman of lofty aims and high purpose. When De Staël wished to give the world a picture of a woman of genius, passion, and poetry, she drew Corinne, and has made the type immortal; Bulwer, in his Lady Florence Lascelles, has perfected the vision he had dreamed of one of the queens of society reigning by sovereign right of beauty, rank, wealth, and brilliant intellect; and Disraeli, when he created "Theodora," gave a magnificent illustration to literature of one of those rare and splendid women who can inspire multitudes and sway nations by the powerful and magnetic force of their passionate convictions. But George Eliot has added no new page to the history of what a woman might be, nor has she created a type, except in "Romola," to interest and inspire. A whole infinity separates her heroine, Dorothea Brooke, from the glowing, impassioned, eloquent Santa Theresa, whose words and works can still kindle an answering fire in human hearts, though the shadow of three centuries rests on them.

George Eliot has a keen insight into ordinary human life and commonplace natures; some humour – a strong trenchant way of describing what lies on a certain low social level, and a sharp, rough power of sarcasm. These are her gifts as a writer, and not without fitness has she assumed a man's name, for she has more of the masculine nature, strong, hard, keen, and somewhat coarse, than of the passionate, glowing, sympathetic woman's intellect. There is a rector's wife in the book who, though described as well-born and bred, utters many of those coarse phrases in which George Eliot's works abound. This lady describes the philosopher as a "great bladder for dried peas to rattle in"; she believes in birth and no birth, "as in game and vermin"; she says, "Some people never know vinegar from wine till they have swallowed it and got the colic"; she calls a gentleman "pulpy." However, there is some humour in the description of the philosopher's family arms, "three cuttle fish, sable, and a commentator rampant." Celia Brooke is rather amusingly drawn – the young lady who hates energy and emphasis, and wonders how well-bred people can distort their faces by excitement and look like turkey cocks. The uncle, also, Mr. Brooke, is cleverly touched off. The man who has travelled in his youth and met many celebrities, and trifled over every science, and who is ready at any moment to take a mental scamper over all countries and all subjects with the most ready and voluble incoherence – he is described as having "a glutinously indefinite mind."

But there is too much exhaustive analysis of all the petty people of the petty town of Middlemarch. Why are we to be bored with the sayings and doings of these very commonplace persons – the mayor and his wife, who was an innkeeper's daughter, and their pseudo-fashionable children, who are ashamed of their mother's English; the old miser with his horrid lot of relations, each striving for his money; and the doctor, and the banker, and the foxhunter, who swears "By God" on the most trivial occasions, which is very offensive – could not the author make him say "By Jove!" it is at least harmless – and she is fond of classic allusions? Indeed, there is one passage about Herodotus and Io so very misty that we should require that "commentator rampant" of whom she speaks to make it intelligible. These provincial people seem in no way connected with the story of the lady who has the "soul-hunger" for exalted deeds, and it would be well, perhaps, to kill them all right off by a railway smash in the early part of the next volume.

Altogether, "Middlemarch" is a dull book, without any development of that mystic working of a gifted woman's mind foreshadowed in the preface. Occasionally there are glimpses of that insight into life for which the author has been celebrated, as in the expression of truths like this: "There is a wonderful frank charm in the intimacy between a man and a woman where there is no passion to hide or to confess." But these passages of simple truth, expressed in clear, lucid language, are few and far between. George Eliot's style in general has the fatal affectation of being learned. There is an illustration, *à propos* of match-making, taken from vortices, hairlets, water-drops, and infusoria, which has too much of a polytechnic flavour; also, her comparison of the mind of a woman to "an irregular solid." Women are very pretty story-tellers, but they are only good writers through sympathy and love. They should know the range of their limited mental powers, and keep within it if they wish to interest. An affectation of learning spoils them, because it is never more than an affectation; no woman is really learned; perhaps she would be very disagreeable if she were so. A logical dogmatic female is detestable. The great charm of the sex is in that light superficiality, which gives sympathy so readily; believes everything through love, and seeks no grounds for belief beyond faith in the one beloved. Our legions of female novelists – and they submerge the land – ought to know that their peculiar mission is to reveal and analyse the working of the heart; in this they may succeed better than men, but they can never expect to vie in power, knowledge of life, in the eloquence that comes by culture, or the wit that comes by nature, with the more richly endowed and more highly educated sex. Men are perpetually adding names to literature that will last for all time – women never. Amongst the male novelists of the day, this age crowns two at least with immortality – Bulwer and Disraeli – but not one woman, though they write by thousands. Not even George Eliot herself, called by the London critics the greatest female writer of the world, can hope to live beyond the passing moment. The fragrance distilled from the glowing feelings, crushed lives, and perhaps broken hearts of literary women may refresh a few idle hours of man's more earnest life. It is enough – the world asks no more from them than to amuse or soften through sympathy the powerful ruling race for whom woman was created only to be the helpmeet; but no one can be expected to care much or long for vanished fragrance, a crushed flower, a faded life, or the wrecks of broken hearts, from which most female writers draw their experiences, unless, indeed, the love tales were embalmed in such prose and verse as men only can write, and which women have never equalled.

Why cannot English novelists see the superior force, beauty, and power of the French style of writing, where a line, a word, is made to unfold a character or express a dramatic situation, and the line or word reveals more of both in a sudden flash than all the long-winded descriptive sentences of English writers, with their numerous clauses and concatenations?

George Eliot has much of this fatal tendency to the insufferably prosy. She is always sermonising in an instructive, parochial way, and giving us her own views, in place of allowing her characters to reveal them by swift, dramatic touches. Nearly all the second volume, for instance, is entirely destitute of incident or scenic effect. It consists simply of a treatise on medical jurisprudence, hard, harsh, and pretentious in style, inspired by a Dr. Lydgate, who seems a pet of the author's, or at least a peg to hang her theories on concerning jurymen, medicines, and medical law. All the characters talk with a ponderous verbosity in sentences of at least twenty lines long, and of the most involved construction, as if, like those of a legal document, they were to be paid for according to their obscurity and length.

There is also much entomology in this portion of the work, and a great deal about anatomy, with incidental phrases too coarse for quoting; so that altogether it is wearisome and disagreeable, and does not in the least tend to the development of the plot. The remainder of the volume has more human interest. We are brought to Rome, where Dorothea (the girl of suppressed passions and undirected intellect) and her grave, philosophic husband are passing the honeymoon, but not too happily; he, still collecting materials for his great work on ancient myths, shut up all day in libraries, writing all the evening; she, weary, listless, solitary, sauntering through picture-galleries with her maid and paid guide; and when at home looking silently and wearily at her husband, walled round by his books and papers, as if on an inaccessible island, far away from her and all her feminine yearnings for love, kind words, and sympathy – for, like all women, Dorothea pined for companionship, for some expressions of gentle, genial interest in her life, pleasures, employments, and pursuits. These would have been more to her than all the picture-galleries in the world; but the grave, silent man, entrenched within his fortifications of manuscript and books, never dreamed that the poor, etiolated plant outside the circumvallation was dying for want of the sunshine of affection and sympathy. Yet he liked her after a fashion – the old literary fashion – that is, he required her not to interrupt him by word or caress, and, in return, he sent her off to do Rome with a hired cicerone, and thought he had thus arranged everything necessary for their mutual happiness. He was an excellent man in every respect; still a suspicion would sometimes rise in his wife's heart that he was withal only a selfish egotist who knew nothing of the needs of a woman's heart. And he, who expected a wife to be a mere passive creature, docile to orders, grateful for small favours, and without any aim beyond ministering to his comforts and securing to him perfect quiet, was startled and troubled at the least claim she made upon his time or attention. In fact, she was in his way, except when he wanted a listener to whom he could expound his views; or someone to sort his papers and arrange his notes. Thus, both began to see their illusions of happiness crumbling to dust. Dorothea was often in tears and her husband looked graver and sterner than ever. In place of the intellectual companion she had expected in a literary husband, she finds that she has wedded only a composing machine whose "blood runs in semicolons." And he feels disturbed at the petulance that sometimes rises to her lips as it interrupts the cohesion of his ideas upon the great subject of the common origin of myths.

It is just at this time that the Polish cousin comes again upon the scene, and the drama begins to be interesting – through the evidently coming conflict of passions and duties. The brilliant, gifted, poetical artist becomes the companion of Dorothea to the studios and picture-galleries, in place of the hired guide, and a new fascination dawns upon her life. "There is a great charm," George Eliot has said, "in the intercourse between a man and woman where there is no passion to conceal or to confess," but the difficulty is to have the intercourse and intimacy without the passion. Few attain to the philosophical balance, especially when genius lights up and intensifies all words and feelings. We perceive at once that these two – Dorothea and the artist – are falling helplessly into a metaphysical passion of so-called friendship, fed with much æsthetic talk over art and poetry and subtle analysis of feelings. But Dorothea is pure as an angel all the while; she does not know that there are some people mystically and mysteriously dangerous to others, who exercise an electric influence over their mind and soul, an influence impossible to resist, for it seems the product of some mystic and eternal law of spiritual affinity; and so she allows this subtle power – call it mesmerism, magnetism, or psychic force – radiated from her companion's presence to enfold her round without an effort at resistance. The husband – when he lifts his head from his books and his history – has some instincts of jealousy, and his manner becomes more stern and sombre than ever. So the second volume ends, leaving a grand opening for a psychological study of human hearts, and a tragic involvement of human lives to be worked out in the concluding part of the work. George Eliot has a deep and penetrating insight into life. And so we leave the three principal actors in the drama to their fate in her powerful hands. Will she save or slay? Probably the latter, for such tragic involvements seldom end happily. Will the husband, from being only stern, become cruel? Will the lover – brilliant, reckless, loving, daring, passionate, and utterly unscrupulous – exert his fatal influence to the utmost? – and the woman, with all her noble resolves, her sacred, saintly sense of wedded vows, her devotion to the good, the beautiful, and the true – her lofty ideal of life – will she suffer herself to be led to the edge of the precipice whose depth is infinite, while all the time she fancies that her soul is springing forward on a path of light to loftier regions and a diviner life? The flame has been kindled, the spell has been woven, and the magnetic circle is closing around these three related lives; but we leave the reader to study the concluding volume, that will give an answer as to the final result.

CHAPTER EIGHTEEN

Jane Wilde, *Social Studies*, 1893

Published in 1893 by Ward & Downey, this was the final collection of Speranza's articles, which also included two new translated stories (from Spanish and German), with titles as diverse and wide-ranging as "Suitability of Dress," "The Bondage of Woman," "The Destiny of Humanity," "Genius and Marriage," "Venus Victrix," and many others. Again, the impressive range and originality of her intellectual interests are evident in these lively and forthright essays, which include her accounts of Australia, American women, and the Vatican.

American Women

The first question propounded to a traveller on returning from a transatlantic tour is usually, "What is your opinion of American women?" for, in truth, the American woman is by far the most important element in the social machinery of the States.

Her reputation for beauty and smartness has spread over the whole earth, and to doubt her fascination would be a heresy even beyond this agnostic age. However, we are, fortunately, not wholly dependent on the crude judgment of awe-struck, startled travellers, saturated as they are with old-world prejudice, and prisoned in its narrow, conventional traditions; for the Americans, having already interviewed and exhausted all Europe, are now laudably engaged in the process of interviewing each other, and that with an acuteness and insight far beyond the observing faculty of the bewildered foreigner.

Nothing, in fact, can be more interesting than the analytical descriptions of their own people to be found in the pages of the great living novelists of America; and we may certainly accept in perfect faith the clever, clearly outlined sketches of eminent writers, such as Howells, Henry James, Cable, Aldrich, Edgar Fawcett, and other leaders of the great modern school of fiction, as the fullest expression of that wonderful product of social progress and advanced intelligence – the nineteenth-century American woman.

Every type is reproduced in their gallery of contemporary portraits – from the fragile, luxurious beauty of the South, to the audacious energetic newspaper woman of the North, who scampers through Europe, notebook in hand, interviewing everyone that has a name, and exhausting every subject, after half-an-hour's study, in letters of pungent criticism for her weekly paper, dated generally from "the express train," "the tunnel," or "the steamboat."

Every city also has its peculiar characteristics, and with these we are made fully acquainted through the novelists. In Boston, for instance, the women are "intense" and transcendental; it is the city of advanced intellects and the emancipated woman. The celebrated Margaret Fuller, the "Zenobia" of Hawthorne's *Blithedale Romance*, gave the first impulse there to psychical progress when she inaugurated the literary *salon* at her own house, selected and announced the subject for the evening's discussion, and brilliantly led the conversation herself. Since then Boston is the accepted exponent of the higher culture; and the intellectual women who gather there under the shadow of the world-soul, treat life with a lofty and serene philosophy, proudly disdaining the fashion, follies and dress of New York.

Philadelphia is the Quaker city – neat, orderly, calm and reserved, where everyone seems to go to bed at ten o'clock, and the ladies make no effort to heighten the charm of their pretty faces by the adventitious aid of rouge or pearl powder. But they cultivate literature, poetry and art; and society is elegant and refined. Among the celebrities of "the flowery city" may be named the late Professor Gross, eminent in medical science, George Boker, one of the leading poets of America, and Mrs Bloomfield Moore, who has earned the gratitude of the citizens by her splendid donations of paintings and artistic works, valued at more than five thousand pounds, to the new Museum of Art established there.

Washington is grand and courtly; a stately city of rank and solemnity. The royal ambassadors set the mode, especially the English embassy, which takes the lead in style and splendour that republicans weakly try to emulate by a display of liveried servants and heraldic emblazonments. Caste and class strive eagerly there for precedence, and every young lady looks forward, confidently, to being elected to the English peerage. In that clever novel, *Democracy*, there are capital sketches of life at Washington, where the officials claim to be ultra aristocrats, and Miss Virginia Dare resolves to become a countess, in which, of course, she succeeds, for what simple English peer could resist her all-compelling energy and smartness; in fact, the American girl is beginning to look on the English peerage as the appanage of her race. Not that she is over-elated at the prospect, for an American woman thinks nothing too good for her that can be had for love or money, no social position too eminent for her merits. If a crowned prince asked her in marriage she would consider it quite right and fitting, and accept her destiny without the least nervous embarrassment.

In every recent American novel there is always an English peer, foolishly devoted to one of these fair enslavers, who snubs him or takes him, according to caprice, evidently of opinion that the favour is all on her side. In one novel, a peer, with an income of a hundred thousand a year, offers his hand, and is refused because he is only a weak, good-natured person, without that strength of intellect required by an American girl in her lover. All women are queens in America, and have no idea of recognising any social position as higher than their own. From men they exact the utmost homage; indeed, the worship of women is the national religion, a sacred law and gospel that none dare infringe. Many types of face and feature may be found in the vast extent of America with its varied climate and diverse races, but the South and West are particularly rich in strongly-marked characteristics. The Mexicans are fine and handsome, with a mixture of Indian and Spanish blood, from which the women derive their superb hair and eyes and graceful figures, and the men their proud Hidalgo bearing.

The miners of the West are strong, bold and picturesque, as the men who may have led the Argonauts or founded Rome, and are worthy of their western land, which is a paradise of beauty, while every woman looks a Penthesilea or a brigand queen. The only one section of America that is wholly deficient in personal beauty is the Mormon settlement. The Mormons own a glorious land, and are industrious and orderly, but the women, it is said, are of ideal ugliness of the colourless Saxon type, with white eyes and eyelashes, sandy hair and shapeless features. It is remarkable that not a single Irishwoman is to be found in the Mormon city, but the bright-eyed daughters of Erin have no objection to intermarry with the Chinese, who are always anxious to obtain Irish wives. Consequently a great colony of Hiberno-Mongolian origin is spreading along the border of the Pacific, and ethnologists will soon have a new type of humanity to study.

In New York there is no distinctive type of race – all races have been fused there into uniformity by the same habits, passions and ambitions, and the influence of Europe on society. The women are dressed by Paris and the men by London, and life is modelled on the English style, but with much more splendour of outlay and effect. New York is the true paradise of women, where they glow and glitter in their gorgeous plumage, while the men toil and work in their dusky offices to amass the wealth that may cover their wives with diamonds to startle Europe – a city of splendour, luxury and pleasure; the third great capital of the world, and equal in wealth to London and Paris put together. Long after America had thrown off the political yoke of England, the bondage to English modes of thought still remained. The awe of England was upon the heads of the people, and social life, in consequence, was provincial and imitative, and wholly wanting in national individuality. America, in fact, was but a suburb of London, an infinite and colourless Bayswater. They did not dare to originate – they copied. They were fed on English ideas, affected English manners, and yearned to find some English ancestor of established lineage to whom they could affiliate themselves. Altogether they were prostrated in humble reverence at the feet of the mighty mother. But steam and the rapid facilities of travel have gradually weakened this awful homage to old social tradition. Modern America now laughs at "the rusty, antiquated usages of England," the rigid distinction of classes, the ridiculous ceremonials, the abject servility of the court life, with the bowings and backslidings of the gold-laced officials, so degrading, in the eyes of a republican, to freeborn humanity. And they mock also at the prosy, dreary, respectable papers, their petty politics, their Hares and Rabbits Bill, and they weary of the dull routine of society, the vapid talk where no large free ideas are ever circulated, and no recognition is apparent of the great fact that democracy is sweeping down monarchy with all its antiquated ritual, to the moles and the bats. London, says an American writer, has two idols – Science and Royalty, and conversation fluctuates between the Electric Light and the last Foundation Stone laid by Royal hands. They find the English slow, ponderous, conventional. A people that would never startle (it would be bad form), who repress all individual assertion, and insist that everything should be done and said according to the custom and usage which has the force of law in English society. They notice the languid crawl of the English accent, the half-finished sentences, as if to complete an idea in the utterance would entirely bore the speaker with fatigue. The English, they say, speak nicely, but they do not know how to converse. They have no fluency, are crude and abrupt in expression, and quite infelicitous in smooth transitions. The girls are dull, diffident and monotonous, with their pale eyes, pale hair and sealskin jackets, one might gather a thousand, or fifty thousand of them together, and they would all be found precisely alike.

The American woman, on the contrary, disdains this colourless uniformity, and revolts against social usages that would limit her bold originality and assertive self-manifestation. She is proud, conscious, strong-souled and self-reliant. "I am an American girl" is answer enough to any timid old-world bigot. And this phrase expresses at once dignity, courage, self-respect and the independence of the emancipated republican. The English girl, in one of the novels, utters her little harmless platitudes in a soft, low monotone of broken sentences. "How nice," she murmurs, "to have pictures on a rainy day – and it rains so often!" and so on, and so on, in a limpid, weak, watery way. Always shy and indistinct with her half utterances, the stiff conventional attitude never changed, nor the level murmur illustrated by gesture or laughter. But the vigorous, vivacious American girl never omits a syllable; she speaks in a loud, clear voice, as if for the reporters, and as one worth hearing, who demands and extorts attention. She accentuates all she says with firm purpose and resolute determination to be heard. She is sharp, smart and terrible at repartee, and may, perhaps, be sometimes fatiguing to the English ear with her voluble flow of words. The English girl never stares, nor asks questions with obtrusive curiosity. She is trained to seem and to be a negation – a dormant soul without volition or an opinion on any subject, felt or expressed. Her American cousin, however, has an aggressive frankness, based chiefly upon interrogatories and bold personalities. Her gaze is clear and direct; not "the stony British stare," but with the large, truthful eyes of childhood – the eager, inquiring glance of a candid nature. Truth is in all her words. This Puritan virtue has indeed remained an heirloom in the American family. They have none of the subtle evasion and graceful mendacities of high life in Europe – the delicate flatteries, so charming and so false. These are stamped out at once by the frank, fearless candour of the American girl. Yet one trembles a little before a candour so uncompromising; for we all shrink from the downright expression of the actual, and the glare of an unshadowed truth makes one nervous. But the Americans have no mercy. Nature meant them for a nation of interviewers. They generalise, describe and label you after ten minutes' inspection, and send off your portrait across the Atlantic, with all your imperfections on your head, for the amusement of the crowd, who must be propitiated by a victim, and who applaud and shout, "Bravo, Toro!" when a "special" has been more than usually successful in tossing the victim from his horns, to be trampled in the dust of the arena. Yet they are by no means an ill-natured or cruel people; on the contrary, they are kind, generous and charming to the passing stranger who enters within their gates, but the Sovereign Demos has no reverence, and finds a subtle pleasure and sense of power in giving pain to sensitive natures; so, like Nero, they sometimes light their gardens with live torches for want of better pastime. They seem also to take pleasure in showing England that they are no longer held in bondage to English opinion; they have even suggested that their native language should in future be called American, not English; and they have already adopted a quite independent system of *othografy*, from which all the superfluous letters are excluded.

It is not improbable, therefore, that a new dialect, which may be called Americanese, will be rapidly formed. Neologism is popular in America; they are perpetually adding new words to their vocabulary, borrowed, perhaps, from the Indians, or the Mexicans, or the Californian miners, or transmuted from the Chinese dialects blended with Gaelic, which the Chinese colony learn from their Irish wives. So that when all these elements have properly simmered together for a reasonable time, the result will be a language widely different from the English of Addison and Ruskin.

Speech is a passion with the Americans. They orate at all times, and on all subjects, with a copious redundancy of expression that is startling to those accustomed only to the slow-moving, hesitating tongue of English speakers, who always seem painfully seeking for the next word, and finding it only by a happy chance after many efforts.

The Americans (men and women alike) are the most voluble of nations, and when trained are the most fluent orators. The women express their ideas with firmness, precision and perfect self-possession, and are admirable speakers on the platform. While men like Wendell Phillips, Doherty, Lowell, Boyle O'Reilly and others would have made their mark as orators in any assembly in the world. This gift of natural eloquence is due, perhaps, to the strain of Irish blood in their veins – for all men of note in America will be found connected, in some way or other, with the fluent, passionate Celtic race. The Saxon basis is the rough block of the nation; but it is the Celtic influence that gives it all its artistic value and finish. A recent President of the United States was the son of an Irishman; the great novelist, Henry James, is the grandson of an Irish emigrant; and the late Mayor of New York, also an admirable speaker, was an Irishman. Ireland has added not a little to the triumph of American genius, and America, in return, has often nobly flung her protecting banner over the desolate exiles.

The Americans are not remarkable as painters or musicians, but as actors, orators and writers they may take a foremost place in the world's pantheon. The power of expression by verbal symbols has certainly been given to them. Emerson is a study of thought crystallised into the most perfect forms; and the leading, living writers, in grace and charm of style, need not fear rivalry with the best English writers. We recognise at once in their work the artist touch, the care in composition, the purity of expression and the entire absence of the Zola element of degrading and degraded language, scenes and images. The American style is acute, fresh and exhilarating, full of quaint humour and gentle satire, which amuses without being malignant, and the pictures of social life, of the statesman and the journalist; the woman of the world, with her perfect grace and superficial culture; the fashionable girl, with her gossamer chatter; and the advanced woman, with her trenchant utterances, are all admirably sketched in the new novels.

We gather from these clever works the full expression of American life, with its strong desires, fierce rivalries, limitless rage for speculation, and energetic will to work, spend, enjoy and make the best of this poor mortal existence, without wasting time on corroding thoughts over transitory pleasures.

Americans are not given to brood over the mysteries of life. They never question the universe for solution of the unknowable; they have no morbid melancholy, no divine discontent, and never worry their heads over agnosticism, positivism or pessimism, but accept religion as it comes to them without any questioning analysis, simply as part of the great whirl of work, dress and fashion, that makes up the sum of daily life.

They like reading, but not study. Everyone in the cars seems furnished with a sixpenny novel or magazine, while newspapers cover the land like snowflakes in midwinter; but above all, they like lectures, because they can thus combine easily acquired information with the excitement of dress and out-door variety, and a crowded lecture is infinitely more amusing than a solitary magazine; besides it is of importance to them to assimilate knowledge rapidly as they eat and live, for life with them is a feverish rush of excitement and enjoyment. They are rapid in speech, in travel, in speculation, in everything. They live, every moment of their lives, an intense, daring, crowded, audacious, reckless and restless life or work, wealth and luxury. The present is enough for them, they take each moment as it comes, and get all the good out of it they can.

There is no girlhood or boyhood; everyone is born grown up, and the life of self-assertion and speculation begins from the cradle. The young girls have perfect freedom at an age when Europe would not allow them out of the nursery. They receive gentlemen alone in the evenings, and go to theatres and public places with them, unaccompanied by any duenna; for the chaperone and lynx-eyed matron of old-world usage and tradition has been quite suppressed in America, along with the superfluous vowels.

In America youth reigns supreme and unfettered, and there is little reference paid to parental authority. Young girls receive and go out alone or with their male friends, as fancy pleases, without any reference to the unwritten law of tradition, which is of such overwhelming force in Europe that to break it would incur the ban of society.

Women in America, whether married or single, rule society, and do not suffer society to rule them. They carry all before them with imperial sway, and are the beautiful despots of the land. Fathers, brothers and husbands are at work all day in the fierce strife and excitement of the ceaseless speculation, which is the national form of gambling. But the men never interfere with the interior management of the house; all the arrangements and expenditure and machinery of social life are left to the taste, judgment and discretion of the wife. The province of the husband is merely to fling down the showers of gold, which the fascinating better half spends right royally.

American women, too, are learned as well as being admirable house-keepers. They can extract square roots as well as pickle them, and think no more of encountering the difficulties of Latin, Greek, and all terrific ologies, than our ladies, those of the crewel or Berlin work.

What, however, is of more consequence than all these elaborate efforts to make women ugly by making them learned – for has not Walter Savage Landor said, that *thought* adds beauty to a man, but takes it from a woman – is the study of that art in which the beautiful Americanese have attained already to a high perfection, the *en touto niko* art for a woman, that of *dress*.

Yet, alas! that grace, intellect and French *tournure* cannot make youth and beauty immortal. These fair and fragile Americans, though possessing all, yet fade as quickly as the night-blowing cereus, reminding one of Goethe's pretty apologue, "Why am I so evanescent, O Zeus?" asked Beauty. "Because I have only made the evanescent beautiful," replied the god. And when youth, beauty, the flowers and the spring heard that, they withdrew themselves weeping from before the throne of Jupiter. Early marriages are consequently much more frequent in America than here, for at twenty these fair destroyers are already in the *mezzo cammin*, or even the *selva oscura*, and at twenty-five they are but traditions. "*Mai jettons une voile sur las passée*," as the Frenchman remarked, while placing a shawl upon one of these sad legends of antiquity. But no matter how many decades she may number, woman is always the great ruling power of America, and the American has become the representative woman of the world. Not crushed down as in Europe by old traditions of mental and legal inferiority, but asserting her sovereign right to equality, and to exact and receive the homage of men. Queens of beauty, lavish and extravagant in all things, gorgeous in toilette, insatiable of pleasure, surrounded by the costly luxuries of often illimitable wealth, the women of fashion bask in a changeless radiance of show and glitter, for money is easily made, and if also easily lost they care little; they enjoy while they can, eat, dress, dazzle and delight; but love is not by any means a leading interest in the life of an American woman, and seldom is scandal heard of in their social circle; for the very freedom of social intercourse trains woman to habits of self-reliance, and encourages so much self-esteem that they are quite insensible to flattery. They know all their perfections thoroughly, and they accept all praise as only a proper acknowledgment of their merits.

Besides, American life is carried on in a perpetual public glare. In their huge hotels and boarding-houses, caravanseries, where hundreds meet and feed and talk together, there is no mystery possible; nor is it needed, for divorce is so easily obtained that passionate dramas of fatal love and remorse form no element in their lives. If the marriage bond is found too galling, it may be broken at once with very little trouble; no one minds these minor family arrangements. Whatever is legal is right; and the divorced pair meet in society, each supplied with a new partner, and they dance in the same set with cool nonchalance, and sometimes even valse together with all that supreme indifference to harrowing sentiment which is the perfection of good manners.

The young girls also, though allowed such entire social freedom, are saved from any compromising entanglement by a certain consciousness of their own value. "They are not coquettes, and have more pride than vanity – a dignity which permits no shadow of disrespect; and their genial cama-raderie with the other sex is often much more allied to friendship than to love. The passion of the American woman is rather for dress, pleasure and display. She loves to live in public, to lead and reign in society. Noto-riety is not displeasing to her, and she attains it easily through the press, for there are hundreds of writing women, though but few really eminent names. Among leading brilliant writers may be named Mrs Julia Ward Howe, whose writings, both in prose and verse, place her in the front rank of gifted women. Her celebrated poem, *The Battle Hymn of the Republic*, is one of the finest lyrics of the age, and deserves a place in the literature of nations. In life and manner she is simple and unaffected. Her brilliancy is all of the intellect. Yet, even in her unpretentious Quaker dress, one can see that she has had remarkable beauty, which her daughter, one of the loveliest girls in America, has inherited.

Mrs Hodgson Burnett, though only a naturalised American, yet may be called an American writer. She was first known in England by her admi-rable novel, *That Lass o' Lowrie's*, of which thirty thousand copies were sold of the first edition. This was followed by her clever work, *Through One Administration*, a brilliant sketch of social, political and official life at Washington, drawn with sharp and rather satirical touches; but her popu-larity was assured by the success of *Little Lord Fauntleroy*, especially in its dramatic form.

An acute American critic remarks of Mrs Burnett, – "She understands suffering and sinning natures, and discovers gracious secrets in forbidding characters."

Mrs Atherton of New York, one of the young band of female writers, has obtained considerable celebrity by her novels, especially by *Los Cerritos*, an interesting and picturesque picture of rude Californian life amongst the squatters, with their strange idiom and fierce, lawless ways, all most vividly described. Another of the young writers, Amelia Reeves, is chiefly remarkable for a very lovely face, an unbridled imagination, with a total disregard of probability in her stories, and a wild, passionate fervour of eloquent expression.

Mrs Platt, wife of the American Consul at Queenstown, Ireland, takes high rank amongst the poetesses of America. Her verse has great strength and beauty, and is always strikingly original, yet simply tender and sympathetic, especially when touching on the subject of children, or the poor and suffering. While Louise Chandler– a poet celebrity in London as well as in America – has set all the soft human emotions to music in her beautiful and cadenced verse. Both Tennyson and Browning extolled her genius, and Mrs Moulton is proud to remember them amongst her best friends.

Literary women hold a high place in American society, and receive more social homage, as a tribute to intellect, than is accorded to literary women in London. Their brilliant circles include all that is eminent in genius, and they inspire, and stimulate with generous praise and true enthusiasm, all that is noble in mind or work. Thus they form an important section of society, and use all the immense power American women possess as social leaders, to uphold the dignity of intellect by refined and high-toned social intercourse. As social writers, they do not indulge in the grotesque sarcasm which so often disfigures the productions of the male contributors; and, as a rule, whatever is best and most appreciative in the society journals of comment or criticism may be safely attributed to a female pen. The most important and successful journalist in the States is a woman – Mrs Frank Leslie. She owns and edits many journals, and writes with bright vivacity on the social subjects of the day, yet always evinces a high and good purpose; and, with her many gifts, her brilliant powers of conversation in all the leading tongues of Europe, her splendid residence and immense income, nobly earned and nobly spent, Mrs Frank Leslie may be considered the leader and head of the intellectual circles of New York.

In former times the Americans lived almost entirely and piratically on English thought; but they are now producing a new and independent literature, of which the style, tone and colouring are quite removed and distinct from English models. While, with regard to technical excellence, the type, paper, binding, illustrations, woodcuts and etchings, they seem far ahead of the old country. They have also brought to the very highest perfection the photographic art, of which Saroni's portraits are an admirable example. All the leading continental works, from Paris to Stockholm and St Petersburg, are translated at once, and in the best style; while works by native writers on science, art, literature, history and archæology are beginning to appear in copious profusion. To these the current literature of England is added. Everything good is appropriated, though, it must be confessed, seldom paid for; a serious injustice to English brain-workers. But the system at least spreads the fame of English writers; while in England scarcely anything is known of the rich and varied literature of America. Hawthorne's *Scarlet Letter* first startled the English mind with a sense of the peculiar intellectual power of America; but it is only recently that the eminent living novelists are becoming known to the reading public of England. A great deal of the popular writing (especially the journalistic) is certainly grotesque, person and impertinent, reckless of giving pain, and wanting in good manners, reverence, reticence and due consideration for others. It seems as if a people that have ceased to fight for liberty still need blood, and must have the arena and the amphitheatre, the fierce lions of the Press, and the victims who are interviewed and slain. In the capricious chances of popular favour the victim may certainly be sometimes crowned, but is too often rent or stoned. The Americans are fond of travel, though the childlike worship of the Old World no longer exists. The have begun to recognise their own immense advantages, and to find out that Europe is "rather a humbug" – a mummy, smothered in bandages of old forms and formulas, that are but the cerements of the dead. The tone of American thought is colossal, their country is colossal, their mode of living, expenditure, wealth and speculations are all of immense proportion. "They consume twice as much of everything as any other people on earth," one of their own writers says. It is not surprising, then, that Europe seems so small to them, after the vastness of their own horizon. The mountains, rivers and plains are as nothing to them after their own, and "the baby-house scenery" of Europe fails to impress people who have looked on the foam and heard the thunders of Niagara. Even the Atlantic is but a mere ferry in their eyes, and they think no more of a run over to Europe than a Londoner of a run down to Brighton. They laugh at the little kings and kingdoms, and, in their large, expansive way, speak of "the Latin countries" generally, as if quite too insignificant for separate notice.

"The Innocents Abroad" are, in fact, ruthless iconoclasts, and mock at legends and ruins, rubbish and relics. They do not find the rail cars as comfortable, the hotels as sumptuous, the champagne as good as the American; nor the women as beautiful as those they left in Baltimore and New York, while to American women, accustomed as they are to admiration and homage, European society seems dull, heavy, monotonous and unappreciative. They do not care to go "moping about galleries or churches." They find Venice slow, and stories of the Falieri rather a bore. They want life, variety, fashion, amusement, picnics and promenades – enjoyment, in a word; not guide-books and routine. They are seeking material for a smart letter to the journals, and they find only formality and the police.

The female tourist is very amusingly drawn in one of the recent novels. She does not care for Turner's landscapes nor Assyrian bulls; she wants the present the actual humanity, not fossil bones. Her fervent aspiration is to meet all the celebrities of London at a dinner-party, to note their peculiarities, faces and features, talk and movements, and then dash off a letter to the journals, with accurate descriptions, marked, no doubt, by all the terrible candour of American nature, which is never glamoured by an illusion, but goes right at the fact with fatal precision.

Americans are amazed at the blind devotion of Europe to the old grooves and the ancient idols of routine and form, apparently unconscious that the pillars of the temple are failing and falling, and that any day a crash may come, bringing down the whole superstructure, built on ceremonial and symbols that have lost their strength since they lost their meaning.

Yet the spell of England, "mystic, mediæval England," is upon them still; and London has a charm for Americans beyond all classic Europe, as the origin of their nation, the founder of their laws, religion and social habits. "Sombre London, the mighty mother of our mighty race," as one of their writers finely designates the great capital of the English people, has an irresistible attraction for them. They love its pleasures and social crowds and stately court functions, with all the awful solemnity and the splendour of visible royalty.

Some even assert a liking for the shrouded atmosphere, the soft, moist air, the veiled skies, and the light, "the ineffable English light," so restful and soothing after the lurid glare and cloudless azure heaven of America.

And the old homage to England is shown in an effort, which is decidedly in progress, to form an aristocracy after the English model, with titled distinctions.

The wives of officials are beginning to arrogate to themselves the prefix of "Honourable," if it belongs by right of office to the husband; and the wife of the next American Minister at London may, perhaps, require to be called "Her Excellency."

The movement, however, has no chance of success, for the good sense of the American public is entirely against it; and already the leading journals have denounced its absurdity, along with the liveries, the fourteen servants, the coat of arms, and four horses of the Republican imitators of the vain glories of a monarchy.

An aristocracy is the growth of a thousand years' feudal lordship, when men had the power of life and death over their vassals; and the English aristos still retain the haughty habits of command, and are treated with traditional reverence, though the power and the feudal rights have passed away.

But an aristocracy cannot be made at once out of men who rise from rude toil or sordid vocations, by dint of fierce competition in trade, or some lucky chance in striking oil.

The Americans should be content to remain as they are, the great republican expression of human progress; where everyone stands on the same level, and is entitled to the same consideration; where the rail-splitter may become the equal of kings, and the daughter of the dry-goods man take her place amid the nobles of Europe, and consider herself quite their equal.

The true dignity of America is in the brain power that has transformed a wild, waste continent into a splendid world of advanced civilisation by the stupendous energy and intelligence of working men.

The old-world nations have been for six thousand years painfully toiling from Ararat to the Atlantic to advance the standard of humanity, and still the triumphs of intellect over ignorance, misery and desolation are incomplete. But in a hundred years the Americans have spread over half the world, furrowed it with iron roads, spanned the mighty rivers, driven paths through the mountains, covered the desolate plains with flourishing cities, and sent the full tide of civilisation from ocean to ocean with a force and power that leaves the old-word kingdoms far behind in the race of progress.

The sixty millions of America are made up of a wonderful medley of heterogeneous elements, but they have all the one watchword "Advance!" They are recruited from the young blood of all nations, for only youth and energy emigrate, and they have the spirit, the courage and the daring of their origin.

Thus the process of fusion goes on rapidly, and already America is becoming strong and assertive with the dignity of a united people. There are no oppressed nationalities, all are equal and have the same privileges, and all uphold the republic with pride and affection, and never dream of giving up the advantages it offers to go back to the bondage of old-world limitations and the chilling influence of class prejudice.

It is remarkable how soon all races become Americanised. No foreign language takes root among them. In a generation foreigners forget their native tongue, and English – the wonderful English language that seems made for the universe – remains triumphant and alone.

American women are not idle in the war of progress against prejudice. They have taken an advanced position in the strife for right and justice, and demand for their sex perfect equality with men – social, legal, professional and political, the right to vote, and even to be elected to Congress, and as they are always terribly in earnest, and have an indomitable will, no doubt they will gain all they demand. And already the women of Europe are following their example. English law has recently made vast concessions, and even English society, prisoned as it is in routine, is making praiseworthy efforts to cast aside many of the stupid old conventions of our false humanity.

The English girl is not so "dull and diffident" as America represents her. She is becoming inspired with a love of freedom and a consciousness of her own mental power, and claims a social, professional and political equality with the other sex. The "matron," hitherto thought so indispensable in society as guide and protector, is becoming an obsolete institution. The English girl is learning independence, and by earnest study, intellectual training and serious life work, is fitting herself for a higher and nobler position in the social organisation than she has hitherto held. Thus she will attain to the self-reliance and dignity that make her American sisters so important as a social power, while at the same time they lose none of their fascination as women.

There is a powerful electric influence in American nature that draws all other nations into its current, and an amount of overflowing nervous energy that is irresistibly stimulating to all who come into contact with it.

The gates of empires cannot be closed against eternal principles, nor can they be warred against by material agencies.

The march of ideas is predestined. Especially when ideas mean a free career for talent, equal chances of work and wealth for all men and women alike, and the fall of ignorance and idleness before enlightenment and industry and education, for on these things the well-being of a people is founded, and the happiness of nations and of humanity.

The Poet as Teacher

It is one of Goethe's profound aphorisms, that "Every day we should in some way renew our impression of the true and the beautiful by a verse from some great poet, the sight of a painting or a statue, or by a noble thought from some heroic mind; for the spiritual within is ever in danger for being choked and suffocated by the rank luxuriance of the weeds and thorns that crowd our daily life." In this country, however, Art has but few temples wherein lessons of grace and beauty can be taught the people; nor can even the glorious book of Nature be enjoyed by those who, with toiling hands and ever lowered eyes, work day and night at the loom of life to earn the scanty bread of subsistence.

The poor in these rough northern climes have little time for the dreamy musings over the illuminated pages of Nature, to which the luxurious indolence of a southern existence gives such full facility. The sunset and the cloud, the spiritual influence of dying day, or of night with starry host; the grandeur of the lonely mountain, the song of waters, the choral music of the waving trees – all the beauty and melody of the world, is, in a great degree, mute and veiled to our weary toiling slaves of civilisation. But literature, in the full plenitude of its ennobling influence, can reach all classes, the lowest as the highest.

The words of man can permeate where the music of the forest trees never can be heard. In the cabin, the cellar, the factory, the mine, amongst the children of the cities or the plains, wherever there is a soul however darkened, the souls of other men can reach him; the divine thinkers of all ages may come in and sit down by him, though his dwelling be the meanest hut. The soul at least can "build herself a lordly pleasure-house," be the poor, toiling, material frame ever so lowly located. The duty of a government, then, is to ameliorate the condition of the people as far as possible by affording every facility whereby these angel ministers may pass to and fro amongst them. It is ignorance that degrades, not poverty or toil. "That one man dies ignorant who has a capacity for knowledge, that I call a tragedy," is the deep and wise utterance of the great thinker and philosopher – Carlyle. "Every man," he adds, "even the meanest, is a priest sent to minister in the Temple of Immensity." And if the masses of men everywhere have fallen from this high birthright, so that the general characteristic of the labouring classes has hitherto been that of the lowest mental and physical degradation, the cause and the consequences must be laid to the charge of the ruling classes who for ages have debarred them from the light and privileges of knowledge. The truth seems only lately to have dawned upon the English mind that education was necessary to build up a noble race of citizens, and that every material advance, without a corresponding moral and intellectual progression, only ensured a vaster amount of crime by increasing the facilities whereby all the tendencies of the lower sensuous nature could be gratified.

Education forms the only counterpoise against the low instincts of a darkened intellect. And a world of gladness and blessedness dawns upon the lowliest human life in proportion as the clouds of ignorance are lifted. A noble thought, then, brings joy, for the moral sense is elevated to comprehend it. The beautiful can be unfolded everywhere from the sepal leaves of the visible, and the awakened intellect finds endless sources of joy in the study of the new-learned harmonies between the laws of nature and of spirit.

But the ignorance and darkness to which Ireland was condemned, up to a very recent period, would be scarcely credible, forming as it does part of an empire whose wealth, power and resources are inexhaustible, if it were not also known that everywhere throughout her colonies and her continents England has at all times manifested the one uniform spirit – a love of gain, and a neglect of souls.

Carleton, our great novelist, in the sketch of his own youth prefixed to the last edition of his *Traits and Stories*, thus speaks of the state of education in his time:–

"In my youth I do not remember a single school in a parish, the extent of which was ten miles by eight. The instruction of the children was a matter in which no one took any interest. Education was wholly left to the hedge school-master."

And we have only to read Carleton's tale of the "Hedge School" for a melancholy proof of what that education was, though the rich humour of his description makes the sketch infinitely amusing. It is indeed coloured from the life, for at this same Hedge School he himself, the "Great Peasant," received all the instruction of his early years. His trials after-wards in pursuit of knowledge were bitter, but one is half selfish enough not to regret them, since they resulted in that most pathetic tale of his *The Poor Scholar*.

Tracing, also, the abject misery and degradation of our people to this systematic neglect, even discouragement of education by all in authority, he says:–

"The Irishman was not only not educated, but actually punished for attempting to acquire knowledge in the first place, and in the second, punished also for the ignorance created by its absence. In other words, the penal laws rendered education criminal, and then caused the unhappy people to suffer for the crimes which proper knowledge would have prevented them from committing. It is beyond question, that from the time of the wars of Elizabeth, and the introduction of the Reformation, until very recently, there was no fixed system of education in the country. The people, possessed of strong political and religious prejudices, were left in a state of physical destitution and moral ignorance, calculated to produce ten times the amount of crime which was committed. Nor is it any wonder if poverty and ignorance combined should give the country a character for turbulence and outrage. The same causes would produce the same effects in any country."

There is truly a deep analogy and intimate connection between morals and education, holiness and intellect. The object of both is the attainment of that ideal perfection which is God's image stamped upon the soul, though obscured for a time by ignorance and vice. Life has no higher meaning than to evolve the inner subjective ideal in word, act and form – that is in Literature, Morals and Art.

And to emancipate this higher nature should be the noblest aim of all education. To remove the mists of sense that stand between the soul and the objects with which it has a natural affinity. To reveal this soul itself in its essential beauty and purity, as the statue becomes revealed slowly from within the block of marble, according as the gross and exoteric is dissevered from it. And as the lower nature is annihilated, the soul will stand forth clearer and clearer, the human life reveal more and more of the beauty, harmony, grace, and gentleness, which is *love*, and the deep and intimate communion with the hidden and profound things of the universe, which is *knowledge*. For all these things are of the essence of the soul – they dwell in it eternally are not created, but revealed through culture and discipline. The thoughts of a great man do not startle us because they are new, but because they wake up what has long lain wordless in the deep infinite of our own souls.

This excellence, however, cannot become the law of a man's life until the lower nature is subdued, and made the slave not the master. This is the mystery of "crucifying the flesh." It is a deep truth which should be ever present to us, that each human being is a compound of two natures, the animal and the God – senses and soul, clay and ether; and the true task of life is to evolve the divine from the earthly.

Education, therefore, must contain a moral idea at the foundation, or it becomes only the ally of the senses. By the effect any work in art of literature produces on the mind, and by that only are we to judge its excellence – by the amount of emotion and the kind of emotion which it excites. Schiller's profound comment on St Peter's at Rome is, that its grandeur consists in making us grander. The proof likewise of the surpassing excellence of Handel's "Hallelujah Chorus" is, that it excites the highest and sublimest emotion of the soul – worship. Our souls are elevated to his own level by a great artist or poet, and we are for the instant equal to Michael Angelo, Handel or Milton. When the intellect and moral nature thus acts in concert, striving together to realise the subjective ideal, the result is the advancement of our entire spiritual nature towards infinite perfection. It is in a word *religion*, for this is the highest, completest term whereby we can express the eternal asymptote or curve of the soul to God. But of all forms in which the thought of man can be incarnated, poetry is the one which produces the most vivid and instantaneous excitement upon the mind of youth. Children may be insensible to the picturesque, to sculpture, music, painting; but no child-heart is proof against a ballad. Impressions which last a life long are often stamped upon the soul by the chantings of a nurse. Thus Carleton's genius was first awakened by the soft, sweet songs of his mother to him in childhood in her own Irish tongue. Poetry, therefore, must always form an important element in education, because it can be made so powerful an auxiliary. It permeates the blood, and tinges a nature for ever after. Amongst the working classes especially, literature of feeling and imagination finds ready access. No world of conventionalities rises up as a wall between them and the spiritual, or crushes them day by day with the dull, leaden weight of its petty forms. Their thoughts rush into space more easily than in higher, fettered, artificial modes of life. Their life-task and God – these are the two poles of their existence. How faithfully and trustfully they seem to realise him as a *Presence* in their daily life! referring all trials, fortunes and events to him alone – never thinking apparently of secondary causes – and this it is which often gives such dignity and pathos to the sorrows of the poor. Out of these elements, faith, simplicity, and an ever-present sense of the spiritual, is the true poetic spirit made, or the true recipient of poetry; and so in the calendar of genius one finds but few noble pedigrees. Here in our own Ireland have not Carleton, Banim, Griffin, Moore, all sprung from the people? The star rests oftener over the manger than the palace. Knowing, then, the influence of poetry upon the people, and how readily they receive impressions through such a medium, one looks with interest on a collection of poems issued by the Irish Commissioners of Education, and intended expressly for the young hearts who are to be the working heads of the advancing age. The collection professes to range over a period of 500 years – from Chaucer to the present time – and from such an ample field one might naturally expect all that could elevate, inspire and invigorate. Into this vast temple of thought, where the words of the great of all ages are collected – it is the office of the teacher to lead the spirit-shrouded child, and guide him to every shrine where the true divinity is worshipped; to all that would excite the emotion which produces noble deeds, all that would appeal to the heart through the history, traditions, sorrows, hopes, aspirations of his native land. After the knowledge of God, a wise teacher would implant a Love of Country in the heart of a child. It is the source of all the noblest virtues, of those most difficult to attain, for they rise on the ruins of narrow self-interest. Thus would a noble, large-hearted race of men be reared, fit to act when duty called them to the great redemptive work of life, and a national spirit fostered, which, re-acting against petty party egoism, would make them one day worthy of being intrusted with national power.

To unfold to the child all that is beautiful in nature, and noble in life, is little, unless, at the same time, you give him an object commensurate with the great duties you teach him. The love kindled for humanity must be concentrated where it can act with power. The knowledge acquired should find channels on every side to benefit others, be a man's station ever so apparently isolated and powerless, for to break down the barrier-walls of self, and diffuse and expand the riches of our own mind amongst thousands around, raising them to the level we have reached, no matter how gained, whether by study or through sufferings, has in it something glorious and godlike as an aim of life, and brings to the soul something of divine felicity.

The true aim of all individual effort should be national advance. Our own land is the sphere of our duties. Here God placed us to dress it and keep it; a vineyard of whose state he will one day demand an account. How a lofty self-denying purpose can ennoble the lowest life, poverty, rags and destitution, we know from the history of many a holy saint:

> Sacrifice and self-devotion hallow earth and fill the skies,
> And the meanest life is sacred whence the highest may arise.

One of the many reasons, perhaps, of Ireland's degradation is, that her gentry were never taught to feel and act as Irishmen! The fact of being placed by God in this particular land, seemed never to suggest the idea that they were to work for it, or would have to render an account of their stewardship. Men and women are dead and dying around us, whose hearts through life never throbbed at the word "Country." By some strange hallucination they strove by vulgar imitation to transform themselves into English, and then assumed they were identical, though England by many a bitter sarcasm showed how she scorned their pretended claim.

In the preface to the *Selections for Irish Children* these views of the paramount importance of inculcating a love of home and fatherland, are distinctly stated; but throughout the whole collection we find no illustrations whatever of so just a theory. In connection with home or country there is not one verse which would strike into the young Irish heart; and for the names even of our leading Irish writers we may search the volumes in vain. The general tone also is didactic and prosy, quite unfitted to attract the attention of youth. At that age fire and energy are demanded, as a translation into words of the first throbbings of the eager, buoyant, daring heart. Ethics must be taught in action, in a vivid picture language, in deeds of heroism that make heroes – of patriotism that kindles a glow which keeps burning a life long; but patriotism is the word which, above all others, is excluded from the national education. Irish children, it seems, may be taught everything but what regards Ireland. An instance of this is given, by the compiler, in his introduction to the Ballad Poetry.

For after going over all ballad history, from Homer to Macaulay, through north and south, east and west of Europe, and even crossing the ocean to pay a tribute to the muse of the native savages of America, he says that the national poetry of *Ireland* is a subject upon which he has left himself *no space* to make any remarks.

Numerous instances have been already brought before the public establishing the existence of this quarantine law against all things Irish in the system of national education, yet one would think that literature was too sacred to be made the tool of politics. The thoughts of genius are for all ages, they are the inheritance, the rightful possession of a people. One is ashamed to see them dovetailed to suit the expediencies of a government.

Is it fair that native shrines should be veiled before the eyes of the young child while he is taught to kneel at those of other lands? Not that sectarianism or one-sidedness in literature should be mistaken for nationality. The mind, like the mystic city of the Apocalypse, should have portals open to all points of earth and heaven, from which a thought, a holy and ennobling thought may come. Heroism from all lands and of any age is still vital and will kindle heroism. We can sympathise with "Horatius Cocles, who kept the bridge so well," or with old King Pharamond, seated calmly by the burning pile to destroy himself if conquered; but in this authorised collection for Irish children, of all the brave deeds our poets sang, of all the wild, beautiful legends of our land, which their verse made more beautiful, not a line is to be found. Holy memories and heroic traditions are the guardian spirits of a people. Why should national commissioners –

Scatter these angel guards, glorious and beautiful?

There is an elevation by induction. Show a child what is worthy in his own race and he will strive to rise to it. Self-reverence is generated, for we reverence our own nature in that of our great men. Different literatures, truly, are but different languages in which one human spirit speaks. But each nation has a peculiar mental organisation. Each heart has its own idiom and ideas thus illustrated, a child will assimilate faster because they are congenial to his nature.

To rear a nation to its full stature upon foreign thought is impossible. Even in an æsthetic point of view, nothing great or original will ever result from it, much less will it awaken the national pride, hereditary heroism or self-respect, at all times necessary in those who would advance their country's glory. Germany tried to live upon foreign thought for a hundred years or more – English and French, or any thought except their own – but nothing came of it. So at last, headed by those grand iconoclasts, Lessing, Herder, Tieck, Goethe and others, they threw down all the foreign idols, and went back to drink at their own holy wells, their Sagas, Mährchen, and wild lays of the Niebelungen. There they found inspiration, and the free, native tide of thought has ever since poured forth in channels created by its own daring force – the only fitting channels for that wondrous German mind, at once the profoundest and most imaginative of Europe; while, on the other hand, by stifling the free utterance of native thought, the literature of modern Italy became the most meagre and artificial of Europe – for the Austrian forbade the words country, independence or freedom to be uttered by the subject people. There is a magic might in song. All rulers and despots know this well. Napoleon found its power, when the chorus, –

Sit sollen ihn nicht haben, derfreie Deutsche Rhien!

made all Germany fly to arms for the War of Liberation. The songs of the poets become swords in the hands of the patriots. Can it be in fear of this transmutation, that Irish song is not flung into the furnace of young hearts? One can only hazard an hypothesis for the *cause* of this singular omission; but the *fact* can be easily proved by merely looking over the index of selections. In the long list of poems on home and country, there is but *one* by an Irishman, and that merely displaying individual, not national feeling – it is, "Our Native Valley," by Griffin – although the compiler states in the Introduction, and justly, that, "On the love of home is founded that of country, and unless this first of affections is inculcated the heart must ever remain selfish, desolate and cold to all social and patriotic feelings." His illustration of these admirable sentiments is by teaching the poor Irish child to chant "The Stately Homes of England." France might as well make "Rule Britannia" her national song, in place of the "Marseillaise," or America rear her youthful population upon "The British Grenadiers."

In the list of "Songs and Lyrics" there is but *one* by Moore, the chief of our poets and our national glory and that the least characteristic of his melodies. However, in compensation, we have "Ye Mariners of England" and "Scots wha hae wi' Wallace bled," which, though excellent poetry, could scarcely vibrate through an Irish heart like Moore's grand and solemn appeal, –

> Let Erin remember the days of old,
> Ere her faithless sons betrayed her.

In the list of the "Social and domestic affections," not one Irish name is to be met with. Not a line from Banim's iron verses, strong and sinewy as a peasant's arm, and passionate as his heart. Nor from Griffin's mournful muse, filled with that deep tenderness yet plaintive orientalism of resignation so characteristic of Irish sorrow. How in that poem of his, "The Mother's Lament," one sees the poor old forsaken, desolate, bereaved-one rocking herself to and fro, by the chill hearth of her ruined home, while she chants –

> My darling, my darling, while silence is on the moor,
> And lone in the sunshine I sit by our cabin door;
> When evening falls quiet and calm over land and sea,
> My darling, my darling, I think of past times and thee!

My darling, my darling, God gave to my feeble age,
A prop for my faint heart, a stay in my pilgrimage;
My darling, my darling, God takes back his gift again,
And my heart may be broken, but ne'er shall my will complain.

Do not these genuine outpourings of an Irish heart call a rush of tender tears to the eyes, which the cold, cultured extracts from "Gertrude of Wyoming," given in the selections, never could awaken?

Amongst the ballads also, a species of composition in which Ireland has won a world-wide fame, there are but two representatives from our country – Moore's "Lake of the Dismal Swamp," and "The Faery Thorn" by Ferguson. The omission of all other distinguished Irish names cannot, however, arise from ignorance; for in his simple way of always making his prose bear testimony against his verse, the compiler assures us of the deserved popularity of Banim, Callanan, Lover, Davis, etc., amongst the modern Irish writers in this particular department, yet no extract appears from any one of them; and throughout the whole work, not a single line from Davis is to be found. The grand and glittering ballad of "Fontenoy," every verse flashing like swords in the sunshine, would give the heart of youth a healthier action, one would think, than "Sweet William's Ghost." Or that other by Davis, where the verse bounds on fierce and beautiful as a panther, –

Oh! For a steed, a rushing steed, and a blazing scimitar,
To hunt from beauteous Italy the Austrian's red hussar,
      To mock their boasts
      And strew their hosts,
   And scatter their flags afar.
Oh! For a steed, a rushing steed, and dear Poland gathered round,
To smite her circle of savage foes, and hurl them to the ground;
      Nor hold my hand
      While on the land
   A foreigner foe was found.

Or is "The Child and Hind," another of the selections, better teaching for the men of the future who are to war and work against the darkness and bigotry of ages than the spirited nationality and noble moral of "The Irish Chiefs," which thrills like a *sursum corda* through the frame.

> Oh! To have lived dear Owen's life, to live for a solemn end,
> To strive for the ruling strength and skill God's saints to the
>   chosen send;
> And to come at length with that holy strength the bondage of
>   fraud to rend,
> And pour the light of God's freedom in where tyrants or slaves
>   are denned.

Or, "The Muster of the North," by Gavan Duffy, with its fast and fiery rhythm, like the rushing of horses over a rocky causeway; or that spirited Orange chant of "The Maiden City," by Charlotte Elizabeth, coloured with the memories of the other Ulster race, beginning, –

> Where Foyle his swelling waters
>   Rolls northward to the main,
> Here, queen of Erin's daughters,
>   Fair Derry, fixed her reign.
> A holy temple crowned her,
>   And commerce graced her street,
> A rampart wall was round her,
>   The river at her feet;
> And there she sat alone, boys,
>   And looking from the hill,
> Vow'd the maiden on her throne, boys,
>   Would be a maiden still.

Ballads like these light up courage and heroism. A great heart speaks in them, and the child, for the moment, is transformed into the hero. But, alas, native heroism is a *taboo'd* subject to the young nation scholar. He may sing of Wallace wight, and the triumph over the Armada, but must not dare to tell how at Fontenoy –

> Right up against the English lines the Irish exiles ran –

and conquered too. But leaving these exciting ballads aside, why is there no illustration of Carleton's thrilling genius given? Would not the exquisite faery music of his legendary ballad of "Sir Turlough" –

> The bride she bound her golden hair –
> Kileevy, O Kileevy!
> And her step was light as the breezy air,
> When it bends the morning flowers so fair,
> By the bonnie green woods of Kileevy! –

have been a bitter poetical model, and more fitted for a place in an authorised collection for national purposes, than the infantile lispings of the Misses Davidson, of America – "The Shouting Cuckoo," or the feeble, flimsy fripperies of the "Keepsake Era"?

Then we have numerous specimens from a poet of Blackwood, called "Delta"; but of the learned, original mind of Clarence Mangan, there is no trace whatever. Poor Mangan; who spent a weary, sad life illustrating all literatures from Ireland to Iran! and who lives consecrated in the martyrology of genius, though allowed no place in the Pantheon of Marlborough Street, amongst the Peabodys and Patersons, and Polehills and Wasthills, and Wiffens, and Wilcoxes, and other poets of such-like strange and uncouth appellations whom the compiler delights to honour, though where he discovered them (particularly Wiffen, author of "The Shouting Cuckoo") is the grand mystery of the book. It is so sad in all the wide world not to know where to look for Wiffen!

But the selections even from the best poets, are as unfortunate as the omissions. Moore, for instance, seems more like an improved version of Isaac Watts than the impassioned bard of Ireland – the quotations from him being principally of sacred pieces, and one "To a Grasshopper." From Keats, "flushed all over with the rich light of poetry," but one poor extract on "Autumn." Were there not "Madeline" and the "Pot of Basil," and these two exquisite odes to "Grecian Urn" and a "Nightingale" to choose from? But of these not word.

Then not a line from Motherwell, but an interminable number from that dull Montgomery, beginning with "Autumn," too. All he ever wrote is not worth Motherwell's "Jeannie Morrison." No rich and gorgeous harmonies of Tennyson's from "Locksley Hall" or the "Lady Godiva." No gleam of that sweet vision the "Queen of the May." Or, "Mariana in the Moated Grange." Only two extracts upon "Autumn" likewise.

'To a Bee," "To a Primrose," "To Autumn," ditto, ditto, ditto, is the staple commodity appended to every name great and small down the index.

We turn to Wordsworth, – but find only Daisies and Daffodils. Not one tinge of sanctuary splendour. No "Intimations of Immortality," not a "Palm Leaf" from Monckton Miles. Yet, how beautiful is his poem, "The Flight of Youth."

> Alas! We knew not how he went,
> We knew not he was going –
> For had our tears once found a vent
> We had stayed him with their flowing.
> It was an earthquake when
> We awoke and found him gone,
> We were miserable men,
> We were hopeless, everyone!
> His impassioned eye had got
> Fire which the sun has not –
> Silk to feel and gold to see
> Fell his tresses full and free,
> And engarlanded with bay
> Must our youth have gone away.
> Through we half remember now,
> He had borne some little while
> Something mournful in his smile –
> Something serious on his brow;
> Gentle heart, perhaps he knew
> The cruel deed he had to do.

And that other sweet poem of his entitled "Moments" –

> I lie in a heavy trance
> With a world of dreams without me,

Shapes of shadows dance
In wavering bands about me;
But, at times, some mystic things
Appear in this phantom lair
That at most seem to me visitings
Of truth known elsewhere.
The world is rich, these things are small,
They may be nothing, but they are all.
A sense of an earnest will
To help the lowly living,
And a terrible heart thrill,
If you have no power of giving
An arm of aid to the weak,
A friendly hand to the friendless,
Kind words, so short to speak,
But whose echo is endless.

These are verses to set as jewels in the heart; but while the noblest poets are ostracised, we find plenty of Mickles and Millars and Mudies, and what they said.

Hogg's name is there, but no bright fragment from his "Bonnie Kilmeny," the sweetest poem of modern Scotland. From Coleridge – the visionary Coleridge – we have only "Lines to a Young Ass," not a line from "Christabel," or "The Ancient Mariner," the poem above all others to excite the heart of youth. And Elizabeth Barrett Browning, the great poetess of England – of the world – is not even named. Yet that noble poem of hers, "The Cry of the Children," so full of beauty and agony, of tenderness and sublimity, is excluded to give room for Miss Eliza Cooke's lines to a Buttercup, and Miss Hannah Golds' to a Crocus.

There are pale young faces enough around us, marred with want, misery and famine, and sad young hearts from desolated homes, to realise Mrs Browning's mournful description:–

Do you hear the children weeping, O, my brothers,
Ere the sorrow comes with years?

They are leaning their young heads against their mothers,
    And *that* cannot stop their tears.
The young lambs are bleating in the meadows,
    The young birds are chirping in the nest;
The young fawns are playing with the shadows,
    The young flowers are blowing toward the west;
But the young, young, children, O, my brothers,
    They are weeping bitterly!
They are weeping in the playtime of the others,
    In the country of the free.

And well may the children weep before you;
    They are weary ere they run;
They have never seen the sunshine or the glory,
    Which is brighter than the sun.
They know the griefs of men, but not the wisdom;
    They sink in the despair without the calm.
Are slaves without the liberty in Christdom,
    Are martyrs by the Pang without the Palm;
Are worn as if by age, yet unretrievingly,
    No dear remembrance keep;
Are orphans of the earthly love and heavenly –
    Let them weep! Let them weep!

Poor L. E. L. is somewhat better treated. But she has written verses more attractive to youth than some we find here; for instance, her spirited, clanging lines on the death of Alexander, surrounded by

His silver-shielded warriors
The warriors of the world!

And "The Graves of a Household," by Mrs Hemans, might surely have claimed a place, of which Monckton Milnes says so beautifully –

There's not a line but hath been wept upon.

Of Shelley's "Sensitive Plant" there are only half-a-dozen verses given. Its fine sensibilities no doubt shrank from keeping company with a Mr Hurdis, who says, –

> I love to see the little goldfinch pluck
> The groundsell's feeble seed, and twit and twit and twit.

Neither is the arrangement the best that could have been chosen for the advantage of students. The classification by subjects is fatiguing in the extreme. One grows wearied by the monotony of a series to similar objects, or on the same subject. Dr Johnson speaks all our feelings when he says, – "One ode, sir, is well enough, but half-a-dozen of them together makes one very sick," Beside the poems ranged under different metaphysical heads, we have an animal series (so long that it seems a rhymed bill of landing from the ark) and a vegetable series, and another to fish. Surely, none but graziers from a cattle show could get through poems to a ram, to a lamb, and to an ass, following in consecutive order as they do here. Then come a great number to cuckoos, but these all appear to be by Wiffen; and amongst the ichthyological specimens we find a sonnet to gudgeon, by some anonymous writer, the compiler actually leaving out the names of such men as Davis, Carleton and Mangan, to make room for a sonnet to a gudgeon!

In addition to the weariness which such an arrangement induces, it deprives the student of the opportunity which a chronological order gives for becoming familiar with the eras of the language, and the mental history of the nation at each successive period. The Saxon, the Latin, the French, and the Teutonic styles of composition in English Literature are as clearly defined as the successive orders of architecture; but these distinctions of style, and the psychological phenomena of which they are the exponent, are wholly lost by the want of a chronological arrangement. The poetry of an age is generally the completest expression of the mind of that age, the ultimate and most perfect formula to express the height to which thought has reached. It incarnates the highest ideal to which the soul of humanity, viewed in its unity, had sprung, and gives definite form to those vague perceptions of the new regions of thought to which it is travelling. It is not merely the result of the spirit of an age, but the spirit itself. Not alone the actual, but the tendencies. Poetry is, in fact, the chanted spiritualism of an age; whether that spiritualism be as full of faith and earnestness as the 16th, and the first half of the 17th century; as frivolous, false and materialised as the 18th; or as daring and transcendental as the philosophic creeds of our own day. Whatever faith or hope exists in any age, will be found condensed or sublimated in the poetry of that era. But from the arrangement of these selections no definite idea can be gained of the peculiar characteristics of each successive century.

The biographies of the poets form the third volume of the work. They are interesting, useful and well executed, and it must be acknowledged that wherever the editor speaks in his own person, it is with sense and judgment. Indeed, his prose displays so much of the qualities in which his selections are deficient, that we must impute the failure of the latter to some stern political necessity; some dark and secret threatenings, some official baton suspended over his head which forced him, in defiance of all good taste, to send forth a collection which almost justifies Hallam's sarcasm on these works in general, that they seem compiled on the principle of excluding everything which is good.

Irish Leaders and Martyrs

The fervent nationality evoked by Moore's music and song at the opening of the century, and formulated afterwards into an immense political force by O'Connell, rose to a fever of enthusiasm in 1848, when a madness of lyrical passion seemed to sweep over the heart of the nation, and "Young Ireland" sprang to manhood, splendid in force and intellect, earnest in aim, and stainless in life and act.

Amongst the new band of workers were powerful organisers like Gavan Duffy; chivalrous leaders like Smith O'Brien, orators like Dillon and Meagher; and fervent apostles of freedom like John Mitchell, one of the boldest, bravest, and most noble-hearted of patriots. But the man, above all, whose words were a tocsin of Revolution, was the poet, orator and leader, Thomas Davis.

His whole public and literary career barely exceeded four years, yet, in that brief time, he created a nation with noble, definite aims, and passionate resolves to achieve success.

A delirium of patriotic excitement raged through the land as these young orators and poets flashed the full light of their genius on the wrongs, the hopes, and the old heroic memories of their country; even the upper classes in Ireland awoke for the first time to the sense of the nobleness of a life devoted to national regeneration.

A *Gott Trunkenheit*, the "Trunkenheit ohne Wein," was on all hearts, the divine fanaticism of youth and genius. The leaders spoke as inspired men, and their words, like the words of the spirit, gave new life and power to every lofty purpose and high resolve. Even Trinity College struck the Irish harp to Hymns of Freedom, and the most popular poem of that era, "Who fears to speak of Ninety-eight?" was written by a young collegian, afterwards a distinguished Fellow of the university; and an eminent Irish Judge, but recently passed away, won his first laurels in literature by songs contributed to the national cause.

Another of the leading spirits of that day was Ferguson, afterwards Sir Samuel Ferguson, who illustrated all that was grand or tragic in the past by his splendid ballads; and who flung the silken singing robes of the bard over the muse of Irish history; while Aubrey de Vere, the most cultured of all the Irish poets, crowned her with the golden diadem of his perfect verse.

The powerful ballads of Charles Gavan Duffy also achieved a rapid fame, and will for ever hold a distinguished place in Irish literature; while as a song writer, John Francis Waller almost rivalled Moore in the melody and music of his words; and his graceful and beautiful lyrics have the true mirth and pathos of Irish nature, blended and united. Denis Florence MacCarthy, the translator of "Calderon," wrote patriot verse that clashed like cymbals; and Clarence Mangan brought treasures from every land and language to weave into the national minstrelsy; while Carleton and Banin proved their claim to rank as poets, as well as the greatest amongst Irish novelists.

Nor was genius unrepresented in the other arts. Frederick Burton, the painter, now Sir Frederick Burton, first drank inspiration at the holy wells of Ireland, and has never known inspiration more fervent and glowing since he left their tree-shadowed mysteries for his English home; and George Petrie's divine soul grew diviner amidst the holy ruins of the ancient abbeys and the purple mist-crowned solitudes of the Irish mountains; for love of country is one of the great motive forces of the mind, and the Irish have ever been singularly susceptible to its influence as a stimulus to action. Nor is the influence evanescent, for the Irish people have been tried through much suffering, yet neither the prison, nor exile, nor broken hearts, not even death itself, could weaken the love and reverence that binds them to their motherland.

In the great outpouring of the Spirit in '48, not only the cultured classes, but the toilers and artisans also, many of them were seized with the poetic frenzy, and wrote and published verses of singular merit and strong, rude power; for Celtic favour always finds its fullest expression in oratory and song. The Irish, especially, have a natural gift for copious and fluent speech. They are orators at all times, but under the influence of strong excitement they become poets, and in that stormy era, when every nation was reading its Rights by the flames of burning thrones, the Irish poets, mad with the magnificent illusions of youth, flashed their hymns of hope and songs of defiance like a fiery cross over land and lake, over river and mountains, throughout Ireland, awakening souls to life that might long have lain dead but for the magic incantation of their words.

Yet, the fate of many of those who made '48 a splendid moment in Irish history, was dark and tragic, and the flame lit up by patriot-passion died out in martyrdom. The brave and brilliant Thomas Francis Meagher, the handsome and gifted young orator of the National party, was drowned in the waters of the Mississippi, and D'Arcy M'Ghee, the poet and statesman, met his death in Canada, murdered by some Irish fanatics who believed that he had given up nationality for place. The high-souled Smith O'Brien, the descendant of kings, and venerated by the people as their chief, was tried and condemned to death, though the sentence was commuted afterwards to exile. He served out his time through the long weary years, disdaining to break his parole, and then returned to Ireland to die. His last words were,– "My heart is broken."

John Dillon, the impassioned orator, who could sway thousands to his will by the magnetism of his presence, looking every inch the magnificent Spanish Hidalgo, with his dark eyes and raven hair, was doomed to prison and exile in the prime of his splendid manhood; and came back only in long after years, a white-haired, mournful wreck, to rest in an Irish grave.

> He looked not like the ruins of his youth,
> But like the ruins of those ruins.

And John Mitchell, the all-powerful advocate of human freedom, suffered also the bitter martyrdom of exile, till youth, hope and energy were all crushed out of his life, and then he was permitted to return and see his native land once more. But the shadow of death was already on him, and he died just as the people, with all their old vivid love for the patriot-martyr unchanged, had elected him as one of their representatives in Parliament.

So they laid him in his Irish grave, with a shamrock on his breast, and never a truer heart, with its scorn of everything false, or a more powerful brain as thinker and writer, could be named amongst all those who have lived and worked and died for Ireland.

Clarence Mangan, one of the most remarkable of the gifted young race of that era, was found almost perishing of want in the streets of Dublin; and he died shortly after in the hospital whither they carried him.

Henry O'Neill, the artist and writer, to whom we are indebted for that truly splendid work "The Sculpted Crosses of Ireland," was sustained chiefly by charity during the closing years of his life, and his family, after his death, were left almost in utter destitution.

But the list is endless of Irish genius left to struggle hopelessly against the corroding cares of life. A natural result when there is no kinship or sympathy between the rulers and the ruled, no pride of race, no heroic memories, no traditions of suffering common to both, yet the word *country* should be for ever sacred, and lie at the base of all individual action and effort; for love of country is the divine force that can alone war against the degrading tendencies of mere material gain; and no mental or moral elevation can be attained by a people who do not, above all, and before all, things, uphold and reverence the hold rights of their Motherland.

Notes

Notes to Introduction: Speranza and William Wilde

1 Oscar Wilde, *De Profundis* (Harmondsworth: Penguin, 1986), 141.
2 Eric Lambert, *Mad with Much Heart* (London: Muller, 1967), vii.
3 I am grateful to Noreen Doody for this point and for referring me to Vyvyan Holland's memoir, *Son of Oscar Wilde* (London: Carroll & Graf, 1999).
4 Eleanor Fitzsimons, *Wilde's Women*, (London: Duckworth, 2015), 8.
5 Speranza, Daniel O'Connell, *Notes on Men and Women*, 185.
6 Lady Wilde, *The American Irish* (Dublin: William McGee, 1878), 2.
7 Colm Tóibín, *Mad, Bad and Dangerous to Know* (London: Viking, 2018), 42.
8 See Joy Melville, *Mother of Oscar: The Life of Jane Francesca Wilde* (London: John Murray, 1994).
9 Emer O'Sullivan, *The Fall of the House of Wilde* (London: Bloomsbury, 2016), 56.
10 Charles Gavan Duffy, *My Life in Two Hemispheres* (Dublin: Unwin, 1898), 75.
11 Peter Froggatt, "The Demographic World of Sir William Wilde," *Irish Journal of Medical Science* 185, no. 2 (2016): 294.
12 Karen Tipper, *Lady Jane Wilde's Letters to Mr. John Hilson, 1847–1876* (New York: Edwin Mellen, 2010), 56.
13 See my novel, *The Diary of Mary Travers* (Bantry: Somerville Press, 2014).
14 Robert Sherard, *Life of Oscar Wilde* (London: T. W. Laure, 1906), 32.
15 Tipper, *Lady Jane Wilde's Letters to Mr. John Hilson*, 49.
16 W. B. Yeats, *Letters to the New Island* (Cambridge, MA: Harvard University Press, 1934), 77.

17   W. B. Yeats, *Autobiographies* (New York: Senate Books, 1995), 278.

18   Charles Gavan Duffy, *Four Years in Irish History* (Dublin: Cassell, 1883), 34.

19   Eleanor Fitzsimons, *Wilde's Women* (London: Duckworth, 2015), 29.

20   See George Bernard Shaw, *The Playwright and the Pirate*, ed. Stanley Weintraub (Gerrard's Cross: Colin Smythe, 1982), 33.

21   Shaw, *The Playwright and the Pirate*, 33.

22   See Eibhear Walshe, *Oscar's Shadow: Wilde and Modern Ireland* (Cork: Cork University Press, 2011).

23   T. G. Wilson, *Victorian Doctor* (London: Methuen, 1942), 1.

24   Wilson, *Victorian Doctor*, 182.

25   Horace Wyndham, *Speranza: A Biography of Lady Wilde* (London and New York: Boardman, 1951), 192.

26   Wyndham, *Speranza*, 162.

27   Wyndham, *Speranza*, 195.

28   St John Ervine, *Oscar Wilde: A Present Time Appraisal* (New York: Morrow, 1952), 35.

29   Lambert, *Mad with Much Heart*, vii.

30   Terence de Vere White, *The Parents of Oscar Wilde* (London: Hodder & Stoughton, 1967), 17.

31   White, *Parents of Oscar Wilde*, 17, 19.

32   Terry Eagleton, *Saint Oscar* (Derry: Field Day, 1989), 6.

33   Eagleton, *Saint Oscar*, 9.

34   Eagleton, *Saint Oscar*, 12.

35   Richard Ellman, *Oscar Wilde* (Harmondsworth: Penguin, 1987), 11.

36   Ellman, *Oscar Wilde*, 17.

37   Davis Coakley, *Oscar Wilde: The Importance of Being Irish* (Dublin: Townhouse, 1994), 3.

38   Melville, *Mother of Oscar*, 270.

39   Colm Tóibín, *Love in a Dark Time: Gay Lives from Wilde to Almodovar* (London: Picador, 2002), 46.

40   Tóibín, *Love in a Dark Time*, 51.

41   Karen Tipper, *A Critical Biography of Jane Wilde* (New York: Edwin Mellen, 2002).

42   Emer O'Sullivan, *The Fall of the House of Wilde* (London: Bloomsbury, 2016), x.

43   O'Sullivan, *The Fall of the House of Wilde*, xi.

44   Eleanor Fitzsimons, *Wilde's Women* (London: Duckworth, 2015), 15.

45   O'Sullivan, *The Fall of the House of Wilde*, 145.

46   Michael O'Doherty, "Sir William Wilde, an Enlightened Editor," *Irish Journal of Medical Science* 185, no. 2 (2016): 298.

47   Melville, *Mother of Oscar*, 8.

48 Michael Cronin, "Lady Jane 'Speranza' Wilde and the Translator's Invisibility," *Claritas* 8 (2002): 86.

49 Amy Martin, "The Skeleton at the Feast: Lady Wilde's Famine Poetry and Irish Internationalist Critiques of Food Scarcity," in *Women and the Great Hunger*, ed. Christine Kinealy, Jason King, and Ciaran Reilly (Hamden, CT: Quinnipiac University Press, 2017), 151.

50 Martin, "The Skeleton at the Feast," 162.

51 Matthew Campbell, "Poetry, 1845–90," in *A History of Modern Irish Women's Writing*, ed. Cliona O'Gallchoir and Heather Ingman (Cambridge: Cambridge University Press, 2018), 82.

52 Eiléan Ní Chuilleanáin, *The Wilde Legacy* (Dublin: Four Courts Press, 2003), 21.

53 Laurence Geary, "William Wilde as Historian: A Bicentennial Appraisal," *History Ireland* 23, no. 5 (2015): 28–31.

54 William Wilde, "The Food of the Irish," *Dublin University Magazine* 43, 1854, 127–28.

55 Cronin, "Lady Jane 'Speranza' Wilde and the Translator's Invisibility," 94.

56 Marjorie Howe, "'Tears and Blood': Lady Wilde and the Emergence of an Irish Cultural Nationalism," in *Ideology and Ireland in the Nineteenth Century*, ed. Tadhg Foley and Seán Ryder (Dublin: Four Courts, 1998), 164.

57 Tipper, *A Critical Biography of Jane Wilde*, 153.

58 Tipper, *A Critical Biography of Jane Wilde*, 161–62.

59 William Wilde, *The Closing Years of the Life of Dean Swift* (Dublin: Hodges and Smith, 1849), 117.

60 Lady Wilde, "Stella and Vanessa," in *Notes on Men, Women, and Books* (London: Ward & Downey, 1891), 88.

61 Lady Wilde, *Ancient Legends, Mystic Charms, and Superstitions of Ireland* (London: Ward & Downey, 1887), ii.

Notes to Chapter 10: Letters from Speranza

1 Melville, *Mother of Oscar*, 97–98.

2 Karen Tipper, *Lady Jane Wilde's Letters to Froken Lotten von Kraemer* (Lampeter: Mellen, 2008), 45–46.

Notes to Chapter 15: Jane Wilde, *Ancient Legends, Mystic Charms, and Superstitions of Ireland*, 1887

1 Melville, *Mother of Oscar*, 199.

Chronology

1815 William Wilde born

1821 Jane Elgee (Speranza) born

1833 William begins studying in Dublin in St. Stevens Hospital

1837 William qualifies as a surgeon, takes his first Mediterranean trip

1838 William's first son, Henry Wilson, born

1840 William's first book, *The Narrative of a Voyage to Madeira, Tenerife, and Along the Shores of the Mediterranean*, published

1843 William's book *Austria* published

1845 Thomas Davis's funeral takes place in Dublin, inspiring Speranza to write nationalist poetry

1846 Jane sends poems into *The Nation* under the name Speranza, Italian for "Hope"

1847 William's first daughter, Emily, born. Speranza publishes her famine poems in *The Nation*

1848 Speranza becomes editor of *The Nation*

1849 *The Nation* trial for treason takes place. William's second daughter, Mary, born

1849 Speranza's translation of *Sidona the Sorceress* published

1850 Speranza's translation of Lamartine's *History of the Girondins* published. William also publishes *The Beauties of the Boyne*, which is then reviewed by Speranza

1851 Speranza and William marry, settle into their first home at Westland Row in Dublin. *The Wanderer and his Home* published by Speranza

1852 Willy, their eldest son, born. Speranza publishes her translation of *The Glacier Land*. William publishes *Irish Popular Superstitions*

1854 Oscar, their second son, born

1857 William publishes his *Catalogue of the Antiquities of the Museum of the Royal Irish Academy*. Their daugher, Isola, born

1858 The family move to Merrion Square

1864 Speranza publishes her collected poems. William knighted. The Mary Travers case takes place

1867 Isola dies. William publishes *Lough Corrib*

1876 William dies

1878 Speranza publishes her essay "American Irish"

1879 Speranza moves to London

1880 Speranza completes and publishes William's last book, *Memoir of Gabriel Beranger*

1884 *Driftwood from Scandinavia*

1887 *Ancient Legends, Mystic Charms, and Superstitions of Ireland*

1890 *Ancient Cures, Charms and Usages*

1891 *Notes on Men, Women, and Books*

1893 *Social Studies*

1895 Oscar Wilde trials in London

1896 Speranza dies

Bibliography of Speranza
and William Wilde

Wilde, William. *The Narrative of a Voyage to Madeira, Tenerife, and Along the Shores of the Mediterranean.* Dublin: Curry, 1840.

Wilde, William. *Austria.* Dublin: Curry, 1843.

Wilde, William. *The Closing Years of the Life of Dean Swift.* Dublin: Hodges and Smith, 1849.

Wilde, Jane. *Sidonia.* London: Reeves and Turner, 1849.

Wilde, William. *The Beauties of the Boyne and the Blackwater.* Dublin: James McGlashen, 1850.

Wilde, Jane. *Pictures of the First French Revolution.* London: Simms and McIntyre, 1850.

Wilde, Jane. *The Wanderer and his Home.* London: Simms and McIntyre, 1851.

Wilde, Jane. *The Glacier Land.* London: Simms and McIntyre, 1852.

Wilde, William. *Irish Popular Superstitions.* Dublin: James McGlashen, 1852.

Wilde, Jane. *The First Temptation.* London: Cautley Newby, 1863.

Wilde, Jane. *Poems.* Dublin: James Duffy, 1864.

Wilde, William. *Lough Corrib.* Dublin: McGlashen and Gill, 1867.

Wilde, Jane and William Wilde. *Gabriel Beranger.* Dublin: Gill, 1880.

Wilde, Jane. *Driftwood from Scandinavia.* London: Richard Bentley, 1884.

Wilde, Jane. *Ancient Legends, Mystic Charms, and Superstitions of Ireland.* London: Ward & Downey, 1887.

Wilde, Jane. *Ancient Cures, Charms and Usages of Ireland.* London: Ward & Downey, 1890.

Wilde, Jane. *Notes on Men and Women and Books.* London: Ward & Downey, 1891.

Wilde, Jane. *Social Studies.* London: Ward & Downey, 1893.

Index